Classics in Linguistics

Chief Editors: Martin Haspelmath, Stefan Müller

In this series:

1. Lehmann, Christian. Thoughts on grammaticalization.

2. Schütze, Carson T. The empirical base of linguistics: Grammaticality judgments and linguistic methodology.

3. Bickerton, Derek. Roots of language.

4. von der Gabelentz, Georg. Die Sprachwissenschaft: Ihre Aufgaben, Methoden und bisherigen Ergebnisse.

5. Stefan Müller, Marga Reis & Frank Richter (Hrsg): Beiträge zur deutschen Grammatik: Gesammelte Schriften von Tilman N. Höhle.

6. Anderson, Stephen R. & Louis de Saussure (eds.). René de Saussure and the theory of word formation.

ISSN: 2366-374X

René de Saussure and the theory of word formation

Edited by

Stephen R. Anderson

Louis de Saussure

Stephen R. Anderson & Louis de Saussure (eds.). 2018. *René de Saussure and the theory of word formation* (Classics in Linguistics 6). Berlin: Language Science Press.

This title can be downloaded at:
http://langsci-press.org/catalog/book/199
© 2018, the authors
Published under the Creative Commons Attribution 4.0 Licence (CC BY 4.0):
http://creativecommons.org/licenses/by/4.0/
ISBN: 978-3-96110-096-5 (Digital)
    978-3-96110-097-2 (Hardcover)

ISSN: 2366-374X
DOI:10.5281/zenodo.1306472
Source code available from www.github.com/langsci/199
Collaborative reading: paperhive.org/documents/remote?type=langsci&id=199

Cover and concept of design: Ulrike Harbort
Typesetting: Stephen R. Anderson, Felix Kopecky, Sebastian Nordhoff
Proofreading: Stephen R. Anderson, Martin Haspelmath, Louis de Saussure, Jingting Ye
Fonts: Linux Libertine, Libertinus Math, Arimo, DejaVu Sans Mono
Typesetting software: XƎLATEX

Language Science Press
Unter den Linden 6
10099 Berlin, Germany
langsci-press.org

Storage and cataloguing done by FU Berlin

Contents

Introduction iii

I The 1911 text

Principes logiques de la formation des mots – Logical principles of the formation of words 3

Reviews of de Saussure 1911 128

II The 1919 text

La structure logique des mots – The logical structure of words 141

III Commentary

1 The Esperantist background of René de Saussure's work
  Marc van Oostendorp 201

2 The morphological theory of René de Saussure's works
  Stephen R. Anderson 209

3 The theory of meaning in René de Saussure's works
  Louis de Saussure 229

René de Saussure

Introduction

In August, 2014, while going through the library of his late father Antoine de Saussure (son of Louis-Octave de Saussure, a younger brother of Ferdinand and René de Saussure), Louis de Saussure discovered a little book of 122 pages entitled "Principes logiques de la formation des mots," written in 1911 by his great-uncle René and obviously dealing in a general way with morphology. René de Saussure was (as discussed below) an engineer and mathematician, not a linguist like his brother Ferdinand. Although he was active in the Esperanto movement in the early years of the 20th century, and wrote on issues concerning the adoption of this proposed international language as discussed in §1 below, he has not been known for the relevance of his work to topics in general linguistics. The book in question seems in particular to have escaped the attention of linguists of the time and later; and indeed, indications of its very existence in the catalogs of major research libraries are quite rare.

While the 1911 book identified itself as the "first part" of a projected work, no second part was ever written as such. In 1919,[1] however, René de Saussure published a further work of 68 pages, "La structure logique des mots dans les langues naturelles, considérée au point de vue de son application aux langues artificielles" (de Saussure 1919), including an initial chapter on much the same topic. While the 1911 work makes no reference to other writings by linguists (such as the author's brother), the 1919 book was composed after the appearance of Ferdinand de Saussure's (1916) *Cours de linguistique générale*, and cites Ferdinand de Saussure's views on general linguistics in places, including a brief but illuminating passage contrasting two possible theories of word structure (de Saussure 1919: 27–28) which will be explored below in §2.

---

[1]Some confusion is produced by the fact that while this work identifies itself as published in 1919 by "Librairie A. Lefilleul, Christoffelgasse, Berne," and the text is signed with the date 17 March, 1919, the title page shows it as having been printed in 1918 by "Imprimerie Büchler & Cie, Berne." As noted below on page 141, the internal evidence argues that the book should be referred to by its 1919 publication date.

Introduction

Both volumes – and especially the second – must be seen as motivated by René's concerns for the design of Esperanto, but their basic premise is that this can only be carried out rationally on a foundation of understanding of the workings of natural languages. As a result, the theoretical framework and general principles proposed should be viewed as a contribution to general linguistics, and not solely in terms of their implications for artificial languages.

René de Saussure

RENÉ DE SAUSSURE (1868–1943), THE SIXTH CHILD AND FOURTH SON of Henri and Louise de Saussure (née de Pourtalès), was eleven years younger than his brother Ferdinand. A mathematician and engineer, he is best known as a prominent figure in the Esperanto movement in the early years of the twentieth century (see §1 below).

He did his undergraduate studies at the École Polytechnique in Paris from 1887 to 1889 before moving to the U.S.A. where he received a PhD from John Hopkins University (Baltimore) in 1895. He was appointed Professor of mathematics at the Catholic University of America at Washington D.C. in 1896 and held this position until 1899 when he came back to Switzerland. He then held positions at the Universities of Geneva and Berne.

During his American years, while he studied mathematics, René de Saussure ran a firm of architects in Virginia with a friend of his and with the partnership of his older brother Horace, a painter. The firm was successful enough to be awarded the building of a musical auditorium, but the partnership did not last (Joseph 2012: 390,391). In 1892 he married Jeanne Davin, an American Roman Catholic woman, and obtained American citizenship. The marriage was tragically ended by Jeanne's death in 1896, at the age of only 24. In 1898, René married Catherine Maurice, from Geneva, who came to live with him in the United States. But a new tragedy was soon to occur: she died after giving birth to their son Jean in April 1899. René then immediately resigned from his position at the Catholic University and came back to Geneva with the baby. He married later for the third time, to Violette Herr from Zurich, who gave birth to another son, Maxime.

His interest in the development of science in America was at the time an original move in the family – his brother Ferdinand was himself mostly connected to the German and French academic worlds – but also an indication of the openness of his intellectual environment towards new horizons, already previously shown by various members of the family.

Figure 1: René de Saussure as a child, as painted by his uncle Théodore (1824–1903). Courtesy of the de Saussure family.

Introduction

Another brother of René and Ferdinand, Léopold, obtained French citizenship (taking advantage of a right granted to members of families who had emigrated during the wars of religion) and became an officer in the French navy. This duty led him to sail in the far East and in particular to China where he became interested in Chinese astronomy and its relation with Western views, as well as the Chinese language, eventually answering questions about Chinese that Ferdinand would ask him in letters. René and Léopold were close to each other in childhood and even 'invented' their own 'language', the grammar of which their older brother Ferdinand tried to crack at the time.

Their father Henri de Saussure, himself a recognized entomologist, went all the way to Mexico in his youth, participated in the cartography of the country and studied traditional artifacts. Later on, Ferdinand's own son Raymond also lived in the USA during WWII after having been in a close intellectual relationship with Sigmund Freud.

René, Ferdinand and the other members of the family were raised in a family with a solid scientific background, tracing back at least to the geologist, meteorologist and alpinist Horace-Bénédict de Saussure in the 18th century. Horace-Bénédict was among the major discoverers of hercynian folding in geology (Carozzi 1989), and his grand-son, the biochemist Nicolas-Théodore was a pioneer in research on photosynthesis. The family provided an environment with a strong incentive to creative thinking and adventurous exploration, certainly qualities to be found in the works of both Ferdinand and René, however opposite the directions they may seem to have taken.

After returning to Switzerland, René taught at the University of Geneva from 1904 to 1910. During this time Ferdinand was also in Geneva, appointed as Adjunct Professor in 1891 and as a full Professor in 1896 following a long teaching career in Paris. Ferdinand gave his famous three courses in general linguistics from 1907 to 1911, thus at a time when the interaction with his younger brother was facilitated by the circumstances. It is likely that René and his famous elder brother pursued an ongoing interaction about language, in the fundamental structure of which both were so much interested; Joseph (2012: 539) for example speculates that René discussed the notion of arbitrariness with Ferdinand in the context of the invention of the Esperantist currency spesmilo and in relation to Ferdinand's famous analogy between language and money as social institutions. It is also clear that René and Ferdinand had a number of occasions to exchange views on Esperanto, in particular regarding the question of whether its artificial nature as a non-native language would preserve it from the usual movements of language diachronic evolution.

Figure 2: René de Saussure (bottom) with (left to right) Leopold de Saussure (brother, 1866–1925), Elizabeth Théodora (sister, 1863–1944), Edmond de la Rive (her husband, 1847–1902), and Louise de Saussure, née de Pourtalès (mother, 1837–1906). Photo courtesy of the de Saussure family.

Ferdinand was not always interested, however, in exchanging ideas with his mathematician brother. In a letter of 1895 to Ferdinand, René complains: "I wish however that we could exchange sometimes some ideas, even though our domains are so different from one another. Sometimes not so bad ideas can be suggested by someone working in a different domain hence conceiving of things from another perspective." They had in fact already exchanged some intellectual correspondence in a number of letters, but in them they discussed mathematics and physics, not language, and Ferdinand seems rather to be lecturing his younger brother about epistemology. A letter by René dated 1890 shows him responding at length to criticisms by Ferdinand about René's hypotheses on a fourth dimension of matter. Whereas René seems to take the discussion to the

Introduction

level of abstract thought experiments, Ferdinand delivers more concrete, empirically anchored arguments. For example, when René explains that a third dimension would be unimaginable to a two-dimensional being, as an illustration of why a 4th dimension may be unimaginable to us, Ferdinand replies that no such being can actually exist.

One might venture to suggest that René's book on morphology was triggered by a desire to oppose Ferdinand's holistic early structuralist view with the help of mathematical, compositional principles and formal arguments, so that their brotherly debate would reach the scientific community outside the closed doors of family discussion. It is noticeable that when René's first book was published in 1911, Ferdinand was just then concluding the delivery of his famous lectures on General linguistics, before he became ill and passed away in 1913. His *Course in General Linguistics* (de Saussure 1916) was only posthumously reconstructed and published in 1916, at which point it – though not its author – was available to René in the preparation of his 1919 continuation of the 1911 work. Whether the debates were fierce between the brothers or not is not known, but they are likely to have been so.

This being said, it might be that René's knowledge about the then recent developments in the Mathematical sciences in relation to philosophy actually did influence Ferdinand's conception of language. In an 1890 letter, René mentions a new treatise on physics (Stallo 1882), on which he comments in details in his own works; it is noteworthy that Stallo develops a conception of physics based on relations of 'identity and differences' and a philosophy where objects are known through their mutual relations only (Joseph 2012: 367), all of which which will sound quite familiar to anyone aware of Ferdinand's theory of value.

René's enduring involvement in the Esperantist movement even led him to teach a course at the University of Geneva in 1910 on the "History of the international language movement from Descartes and Leibniz to Esperanto" (Joseph 2012: 566).

From 1920 to 1925 René was a professor at the University of Berne. In 1934 he was nominated as the official representative of American universities during the celebrations of the University of Berne's jubilee. The same year, René was awarded a doctorate *honoris causa* from the Faculty of Sciences in Geneva for his contribution to the geometry of movement, work which had also been recognized by a prestigious French prize in geometry in 1917. According to M. E. Briner, Dean of the Faculty at that time, René de Saussure "addressed geometry of movement from a new, original and fruitful perspective."[2] A review of his

---

[2] *Journal de Genève*, 17 March, 1943.

work on the geometry of movement (Bricard 1910) is enlightening in terms of method: just as in his treatment of morphology, René de Saussure develops a novel theory where only a limited number of parameters (actually, five parameters) may enter into the calculation of the forms of an object in space, but more importantly he proposes a number of "conditions" to which the solid object in movement is subjected. As a result, his theory, developed in the published version of his thesis on metageometry (in 1921), allows for relatively simple calculations of movement based on a number of dimensions besides mass, time, and energy. Joseph (2012: 366) suggests that René's research on the boundaries of physics and geometry prefigures Einstein's subsequent Theory of Relativity.

It is apparent that René de Saussure's work was very creative, even though it did not lead to significant continuations. At the same time, he was very concerned with the aim of finding the commonalities, and therefore the universality, of the various domains of geometry, his specialty – movement –– being conceived as a mere extension of 'classical' geometries. Perhaps the search for universal grounds, i.e. the essentialist perspective, is what unites the two brothers' remarkable minds, despite the clearly different perspectives they adopt on language, one from a scholar originally specialized in the history of languages and the other from a mathematician.

The present volume

René de Saussure's works on word formation present a number of points of interest, partly for general historical reasons and especially for an understanding of the history of theorizing about the analysis of words within modern linguistics. Neither has been made available previously in English, and even the French originals are difficult to obtain. The present volume contains the original French texts[3] and two reviews of the 1911 volume, with English translations (by S. R. Anderson), preserving the original pagination and (so far as possible) typography. These are followed by commentaries on some interesting aspects of the work and its history: discussions of the background of this work in René de Saussure's involvement with the design of the international auxiliary language Esperanto (by Marc van Oostendorp), and of the morphological and semantic theories (by Stephen R. Anderson and Louis de Saussure, respectively) that underlie the texts.

---

[3] Pages 29–68 of de Saussure (1919) are devoted to the application of de Saussure's ideas to artificial languages, followed by a description of the grammar of a variatnt of Esperanto written in that language, and these sections of the work are not included here.

Introduction

PDF copies of scanned images of the two original works (including the portions of de Saussure 1919 not included here) have been deposited in the Zenodo online archive, and can be consulted at https://doi.org/10.5281/zenodo.1217635.

We are grateful to the de Saussure family for their permission to reproduce the photographs used here as the frontispiece and Figure 2, and the oil painting of René de Saussure as a child in Figure 1. We are also grateful to Prof. David Pesetsky for locating and photocopying the copy of de Saussure 1919 from which the edition in Part II was prepared, and to Prof. S. Jay Keyser for having donated this to the MIT library. Anonymous referees for Language Science Press and also for other publishers who considered early versions of our project provided useful comments which we have attempted to incorporate, as did Prof. Thomas Leu, who read a more recent version of the manuscript.

References

Bricard, Raoul. 1910. Sur la géométrie des feuillets de M. René de Saussure. Étude analytique. *Nouvelles annales de mathématiques* 4(10). 1–21.

Carozzi, Albert. 1989. Forty years of thinking in front of the Alps: Saussure's (1796) unpublished theory of the earth. *Earth Sciences History* 8(2). 123–140.

de Saussure, Ferdinand. 1916. *Cours de linguistiique générale*. Lausanne: Librairie Payot. Edited by Charles Bally and Albert Sechehaye, with the collaboration of Albert Riedlinger.

de Saussure, René. 1919. *La structure logique des mots dans les langues naturelles, considérées au point de vue de son application aux langues artificielles*. Berne: Librairie A. Lefilleul.

Joseph, John E. 2012. *Saussure*. Oxford: Oxford University Press.

Stallo, John Bernhard. 1882. *The concepts and theories of modern physics*. New York: D. Appleton.

Part I

The 1911 text

Principes logiques de la formation des mots – Logical principles of the formation of words

The text of René de Saussure's first little book follows here together with an English translation. In the translation, French words cited as examples have been preserved as such and italicized, with the first instance of a given word on a page provided with an English gloss in the early pages. Since the range of French examples cited by de Saussure is quite limited, however, glosses are dispensed with in later portions of the work for words that should be familiar. French words cited as concepts or ideas, in contrast, have generally been translated except where this would impair the sense of the text (in which case they have been treated in the same manner as examples). Words from other languages (in particular, German) presented without glosses by de Saussure have been left in that form.

The translation has attempted to follow the original as closely as possible: Our goal is to make the French original accessible to the English reader, rather than to recreate the work as René de Saussure might have written it in English. The pagination of the original text has been preserved and indicated at the top of each page, although no attempt has been made to maintain the division of pages into lines. We have retained the original typography to the extent possible. Inserted material (e.g. opening or closing quotes missing in the original) is enclosed in square brackets; we trust no confusion will result from confusion with the use of such brackets in the text.

The volume is dedicated to "M. le Professeur Th. Flournoy", without further elaboration, and some remarks on this scholar are in order here. Théodore Flournoy was born in Geneva in 1854 and died there in 1920. He studied philosophy and medicine before turning to psychology, and held a chair in Experimental Psychology at the University of Geneva from 1891 until his death. A member of another of Geneva's socially prominent protestant families (the Claparèdes), he would naturally have come into contact with the de Saussures, and in particular with René's brother Ferdinand. The two attended the same schools, and both eventually held chairs at the University, although since Flournoy was three years older, they were not particularly close in their youth.

Figure 3: Théodore Flournoy (1854–1920)

Flournoy was a significant figure in the early development of psychology in Europe, and his best known work, *From India to the Planet Mars* (Flournoy 1900) was a major influence on Carl Jung. This book involved a detailed recounting and analysis of a series of séances with a Geneva medium Cathérine-Élise Müller (identified in the book by the pseudonym Mlle. Hélène Smith). Mlle. "Smith" in a series of trances over a five year period recounted a series of supposed experiences in past lives, including a life on Mars, life as Marie Antoinette, and a life in India. Flournoy takes her experience quite seriously and does not treat it as fraudulent, but rather works out in detail the ways in which what she describes originates in her own early experience and reflects the operations of a subconscious mental life. All of this was quite congenial to those such as Jung (and William James, with whom he was also in contact) developing similar views of the mind (Witzig 1982).

Important to Flournoy's connection with the Saussures, however, is the fact that he involved Ferdinand with the analysis of the series of the medium's "Hindoo Cycle" séances, several of which he attended (Joseph 2012: 426ff.). Ferdinand was consulted especially with regard to the idea that some of Mlle. "Smith's" utterances on these occasions were in (some form of) Sanskrit, since Ferdinand was an authority on that language. Flournoy had also consulted Ferdinand earlier in connection with his ideas about synæsthesia, and indeed they maintained cordially collegial relations for much of their joint careers at the University of Geneva. Apart from this, however, and the connections between the families

(Flournoy's daughter Ariane married Ferdinand's son Raymond in 1919), there is little evidence for a close association specifically between Flournoy and René, apart from one point: in 1909, Flournoy hosted the International Congress of Psychology at the University of Geneva, and René was one of the plenary speakers, speaking on the advantages of Esperanto (Joseph 2012: 561). René's dedication of the 1911 book, therefore, appears to reflect more in the way of general respect for a notable figure in the science of the mind than a more specific and more personal link.

References

Flournoy, Théodore. 1900. *From India to the planet Mars.* New York: Harper & Bros. [translation by Daniel B. Vermilye of *Des Indes à la planète Mars*].

Joseph, John E. 2012. *Saussure.* Oxford: Oxford University Press.

Witzig, James S. 1982. Theodore Flournoy – a friend indeed. *Journal of Analytical Psychology* 27. 131–148.

René de Saussure

PRINCIPES LOGIQUES
DE LA
FORMATION DES MOTS

par
René DE SAUSSURE
Privat-docent à l'Université de Genève

GENÈVE
IMPRIMERIE ALBERT KÜNDIG

À M. le Professeur Th. Flournoy

René de Saussure

PRINCIPES LOGIQUES
DE LA
FORMATION DES MOTS

Un mot est le symbole d'une idée. Les idées simples, ou considérées comme telles, sont représentées généralement par des *mots simples*, tels que : «homme», «grand», «table», etc., c'est-à-dire par des mots indécomposables en plusieurs parties. Les idées plus complexes sont représentées par des *mots composés*, tels que : «porte-plume» en français, «Dampfschiff» en allemand, etc., ou par des *mots dérivés*, tels que : «grandeur», «humanité», etc., décomposables en plusieurs parties («hum-an-ité»)

On est donc naturellement conduit à examiner les deux questions suivantes :

1° Etant donné un mot composé, quelle est l'idée complexe représentée par ce mot ? C'est là le problème de *l'analyse des mots composés*.

LOGICAL PRINCIPLES
OF THE
FORMATION OF WORDS

A word is the symbol of an idea. Ideas that are simple, or regarded as such, are generally represented by *simple words,* such as *homme* 'man', *grand* 'tall', *table* 'table', etc. — that is, by words that cannot be decomposed into several parts. More complex ideas are represented by *compound words,* such as *porte-plume* 'penholder' in French, *Dampfschiff* 'steamship' in German, etc., or by *derived words* such as *grandeur* 'size, height', *humanité* 'humanity', etc. which can be decomposed into several parts (*hum-an-ité*).

We are thus naturally led to examine the following two questions:

1° Given a compound word, what is the complex idea that this word represents? This is the problem of *the analysis of compound words.*

2° Etant donnée une idée complexe, quel est le mot composé qui la représente ? C'est le problème de la *synthèse des mots composés*.

Pour résoudre ce double problème, il faut des données ; ces données sont les mots simples. Peu importe, du reste, la forme de ces mots simples : que l'on dise «homme», comme en français, ou «Mensch», comme en allemand, pour symboliser l'idée «homme», cela ne modifie en rien les lois qui régissent la formation des mots. Peu importe aussi l'étymologie des mots simples ; ces questions peuvent intéresser le linguiste, mais pour le logicien les mots simples sont des données conventionnelles analogues aux symboles mathématiques, et ce qui importe, c'est la définition de chaque symbole, c'est-à-dire l'*idée* représentée par chaque mot simple.

Les principes logiques de la formation des mots sont donc les mêmes pour toutes les langues, du moins pour toutes celles qui partent des mêmes éléments primitifs. Ainsi, dans nos langues européennes (les seules dont je m'occuperai), il y a deux sortes d'éléments primitifs : les *mots-radicaux*, tels que : «homme», «grand», etc., et les *affixes*, tels que : «iste» (dans «violoniste»), «pré» (dans «prévenir»), etc. Au point de vue logique, il n'y a pas de différence essentielle entre un radical et un affixe ; ceux-ci sont, du reste, souvent

2° Given a complex idea, what is the compound word that represents it? This is the problem of *the synthesis of compound words*.

To resolve this double problem, data are required: these data are the simple words. Apart from that, the form of the simple words does not matter: whether one says *homme* 'man' as in French or *Mensch* as in German to symbolize the idea "man", it does not at all change the laws that govern the formation of words. The etymology of simple words also does not matter; those questions may interest the linguist, but for the logician simple words are conventional givens analogous to mathematical symbols, and what matters is the definition of each symbol, that is the *idea* represented by each simple word.

The logical principles of the formation of words are thus the same for all languages, or at least for all those that begin from the same primitive elements. Thus, in our European languages (the only ones with which I will be concerned), there are two kinds of primitive element: *root words*, such as *homme* 'man', *grand* 'tall', etc., and *affixes*, such as -*iste* (in *violoniste* 'violinist'), *pré* (in *prévenir* 'forwarn' [literally 'precede']), etc. From the logical point of view, there is no essential difference between a root and an affix: these are often

d'anciens radicaux. Il est vrai que la soudure entre un affixe et un radical n'est pas, en général, de meme nature que la soudure entre deux radicaux, mais cela ne tient pas à une différence spécifique entre les affixes et les radicaux; cela tient à d'autres causes que nous examinerons plus loin.

On peut donc considérer les affixes comme des mots simples, et les mots dérivés au moyen d'affixes, comme de véritables mots composés. Il n'y a plus alors que deux sortes de mots : les *mots simples* (radicaux, préfixes, suffixes), et les *mots composés* par combinaison de mots simples.

On peut comparer un mot composé à une molécule construite au moyen de trois sortes d'atomes (radicaux, préfixes, suffixes); l'analyse et la synthèse logique des mots est alors comparable à l'étude d'une molécule dont les atomes sont connus, et le double problème que nous cherchons à résoudre peut s'énoncer : «Trouver l'idée exprimée par une molécule donnée», ou réciproquement «construire la molécule représentant une idée donnée».

Or, la condition essentielle pour que ce problème soit susceptible d'une solution logique et précise est que *les atomes* (radicaux, préfixes et suffixes) *qui représentent les matériaux primitifs de la formation des mots soient des éléments absolument invariables et indépendants*, dont on connaît exactement le contenu individuel, c'est-à-dire qu'il faut

former roots. It is true that the juncture between an affix and a root is not in general of the same type as the juncture between two roots, but that has nothing to do with a specific difference between affixes and roots; it has other causes that we will examine below.

We can therefore consider affixes as simple words, and words derived by means of an affix as real compound words. There are then only two sorts of word: *simple words* (roots, prefixes, suffixes) and *compound words* formed by combining simple words.

A compound word can be compared to a molecule built by means of three sorts of atoms (roots, prefixes, suffixes); the analysis of the logical synthesis of words is thus comparable to the study of a molecule of which the atoms are known, and the double problem which we are trying to solve can be formulated as "Find the idea that a given molecule expresses" or inversely "construct the molecule that represents a given idea."

Now the essential condition for this problem to be subject to a logical and precise solution is that *the atoms* (roots, prefixes, suffixes) *that represent the basic material for word formation should be absolutely invariant and independent elements,* whose individual content is known exactly. That is, it is necessary

que le sens et le contenu de chaque radical ou affixe reste toujours le même, quelles que soient les circonstances particulières où il se trouve. Cela signifie que dans une molécule comme, par exemple, «grandeur», composée de plusieurs atomes (radical «grand», suffixe «eur»), l'atome «grand» est exactement le même mot que l'adjectif «grand» considéré isolément[1].

Le but de la présente étude est précisément de montrer qu'à part quelques exceptions qui, du reste, ne sont qu'apparentes, il en est bien ainsi dans les langues naturelles et que, par conséquent, il est possible d'établir une théorie logique et précise du mécanisme de la formation des mots.

---

[1]Il est bien entendu que le principe de l'invariabilité des atomes se rapporte non à la forme extérieure, mais au sens de ces atomes. Ainsi, dans les mots *homme, humain, humanité,* l'atome *homme* se transforme en *hum* et l'atome *ain* devient *an* ; mais ces atomes, variables de forme, sont invariables de sens, c'est-à-dire que dans le mot *hum-an-ité,* l'atome *hum* est exactement le même mot que le substantif *homme* considéré isolément. Les causes qui ont ici transformé les atomes réguliers *homme, ain* en *hum* et *an* sont d'ordre purement physiologique et peuvent intéresser le philologue, non le logicien. Du reste, cette variation de forme des atomes ne se produit guère que dans les langues latines. Dans les langues germaniques, slaves, etc., les atomes restent presque toujours invariables de sens et de forme. Ex. : *Mensch, mensch-lich, Mensch-lich-keit.*

that the sense and content of each root or affix should always remain the same, whatever the particular circumstances in which it is found. This means that in a molecule such as, for example, *grandeur* 'size, height', composed of multiple atoms (root *grand* 'large, tall', suffix *eur* '-ness'), the atom *grand* is exactly the same word as the adjective *grand* considered in isolation.[1]

The aim of the present work is precisely to show that apart from some exceptions which are, however, only apparent, this is indeed the case in natural languages, and that consequently it is possible to establish a logical and precise theory of the mechanism of word formation.

---

[1]It is to be understood that the principle of the invariability of atoms relates not to the exterior form, but to the sense of these atoms. Thus, in the words *homme* 'man', *humain* 'human', *humanité* 'humanity', the atom *homme* is transformed into *hum* and the atom *ain* becomes *an*; but these atoms, while variable in form, are invariant in sense. That is, in the word *hum-an-ité*, the atom *hum* is exactly the same word as the noun *homme* considered by itself. The causes that have transformed the regular atoms *homme, ain* into *hum* and *an* are of a purely physiological order, and may interest the philologist but not the logician. On the other hand, this variation in form of atoms is almost exclusive to the Romance languages. In the Germanic, Slavic, etc. languages, the atoms are almost always invariable in sense and in form. E.g. *Mensch* 'man', *mensch-lich* 'human', *Mensch-lich-keit* 'humanity'.

CHAPITRE PREMIER

ANALYSE DES MOTS

Le problème principal à résoudre est le suivant : *Etant donne un mot composé* (c'est-à-dire une combinaison de radicaux, de préfixes et de suffixes), *trouver l'idée totale représentée par ce mot.*

Invariabilité des éléments. — De même qu'un tout est l'ensemble de ses parties, *l'idée totale représentée par un mot composé est l'ensemble ou, si l'on veut, la résultante des idées partielles représentées par les différentes parties de ce mot.* Cette vérité semble évidente, mais il ne faut pas oublier qu'elle présuppose *l'invariabilité* de sens et *l'indépendance* des divers éléments ou atomes qui entrent dans la composition du mot à analyser. L'analyse logique des mots n'est possible que si les symboles sur lesquels on opère sont des éléments invariables ; ainsi le sens, la valeur d'un atome, ne doit dépendre que de lui-même et nullement du sens ou de la valeur des atomes qui l'environnent. On peut dire

FIRST CHAPTER

THE ANALYSIS OF WORDS

The principal problem to be solved is the following: *Given a compound word* (that is, a combination of roots, prefixes and suffixes), *find the total idea this word represents.*

Invariability of the elements. — Just as a whole is the totality of its parts, *the entire idea represented by a compound word is the totality, or if you will, the resultant of the partial ideas represented by the different parts of the word.* This truth seems obvious, but it is necessary not to forget that it presupposes the *invariability* of sense and the *independence* of the various elements that enter into the composition of the word to be analyzed. The logical analysis of words is only possible if the symbols with which we work are invariant elements; thus the sense, the value of an atom, must depend only on itself and not at all on the sense or the value of the atoms that surround it. It can be said

alors que *le sens d'un mot composé ne dépend que de son propre contenu et de tout son contenu,* c'est-à-dire du contenu de ses différentes parties considérées isolément.

RÈGLES DE DÉRIVATION. — Il n'est donc pas besoin d'établir des *règles de dérivation* reliant l'un à l'autre le sens des mots d'une même famille (comme «homme», «humain», «humanité»; «couronne», «couronner», «couronnement»), car on crée ainsi des liens artificiels entre des atomes qui devraient rester indépendants et interchangeables comme les différentes pièces d'une machine.

Il faut chercher le sens logique d'un mot quelconque dans le mot lui-même et non pas dans la manière dont ce mot semble dérivé d'un autre mot. Dériver un mot d'un autre, c'est simplement ajouter un ou plusieurs atomes au mot primitif ; par exemple, substantifier un adjectif, c'est ajouter à cet adjectif un atome contenant l'idée substantive ; ainsi, en ajoutant au mot «homme» les atomes «ain» et «ité», on obtient le mot «humanité», dont le sens est connu dès que l'on connaît le sens et la valeur des trois atomes qui composent ce mot et sans que l'on ait à se préoccuper d'autre chose.

then that *the sense of a compound word depends only on its own content and on all of its content,* that is on the content of its different parts considered in isolation.

RULES OF DERIVATION. — There is thus no need to establish *rules of derivation* linking to each other the senses of words belonging to the same family (such as *homme* 'man', *humain* 'human', *humanité* 'humanity'; *couronne* 'crown (n.)', *couronner* '(to) crown', *couronnement* 'coronation'), because that would create artificial links between atoms that must remain independent and interchangeable like the different parts of a machine.

It is necessary to look for the logical sense of any word whatsoever in the word itself, and not in the way the word seems to be derived from another word. To derive one word from another is simply to add one or more atoms to the basic word; for example, to nominalize an adjective is to add to the adjective an atom that contains a nominal idea; thus, in adding to the word *homme* the atoms *ain* and *ité*, we get the word *humanité*, whose sense is known once we know the sense and the value of the three atoms which compose this word and without having to be concerned with anything else.

13

§ 1. — The study of atoms.

Atoms are the simple words (roots, prefixes and suffixes) that constitute the invariable elements by means of which compound words are built.

Every simple word represents an idea. This idea is more or less specific, more or less general,[1] but the different ideas are not independent of one another; they are not juxtaposed like beads on a string; they form hierarchies, or more precisely, they fit together with one another in passing from the specific to the general. That is, every specific idea contains *implicitly* in itself a series of more and more general ideas that it leads to as soon as one apprehends it. An atom thus does not represent simply an isolated specific idea, but an entire series of more general ideas, even though these are not explicitly expressed. This remark is important: it is this that makes it possible to consider the sense of a compound word

---

[1] We can say roughly that affixes represent more general ideas than roots. Effectively, the more general an idea, the more frequent it is in discourse. Words that represent general ideas thus tend to be transformed into suffixes or prefixes, precisely because of their frequent repetition.

composé comme ne dépendant que du sens individuel de ses différents éléments, car nous verrons que les idées générales sous-entendues jouent, dans l'analyse des mots, un rôle aussi important que les idées particulières exprimées par les mots simples. Il est donc nécessaire de bien se rendre compte de tout ce que contient un atome, soit extérieurement, soit intérieurement.

Prenons, par exemple, le mot radical «cheval» : ce mot représente une idée particulière ; c'est la partie *apparente* de l'atome. Mais cette idée particulière contient en elle-même d'autres idées plus générales. Ainsi, si nous nous plaçons, par exemple, au point de vue zoologique, l'idée «cheval» contient celle de «animal mammifère», qui contient elle-même celle de «animal vertébré», qui contient à son tour celle de «animal», qui contient celle de «un être réel» (personne ou chose), qui contient enfin l'idée de «un être» tout court, de «quelque chose qui est, qui existe», soit réellement, soit idéellement. L'idée d'«un être» est tellement générale qu'elle n'en contient plus d'autres ; c'est ce qu'on appelle *l'idée substantive* .

Ainsi, dire que le mot «cheval» est un substantif, c'est dire simplement que l'idée la plus générale sous-entendue dans le mot «cheval» est l'idée de «un être», de «quelque chose qui est». Mais il faut remarquer, à ce propos, que cette idée comprend

as depending only on the individual sense of its different elements, because we will see that the understood general ideas play a role in the analysis of words that is as important as the specific ideas expressed by the simple words. It is thus necessary to take account of everything that is contained in an atom, either externally or internally.

Let us take, for example, the root word *cheval* 'horse': this word represents a specific idea, which is the *evident* part of the atom. But that specific idea contains other more general ideas within it. Thus, if we take for example the zoological point of view, the idea *cheval* contains that of *animal mammifère* 'mammalian animal', which itself contains that of *animal vertébré* 'vertebrate animal', which in turn contains the that of *animal* 'animal', which contains that of *un être réel* 'an actual being' (person or thing), which finally contains the idea simply of *un être* 'a being', *quelque chose qui est, qui existe* 'something that is, that exists' either in reality or ideally. The idea of *un être* is so general that it does not contain anything further: it is what we call *the nominal idea*.

Thus, to say that the word *cheval* is a noun is simply to say that the most general idea understood in the word *cheval* is the idea of *un être, quelque chose qui est*. But it is necessary to note in that connection that this idea includes

not only entities that are real, or concrete by nature (such as *homme* 'man', *table* 'table', etc.) but also entities that are ideal, or abstract in their nature[1] (such as for instance *théorie* 'theory', *genre* 'type', *science* 'science'), that is mental entities created by man, who has abstracted them from reality for the purposes of language. In other words, nouns correspond not only to the entities that form the substance of the Cosmos, but also to those that form that of language.[2]

---

[1] I use the words "real" and "ideal" because we cannot classify nouns by the notions of "concrete" and "abstract", notions that have only relative value (like the notions "specific" and "general"), since the same word can always be taken in a concrete sense and in an abstract sense. We can say, however, that *real* beings (persons or things) are concrete in their nature; their basic sense is concrete and the abstract sense is only derived. On the other hand, for *ideal* beings the basic sense is abstract and the concrete sense is only derived.

[2] The nominal idea can itself be generalized, like any specific idea: the idea of "an entity", real or ideal, contains in itself the more general idea of "an entity" in general, "abstract entity, existant", just as the specific idea "man" contains the more general idea of "man in general", "man" in the abstract sense. We can thus distinguish the specific nominal idea "an entity" from the general nominal idea "entity"; the first contains the second, and thus the final idea which by reason of its generality contains no other is the general nominal idea of "entity in general, abstract entity".

L'idée substantive, l'idée adjective et l'idée verbale sont donc des idées tout à fait semblables aux autres idées ; ce sont seulement celles de nos idées qui sont *les plus générales* et, par conséquent, les plus abstraites. A ce titre, et à ce titre seulement, elles méritent une dénomination spéciale : je les appellerai les *idées grammaticales*. Ces idées sont évidemment abstraites ; l'idée adjective, par exemple, est l'idée générale abstraite des adjectifs particuliers.

Nous venons de voir que lorsqu'on examine les idées de plus en plus générales contenues dans un mot simple comme «cheval», on arrive finalement à une idée grammaticale. *Cette idée caractérise le mot considéré*, c'est-à-dire que le même mot conduit toujours à la même idée grammaticale, quelle que soit la série des idées intermédiaires que l'on interpose. Ainsi, au lieu de considérer un «cheval» comme un animal vertébré, on peut le considérer comme un animal quadrupède, par exemple ; le mot «cheval» n'en restera pas moins substantif, car l'idée «animal quadrupède» est aussi substantive ; elle contient l'idée de «animal» et, par conséquent, aussi celle de «un être réel», et enfin celles de «un être» tout court et de «l'être» en général.

On arrive donc au même résultat final, c'est-à-dire à la même idée grammaticale, que l'on considère l'une ou l'autre des deux séries d'idées sous-entendues :

The nominal idea, the adjectival idea and the verbal idea are thus ideas completely like other ideas: they are simply those of our ideas that are *the most general* and as a consequence, the most abstract. On that basis, and on that basis alone, they deserve a special terminology: I will call them the *grammatical ideas*. These ideas are obviously abstract: the adjectival idea, for example, is the general idea abstracted from specific adjectives.

We have just seen that when we examine the increasingly general ideas contained within a simple word like *cheval* 'horse', we arrive in the end at a grammatical idea. *This idea characterizes the word under consideration*, that is the same word leads always to the same grammatical idea, regardless of the series of intermediate ideas that we put in between. Thus, instead of considering a "horse" as a vertebrate, we could consider it as a quadruped, for example: the word *cheval* would remain nonetheless a noun, since the idea "quadruped animal" is also nominal: it contains the idea "animal" and consequently "real entity", and finally just "an entity" and "entity" in general.

We thus arrive at the same final result, that is at the same grammatical idea, whether we consider the one or the other of the two series of understood ideas:

17

cheval	cheval	horse	horse
(animal mammifère)	*(animal quadrupède)*	*(mammalian animal)*	*(quadruped animal)*
(animal vertébré)	*(animal)*	*(vertebrate animal)*	*(animal)*
(animal)	*(un être réel)*	*(animal)*	*(a real entity)*
(un être réel)	*(un être)*	*(a real entity)*	*(an entity)*
(un être)	*(l'être)*	*(an entity)*	*(entity)*
(l'être)		*(entity)*	

Cette remarque montre que *l'analyse des mots est indépendante de la manière dont on subdivise les idées*; elle est donc aussi indépendante des diverses théories scientifiques ou philosophiques, et dans chaque cas particulier, on emploiera la subdivision qui convient le mieux au point de vue auquel on s'est momentanément placé.

La seule condition nécessaire (et qui d'ailleurs est forcément remplie) est que toutes les idées intercalées entre une idée particulière et l'idée grammaticale correspondante, contiennent elles-mêmes cette idée grammaticale. Autrement dit, si l'idée particulière donnée est, par exemple, substantive, toutes les idées plus générales intercalées entre cette idée et l'idée substantive sont forcément représentées aussi par des substantifs. C'est pourquoi j'ai écrit sous le mot «cheval» : «animal mammifère», «animal vertébré», etc., et non pas simplement «mammifère», «vertébré», etc., car ces mots sont des adjectifs.

This observation shows that *the analysis of words is independent of the way we subdivide the ideas*; it is thus also independent of the various scientific and philosophical theories, and in each specific case we make use of the subdivision that is most suitable from the point of view taken at the moment.

The only necessary condition (which, however, is necessarily fulfilled) is that all of the ideas interposed between a specific idea and the corresponding grammatical idea should themselves contain that grammatical idea. In other words, if the given specific idea is, for example, nominal, all of the more general ideas by which one passes from that idea and the nominal idea should also necessarily be represented by nouns. This is why I have written under the word *horse* "mammalian animal", "vertebrate animal, etc. and not just "mammalian", "vertebrate", etc., since these words are adjectives.

Ce qu'il faut surtout ne pas oublier, c'est que pour l'analyse des mots, *ce sont les idées générales qui sont contenues implicitement dans les idées particulières et non pas les idées particulières qui sont contenues dans les idées générales*, comme on pourrait quelquefois être tenté de le croire. Ainsi, par exemple, c'est l'idée «cheval» qui implique l'idée de «animal» et non pas l'idée «animal» qui implique l'idée «cheval», car tous les chevaux sont des animaux tandis que tous les animaux ne sont pas des chevaux. Dire que l'idée «cheval» contient celle de «animal», cela signifie qu'on n'ajoute rien à l'idée «cheval» en disant «cheval animal»; au contraire, en disant «animal cheval», on ajoute à l'idée «animal» une nouvelle idée qui spécialise la première, car elle signifie «animal, espèce particulière cheval»; on ne doit donc pas considérer l'idée «cheval» comme impliquée dans celle de «animal». En résumé, on peut comparer le dispositif des idées à une carte géographique : représentons les idées grammaticales par des pays indépendants, par exemple l'idée substantive par la France, l'idée adjective par la Grande-Bretagne et l'idée verbale par l'Allemagne. Alors toute idée substantive sera représentée par un endroit ou une région de la France; cet endroit étant d'autant plus petit que	What must especially not be forgotten is that for the analysis of words, *it is the general ideas that are contained implicitly in specific ideas, and not the specific ideas that are contained in general ideas,* as one is sometimes tempted to believe. Thus, for example, it is the idea "horse" that implies the idea "animal", and not the idea "animal" that implies the idea "horse", because all horses are animals but not all animals are horses. To say that the idea "horse" contains that of "animal" means that one adds nothing to the idea "horse" by saying "animal horse": on the contrary, in saying "animal horse" one adds to the idea "animal" a new idea that specializes it, because this means "animal of the particular species horse"; one must thus not consider the idea "horse" as implied in that of "animal". In sum, we can compare the system of ideas to a geographic map: we represent the grammatical ideas by independent countries, for example the nominal idea by France, the adjectival idea by Great Britain and the verbal idea by Germany. Then every nominal idea will be represented by a place or region of France; and the smaller the place,

l'idée en question est plus particulière ; ainsi les villages, les bourgs, les villes de France pourront figurer les idées substantives les plus particulières, tandis que les communes, les départements, les provinces, etc., figureront les idées substantives plus générales.

De même que l'idée «cheval» contient l'idée substantive de «un être», quelles que soient les idées intermédiaires intercalées, de même toute ville française, comme «Caen», contient l'idée «France» quelle que soit la manière dont on subdivise ce pays : si l'on divise la France en provinces, l'idée «Caen» contient l'idée «Normandie» ; si on la divise en départements, l'idée «Caen» contient l'idée «Calvados» ; mais, dans les deux cas, l'idée «France» reste contenue dans «Caen», parce que soit la Normandie, soit le Calvados sont des subdivisions de la France, et les deux schémas :

Caen   Caen
(Normandie)   (Calvados)
(France)   (France)

sont analogues aux deux schémas que nous avons construits pour le mot «cheval». L'analyse des mots est indépendante de la manière dont on subdivise les idées.

the more specific the idea; thus the villages, towns, cities of France can represent the most specific nominal ideas, while the communes, the departments, the provinces will represent more general nominal ideas.

Just as the idea "horse" contains the nominal idea of "an entity" whatever intermediate ideas come between them, so every French city, such as "Caen" contains the idea "France" in whatever way we subdivide this country. If we divide France into provinces, the idea "Caen" contains the idea "Normandy"; if we divide it into departments, the idea "Caen" contains the idea "Calvados"; but in both cases the idea "France" remains contained in "Caen", because either Normandy or Calvados are subdivisions of France, and the two patterns:

Caen   Caen
(Normandy)   (Calvados)
(France)   (France)

are analogous to the two patterns we constructed for the word *cheval* 'horse'. The analysis of words is independent of the way in which we subdivide the ideas.

*
* *

CLASSIFICATION OF ATOMS. — We can classify all atoms (roots and affixes) according to the nature of the most general idea that each contains.

If that most general idea is that of "entity", of "that which is" (the nominal idea), the atom will be classified as a *noun*. For example, *cheval* 'horse' is a nominal atom according to the analysis given above. The suffix *iste* '-ist' (in *violoniste* 'violinist', *artiste* 'artist', etc.) is also a nominal atom, because this suffix designates a "person" (whose profession or habitual occupation is specified by the root to which it is attached); this suffix thus implicitly contains the idea of "a living being", an idea which contains in turn that of simply "an entity" and of "entity" in general (the nominal idea).

When the most general idea contained in an atom is that of "qualifying", the atom will be classified as an *adjective*, because adjectives *qualify* nouns. The abstract adjectival idea is thus the idea expressed by the root word "qual"[1] or by the word

---

[1] From Latin *qualis* 'what sort', from which the noun *qual-ité* 'quality' derives, as opposed to *quantum* 'how many', from which the noun *quant-ité* 'quantity' derives. We manage thus to express the general adjectival idea by an irreducible atom.

«propre», dans le sens[1] de «propre à», «propre à un être»[2].

Pareillement aux atomes substantifs, les atomes adjectifs ont tantôt la forme de radicaux, comme «grand», «riche», «sage», etc., tantôt la forme de suffixes, comme l'atome «able» (dans «louable»). En effet, «able» signifie «pouvant (être)», «digne (d'être)» [loué]; ce suffixe contient donc bien une idée qualificative, car «pouvant», «digne», sont des adjectifs.

Enfin, si l'idée la plus générale contenue dans un atome est l'idée *dynamique* de «faire une action» ou l'idée *statique* de «être dans un état», l'atome sera classé comme *verbal*[3]. On peut représenter ces deux formes de l'idée verbale par les simples mots «agir» (ou «faire») et «être» (au sens statique, en

"characteristic, proper" in the sense[1] of "characteristic of, proper to", "characteristic of an entity"[2].

Parallel to nominal atoms, adjectival atoms have sometimes the form of roots, such as *grand* 'large, tall', *riche* 'rich', *sage* 'wise', etc., and sometimes the form of suffixes, such as the atom *able* (in *louable* 'commendable'). Actually, *able* means "capable (of being)", "worthy (of being)" [praised]. This suffix thus does contain a qualifying idea, since "capable", "worthy", are adjectives.

Finally, if the most general idea contained in an atom is the *dynamic* idea of "perform an action" or the *static* idea of "be in a state", the atom will be classed as *verbal*[3]. We can represent these two forms of the verbal idea by the simple words "(to) act" (or "(to) do") and "(to) be" (in the static sense of

---

[1] Il n'y a, en effet, guère de différence entre les «qualités» et les «propriétés» d'un être. Elles désignent «ce qui est qual» dans cet être, ou «ce qui est propre» à cet être. En allemand, «propre» se dit «eigen» et l'*adjectif* est dénommé «Eigenschaftswort».

[2] Dans l'expression «propre à un être», l'idée adjective est exprimée par le seul atome «propre»; le reste n'est qu'explicatif et indique simplement comment l'adjectif «propre» doit être uni au substantif, à l'être qu'il qualifie.

[3] Dans toute cette étude, je n'emploierai le mot verbal que comme adjectif du mot «verbe» opposé à «substantif» ou «adjectif», et non du mot «verbe» dans le sens de «parole» (λογος).

[1] In fact, there is hardly any difference between the "qualities" and the "properties" of an entity. They designate "that which is qual" in this entity, or "that which is characteristic" of this entity. In German, "characteristic" is *eigen* and the *adjective* is called *Eigenschaftswort*.

[2] In the expression "proper to an entity", the adjectival idea is expressed by the single atom "proper"; the rest is only explanatory and simply indicates how the adjective "proper" must be linked with the noun, with the entity which it qualifies.

[3] Throughout this work, I will only use the word verbal as the adjective related to the word "verb" as opposed to "noun" or "adjective", and not to the homophonous French word with the sense "language" (λογος).

Latin *stare*), but these words still contain the verbal endings *ir* and *re* which indicate only the infinitive, such that they have no use from the perspective of logic: to express the idea contained in these words, the roots *ag* 'act' (or *fai* 'do') and *sta* (or *êt*) 'be' are sufficient. We thus come to represent the abstract verbal idea by the irreducible atom *act* for active verbs and *be* for neuter (stative) verbs. We will show below, besides, that the idea "to perform an action" reduces to the atom *act* (to act) and that the idea "to be in a state", or literally, in a "station", reduces to the atom *be* (*stare*)[1].

Just as with nominal atoms and adjectival atoms, verbal atoms are sometimes roots, such as *abonn* (*abonner* 'to subscribe'), *écri* (*écrire* 'to write'), *dorm* (*dormir* 'to sleep'), etc., and sometimes suffixes, such as *is* '-ize' (in *modern-is-er* 'to modernize'), or *ifi* '-ify' (in *béat-ifi-er* 'to beatify'), etc. These suffixes actually contain a dynamic idea: *moderniser* means 'to make modern', *béatifier* 'to make holy'.

We are thus led naturally to classify atoms (roots and affixes) as belonging to three main classes: the class of nominal atoms,

---

[1] There is the same logical relation between *état* (or *estat*) 'state' and *station* (or *estation*) 'station' as between *acte* 'act' and *action* 'action'. Furthermore, in English one says regularly "state", "station" and "act", "action".

qui contiennent implicitement l'idée de «l'être» ou «ce qui est»; celle des atomes adjectifs, qui contiennent l'idée «qual» ou «propre (à)», et celle des atomes verbaux, qui contiennent l'idée «ag» ou «sta».

Ceci revient à considérer tous les atomes substantifs comme des cas particuliers de l'atome substantif général «l'(être)», «un être», en latin *ens*, ou «ce (qui est)»; tous les atomes adjectifs comme des cas particuliers de l'atome adjectif général «qual» ou «propre (à)», et tous les atomes verbaux comme des cas particuliers de l'atome verbal général «ag» ou «sta». On peut donc établir une classification des mots simples en trois colonnes correspondant respectivement aux trois rubriques : «ens», «qual» et «ag». Cette classification est indispensable pour l'analyse et la synthèse logique des mots. Elle a pour but d'associer à l'idée particulière exprimée explicitement par un atome, une idée grammaticale (implicite) et *une seule*.

Il y a, en effet, des cas où l'on serait tenté d'attribuer à un même atome deux idées générales différentes : on prend souvent, par exemple, un adjectif dans un sens substantif, en disant «un riche» pour «homme riche», «le beau» pour «l'être idéel *beau*», «abstraction *beau*» (beauté), etc. Mais il est bien évident que dans ces expressions l'article «un» est l'atome substantificateur, car il remplace un substantif sous-entendu; on dit, par exemple,

which contain implicitly the idea of "entity" or "that which is"; that of adjectival atoms, which contain the idea "qual" or "property of", and that of verbal atoms, which contain the idea "act" or "be".

This comes down to considering all nominal atoms as special cases of the general nominal atom "entity", "an entity", in Latin *ens*, or "that which is"; all adjectival atoms as special cases of the general adjectival atom "qual" or "property (of)", and all verbal atoms as special cases of the general verbal atom "act" or "be". We can thus set up a classification of simple words in three columns corresponding respectively to the three rubrics "ens", "qual" and "act". This classification is indispensable for the logical analysis and synthesis of words. Its goal is to associate with the specific idea expressed explicitly by an atom an (implicit) grammatical idea and *only one*.

There are actually cases in which we would be tempted to attribute to the same atom two different general ideas: an adjective is often used, for example, in a nominal sense, as when we say *un riche* 'a rich (person)' for *homme riche* 'rich man', *le beau* 'the beautiful' for *l'être idéel beau*, *abstraction beau* (*beauté* 'beauty'), etc. But it is quite obvious that in these expressions the article *un* 'a' is the nominalizing atom, because it replaces an understood noun; we say, for example,

«*un* avare» (pour «homme avare»), «*un* vertébré» (pour animal vertébré»), «*un* désert» (pour «lieu désert»), «*un* vide» (pour «espace vide»), etc. Ces formes échappent à l'analyse logique, parce que l'article «un» ne peut représenter par lui-même que l'idée substantive «un être» (réel ou idéel), et non pas un être particulier comme «homme», «lieu», etc.; l'analyse logique n'est possible que si l'on rétablit le substantif sous-entendu. Si, au contraire, on emploie l'article défini «le» devant un adjectif, l'analyse logique est facile, car «le» équivaut à «l'(être)» en général, «l'être idéel», abstrait de la réalité, par exemple «*le* beau», «*le* noir», etc.; de même dans les expressions substantives tirées de verbes, comme «*le* manger», «*le* boire», «*le* dormir»[1].

---

[1]Pour trouver la vraie signification d'un mot, simple ou composé, il faut considérer ce mot *isolément*, sans y ajouter ni article, ni autre chose. On voit alors clairement que les atomes «beau», «riche», etc., sont des atomes adjectifs. Il y a cependant quelques cas douteux (comme le mot «logique» par exemple), que nous examinerons plus loin.

De même, quand nous disons que «le beau» signifie «l'être idéel, l'être abstrait beau» ou «beauté», nous entendons par là l'expression «le beau» prise isolément et sans contexte, car il est bien entendu que si dans le contexte on a parlé d'un «homme beau» ou du «beau temps», l'expression «le beau» pourrait se rapporter à cet homme ou au temps. En résumé, lorsqu'il n'y a pas de contexte, l'article «le» ne peut signifier que «l'être» en général et l'article «un», «un être quelconque» (réel ou idéel).

<u>un</u> avare 'a miser' (for *homme avare* 'miserly man'), <u>un</u> vertébré 'a vertebrate' (for *animal vetébré* 'vertebrate animal'), <u>un</u> désert 'a desert' (for *lieu désert* 'deserted place'), <u>un</u> vide 'an emptiness' (for *éspace vide* 'empty space'), etc. These forms elude logical analysis, because the article *un* 'a' by itself can only represent the nominal idea "an entity" (real or ideal), and not a specific entity such as "man," "place," etc. The logical analysis is only possible by re-establishing the understood noun. If by contrast the definite article *le* 'the' is used before an adjective, the logical analysis is straightforward, because *le* is equivalent to *l'être* 'the entity' in general, the ideal entity, abstracted from reality, such as <u>le</u> *beau* 'the beautiful', <u>le</u> *noir* 'the black', etc.; similarly for nominal expressions derived from verbs, such as <u>le</u> *manger* '(the) food', <u>le</u> *boire* '(the) drink', <u>le</u> *dormir* '(the) sleep'.[1]

---

[1]To determine the true meaning of a word, simple or compound, it is necessary to consider the word *in isolation*, without adding an article or anything else. It is then clearly to be seen that the atoms *beau* 'beautiful', *riche* 'rich', etc. are adjectival atoms. There are, however, some doubtful cases (like the word *logique* 'logic(al)' for example) which we will examine below.

Similarly, when we say that *le beau* means 'the ideal entity, the abstract beautiful entity' or 'beauty', we mean thereby the expression *le beau* taken in isolation and without context, because it is clear that if in context there has been talk of an *homme beau* 'handsome man' or of *beau temps* 'nice weather', the expression *le beau* can refer to that man or that weather. In brief, when there is no context, the article *le* can only mean 'the entity' in general, and the article *un* 'any entity' (real or ideal).

There are no specific ideas assumed here: the article *le* 'the' contains only the general, and therefore abstract, nominal idea, and *by virtue of the principle of the invariability of atoms,* the expression *le beau* 'the beautiful' must be considered as a compound word, that is, as a bi-atomic molecule equivalent to *beau-té* 'beau-ty'. The affixes *le* and *té* are both effectively atoms that represent only the general nominal idea, that of 'entity in general,' 'entity' abstracted from reality. We can say that the word *beauté* is a *condensed* molecule (the synthetic form), while the expression *le beau* is a *dissociated* molecule (the analytic form). We will see what relations there are between a dissociated molecule and the same molecule in the condensed state; for the moment, let us only note that the principle of the invariability of atoms is applicable to dissociated molecules just as it is to condensed molecules, that is, in the molecule *le beau* as in *beau-té*, the atom *beau* is and remains purely adjectival. This atom contains in itself only the adjectival idea "qual"; it is not an entity, but only an attribute proper to an entity.

We thus see how important the classification of atoms is, since the general idea contained in an atom depends on that classification and thus also the internal sense of the atom.

This classification has a character that is more or less arbi[trary:]

[arbi]trary: thus, the word *gaieté* 'gaiety' is derived from the adjective *gai* 'gay'; the word *joie* 'joy', however, is a noun root; but once the classification is made, it must be definitive, since the sense of derived words in which this atom plays a part depends in part on that classification.

THE BASIC ATOMS — Before classifying all specific atoms according to the general (or grammatical) idea contained in each, it is best to classify separately all those atoms which contain no specific idea, but only one of the three grammatical ideas (nominal, adjectival or verbal), since the three atoms *le* (entity), "qual" and "ag" are not the only ones that can express these three general ideas. These are often also expressed by suffixes or otherwise: those suffixes are thus *synonyms* of one of the three root atoms *le*, "qual" or "ag".

The three grammatical ideas are the basic ideas, by virtue of their generality. I will thus designate as *basic atom* any atom (root or affix) which contains nothing but a grammatical idea. These atoms serve as types for the others, because their composition is completely simple. In effect, the more general an idea is, the less it contains understood ideas that are more general. The basic atoms thus contain only a single idea (the grammatical idea), and can

contenir rien d'autre, puisqu'il n'existe pas d'idée plus générale, plus abstraite, que les idées grammaticales.

Examinons séparément chacun des trois groupes d'atomes fondamentaux :

1. *Atomes fondamentaux adjectifs* : les suffixes «ain» (dans «humain»), «el» (dans «industriel»), «ique» (dans «périodique»), «eux» (dans «fameux»), etc., ne contiennent que l'idée adjective générale. Ce sont donc des synonymes du radical adjectif général «qual», c'est-à-dire qu'ils sont interchangeables avec ce radical ; ainsi, par exemple, «hum-ain» = «hom-qual» et «hum-an-ité» = «hom-qual-ité».

Il y a encore d'autres atomes équivalents à l'idée adjective. L'adjectif est souvent un simple génitif ; ainsi «une main humaine» signifie «une main d'homme», de sorte que la préposition génitive «de», «d'(un être)[»], doit être traitée comme un atome adjectif fondamental. Cet atome ne diffère des suffixes «ain», «eux», etc., que par sa position dans la molécule, car il précède, au lieu de suivre, l'atome qu'il qualifie. D'autre part, la préposition «de» n'est pas un préfixe, car elle n'est pas soudée au mot auquel elle se rapporte ; on peut dire que c'est un *suffixe dissocié*, car cette préposition forme des molécules dissociées comme «d'homme», molécules dans lesquelles elle joue le même rôle que le

contain nothing more, since there is no idea that is more general, more abstract than the grammatical ideas.

Let us examine separately each of the three groups of basic atoms:

1. *Basic adjectival atoms*: The suffixes *ain* (in *humain* 'human'), *el* (in *industriel* 'industrial'), *ique* (in *périodique* 'periodic'), *eux* (in *fameux* 'famous'), etc. contain only the general adjectival idea. They are thus synonyms of the general root adjective "qual"; that is, they are interchangeable with that root. Thus, *hum-ain* = "hom-qual" and *hum-an-ité* = "hom-qual-ité".

There are still other atoms that are equivalent to the adjectival idea. The adjective is often a simple genitive: thus, *une main humaine* 'a human hand' means *une main d'une homme* 'a hand of a man', such that the genitive preposition *de* 'of', *d'(un être)* 'of (an entity)' must be treated as a basic adjectival atom. This atom differs from the suffixes *ain, eux,* etc. only by its position within the molecule, since it precedes rather than following the atom that it qualifies. On the other hand, *de* is not a prefix, because it is not bound to the word it relates to. We can say that it is a *dissociated suffix*, since this preposition forms dissociated molecules like *d'homme* 'of man', molecules in which it plays the same role as the

suffix *ain* in the condensed molecule *humain* 'human'. Effectively, we have *d'homme* = *humain*, just as *de qualité* 'of quality' is the adjective from the noun *qualité* 'quality', which is itself taken from the adjective "qual"; we thus have *de qualité* = "qual[1]". Thus, for example, *un bâton de fer* 'a stick of iron' = *un bâton ferr-eux* 'an iron stick' or also *de qualité fer (fer-qual)* '[a stick] with iron properties'.

Finally, as a basic adjectival atom, there is the word *qui* 'who, which', *qui (est)* 'which (is)', *qui (a l'être)* 'which (the entity has)'. Thus, *ac-tif* 'active' = *qui ag(-it)* 'which acts', *pallia-tif* 'palliative' = *qui pallie* 'which allays, moderates'. The word *qui* is also equivalent to the ending of the participle when this is taken in an adjectival sense: thus, *aim-ant* 'lov-ing' = *qui aime* 'who loves', *diffèr-ent* = *qui diffère* 'which differs'. *Aimant* is the condensed form, *qui aime* is the dissociated form, and we see that the atom *qui* is another dissociated or displaced suffix, like the preposition *de*. Further proof that the atom *qui (est)* contains only the general adjectival idea is that nothing is added to an adjective when this atom is attached: thus, we have *beau* = *qui (est) beau*, *le grand arbre* 'the tall tree' = *l'arbre qui (est) grand* 'the tree which (is) tall'[2], etc.

---

[1] Effectively, the family "qual", *qualité, de qualité* is analogous to the family *beau* 'beautiful', *beauté* 'beauty', *beautiful* (in English). We have *de qualité* = "qual", just as *beautiful* = *beau*, because the second derivation (adjectivalization of a noun) is exactly the inverse of the first (nominalization of an adjective).

[2] Or again *l'arbre qui (a l'être) grand, qui a de la grandeur,* 'the tree which (has) tallness, which has height', since *le grand, l'être ideel "grand"* = *grandeur* 'height'.

Même dans une phrase comme «Socrate est sage», il suffit de remplacer ce qui est sous-entendu [«Socrate est un (homme) sage»] pour pouvoir ajouter l'atome «qui (est)» sans rien changer au sens de la phrase : «Socrate est un (homme) qui est sage».

L'expression «qui est» placée devant un adjectif est un simple pléonasme, une répétition de l'idée adjective générale, tout comme un suffixe verbal placé après un radical verbal n'est qu'une répétition de l'idée verbale déjà contenue dans ce radical, c'est-à-dire que *beau* = *qui est beau*, comme *écri* = *écri-re*. Au contraire, devant un verbe ou un substantif, l'atome adjectif «qui» ou «qui (est)», «qui (a l'être)», reprend toute sa valeur qualificative ; ainsi «qui aime» ne signifie pas «aim» ou «aimer», mais «aim-ant», de même «qui est homme» ne signifie pas «homme», mais «humain» ; par exemple, *un être humain* = *un être qui est homme*. Il faut seulement ne pas confondre l'atome adjectif «qui (est)» avec l'atome substantif «ce (qui est)» ; ce dernier désigne «l'être», tandis que le premier ne désigne qu'un attribut de l'être ; il y a la même différence entre «qui est» et «ce qui est» qu'entre «beau» et «le beau».

On voit que l'idée adjective générale peut être représentée par beaucoup d'atomes différents, tous synonymes entre eux, c'est-à-dire interchangeables les uns avec les autres au point de vue logique. Si

Even in a sentence like "Socrates is wise," it suffices to replace what is understood ["Socrates is a wise (man)"] to be able to add the atom *qui est* 'who (is)' without changing anything in the meaning of the sentence: "Socrates is a (man) who is wise."

The expression *qui est* 'who/which is' before an adjective is simply a pleonasm, a repetition of the general adjectival idea, just as a verbal suffix placed after a verbal root is only a repetition of the verbal idea already contained in the root. That is, *beau* 'beautiful' = *qui est beau* 'who is beautiful', just as *écri-* 'write (root)' = *écrire* '(to) write (infinitive)'. In contrast, before a verb or a noun, the adjectival atom *qui* or *qui (est), qui (a 'l'être)* 'who/which (is), which (the entity has)' recovers all of its qualifying value. Thus *qui aime* 'who loves' does not mean *aim-* 'love (root)' or *aimer* 'to love', but rather *aim-ant* 'loving', just as *qui est homme* 'who is (a) man' means not *homme* 'man', but *humain* 'human'; for example, *un être humain* 'a human being' = *un être qui est homme* 'a being that is (a) man'. It is only required not to confuse the adjectival atom *qui (est)* with the nominal atom *ce (qui est)* 'that (which is)'. The latter designates an "entity", while the former designates only an attribute of an entity. The difference between *qui est* and *ce qui est* is the same as between *beau* 'beautiful' and *le beau* 'the beautiful'.

We see that the general adjectival idea can be represented by a number of different atoms, all synonyms of each other, that is, interchangeable with one another from the point of view of logic. If

donc on représente l'idée adjective par le symbole spécial **a**, on peut écrire :

Idée adjective a=atomes-radicaux : *qual, propre* (à);
        = » suffixes : *ain, el, ique, eux,* etc.;
        = » suffixes dissociés : *de, qui* (est), *qui* (a l'étre).

Ces atomes sont interchangeables : ainsi l'idée adjective **a** ajoutée au substantif *homme* donne l'une quelconque des molécules bi-atomiques suivantes : **hom-a** = *hum-ain* = *hom-qual* (molécules condensées) ou : *propre* (à l')*homme, d'homme, qui* (est) *homme, qui* (a l'être) *homme* (molécules dissociées).

2. *Atomes fondamentaux substantifs.* — Jusqu'ici nous avons représenté l'idée substantive par les expressions «l'être» ou «ce qui est». Ces expressions contiennent ou semblent contenir plusieurs atomes, c'est-à-dire qu'elles ont l'apparence d'une molécule. Or, les idées grammaticales, servant de base aux idées particulières, doivent être représentées par des atomes irréductibles (radicaux ou suffixes) pouvant servir de modèles aux atomes particuliers. Ce n'est qu'après avoir défini et classé tous les atomes, que l'on peut entreprendre la construction des molécules composées de plusieurs atomes pour exprimer des idées plus complexes. La théorie

therefore we represent the adjectival idea by the special symbol **a**, we can write:

Adjective idea a=atom-roots: *qual, specific* (to);
        = " suffixes: *an, ial, ic, ous,* etc.;
        = " dissociated suffixes: *of, which* (is), *which* (it has).

These atoms are interchangeable: thus, the adjectival idea **a** added to the noun *homme* 'man' gives any one of following bi-atomic molecules: **hom-a** = *hum-ain* 'human' = *hom-qual* (condensed molecules) or *propre* (a l')*homme* 'specific (to the) man', *d'homme* 'of man, *qui (est) homme* 'which (is) man', *qui (a l'être) homme* 'which (the entity) man (has)' (dissociated molecules).

2. *Basic nominal atoms.* — Up to this point we have represented the nominal idea by the expressions *l'être* 'the entity' or *ce qui est* 'that which is'. These expressions contain or appear to contain several atoms, that is, they have the appearance of a molecule. Now the grammatical ideas, serving as the bases of specific ideas, must be represented by irreducible atoms (roots or suffixes) capable of serving as models for specific atoms. It is only after having defined and classified all of the atoms that we can undertake the construction of molecules composed of several atoms to express more complex ideas. The [atomic] theory

atomic [theory] of the formation of words only has force if we start from irreducible atoms. Indeed, if we were to define the fundamental ideas by polyatomic molecules, we would fall into a vicious circle and the theory itself would collapse, because we cannot define word-atoms by word-molecules. It is the molecules that must be defined by the atoms that they contain. As there are specific atoms and general atoms, we can fit specific atoms into the general atoms, but that is all. Thus in the end, the last resort, the irreducible basis of the analysis of words is the [set of] general or basic atoms which represent the grammatical ideas. These atoms must have a completely simple form: that is why we have shown that the expression *de qualité* 'with the quality', which represents the general adjectival idea, only has the appearance of a polyatomic molecule: in reality this expression reduces to the atom "qual". The adjectival idea has thus been defined by completely irreducible elements, such as the roots "qual", *propre* 'proper (to)', or the suffixes *ain, ique, eux* etc.

Similarly, the expressions *l'être* 'the entity', *ce qui est* 'that which is', which express the nominal idea, only have the appearance of dissociated polyatomic molecules. In reality, the verb *être* 'to be' in these expressions has only an explanatory role; it is the atoms *le* 'the'

(article) et «ce» (pronom) qui indiquent vraiment l'idée substantive ; ces atomes sont des substantificateurs : dans l'expression «l'être», l'affixe «l'» ou «le» substantifie le verbe «être» (exister), comme il substantifie l'adjectif «beau» dans l'expression «le beau» (beau-té).

Mais il y a beaucoup d'autres atomes représentant l'idée substantive. Les atomes «le», «ce» représentent l'idée substantive sous sa forme la plus générale, la plus abstraite (l'être). Pour représenter l'idée substantive particulière sous sa forme concrète (un être), on emploie l'article indéfini «un». Cette forme de l'idée substantive est moins générale, car l'idée concrète «un» implique l'idée abstraite «le», tandis que la réciproque n'est pas vraie. Cependant, l'atome «un» représente encore l'idée substantive pure (un être), à condition de ne pas l'employer pour représenter un être spécial. Les expressions «un riche», «un beau», dans le sens de «homme riche», «homme beau» sont des expressions incomplètes, car on donne ici à l'article «un», non pas le sens de «un être quelconque» (réel ou idéel), mais le sens spécial de «un être réel» (par opposition à un être de langage), et même les sens encore plus spéciaux de «un être réel vivant», «un être réel vivant humain». Le sens logique total de l'expression «un beau», prise isolément et sans contexte, ne peut être que «un

(article) and *ce* 'this' (pronoun) that really indicate the nominal idea. These atoms are nominalizers: in the expression *l'être* '(the) entity', the affix *l'* or *le* nominalizes the verb *être* (to exist), just as it nominalizes the adjective *beau* 'beautiful' in the expression *le beau* (*beau-té* 'beau-ty').

But there are many other atoms that represent the nominal idea. The atoms *le, ce* represent the nominal idea in its most general and most abstract form (entity). To represent the specific nominal idea in its concrete form (an entity), the indefinite article *un* 'a' is used. This form of the nominal idea is less general, because the concrete idea *un* 'a' implies the abstract idea *le* 'the', while the inverse is not true. However, the atom *un* still represents the pure nominal idea (an entity) so long as it is not used to represent a particular entity. The expressions *un riche* 'a rich (one)', *un beau* 'a handsome (one)' in the sense of *homme riche* 'rich man', *homme beau* 'handsome man' are incomplete expressions, because here the article *un* is given not the sense of *un être quelconque* 'any entity' (real or ideal), but the specific sense of *un être réel* 'a real entity' (as opposed to a linguistic entity), and even the yet more specific sense of *un être réel vivant* 'a real living being', *un être réel vivant humain* 'a real living human being'. The entire logical sense of the expression *un beau*, taken in isolation and without context, can only be *un*

être beau», cet être étant d'ailleurs quelconque, réel ou idéel; et, en effet, comme l'atome «un» contient en lui-même l'atome plus général «le», on a «un beau» = «un—le beau» = «une beauté»[1] (puisque le beau = beau-té), expression qui s'applique bien à un être quelconque. En résumé, on peut considérer l'atome «un» comme atome fondamental substantif représentant l'idée particulière «un être»; il faut seulement faire attention qu'il y a souvent, dans cet atome, une idée substantive spéciale sous-entendue, idée qu'il faut rétablir sous une forme explicite avant de procéder à une analyse quelconque. Ainsi, au lieu de «un riche» on doit écrire «homme riche»; par contre, dans l'expression «un tout» il n'y a rien de sous-entendu, parce que l'atome «un» peut être appliqué ici à un être quelconque.

L'idée substantive générale peut aussi être représentée par le mot «entité» (du latin ens), qui équivaut à l'expression «l'(être)», «un être abstrait de la

être beau 'a beautiful being', this entity being, however, any entity, real or ideal. Indeed, since the atom *un* contains the more general atom *le* within it, we have *un beau* 'a beautiful (one)' = *un—le beau* = *une beauté* 'a beauty'[1] (since *le beau* = *beau-té* 'beauty'), an expression completely applicable to any being. In sum, we can consider the atom *un* as a basic nominal atom representing the specific nominal idea *un être* 'an entity'; it is only necessary to attend to the fact that there is often understood, within this atom, a specific nominal idea that must be restored in explicit form before proceeding to any analysis. Thus, instead of *un riche* 'a rich (one)' we have to write *homme riche* 'rich man'; on the other hand, in the expression *un tout* 'a totality' there is nothing understood, because the atom *un* can here be applied to any entity.

The general nominal idea can also be represented by the word *entité* 'entity' (from Latin *ens*), which is equivalent to the expression *l'être* 'an entity abstracted from

---

[1] On se rend mieux compte du sens logique de la molécule formée par un adjectif précédé de l'article indéfini en choisissant un adjectif qui n'évoque pas d'idée substantive spéciale; par exemple, «un vrai» = «une chose vraie» = «une vérité» = «un—le vrai». Ou encore: «un blanc» peut, signifier soit «un homme blanc», soit «un objet-unité blanc» (sens concret), soit «un blanc de l'esprit» (sens abstrait).

[1] The logical sense of the molecule formed by an adjective preceded by the indefinite article is better shown by choosing an adjective that does not evoke a specific nominal idea: for example, *un vrai* 'a true (one)' = *une chose vraie* 'a true thing' = *une vérité* 'a truth' = *un—le vrai*. Or again: *un blanc* 'a white (one)' can mean either *un homme blanc* 'a white man' or *un objet-unité blanc* 'a white object' (concrete sense) or *un blanc d'esprit* 'a mental blank' (abstract sense).

réalité». (Voir plus loin l'analyse du mot «entité»).

Enfin, il y a beaucoup de suffixes qui représentent l'idée substantive générale : ainsi les suffixes «ité» (dans «égalité»), «esse» (dans «richesse») «eur» (dans «grandeur»), «ment» (dans «abonnement»), «ture» (dans «écriture»), «tion» (dans «abdication»), etc., sont des atomes fondamentaux, car ce sont de simples substantificateurs d'adjectifs ou de verbes.

Si donc on représente l'idée substantive générale par le symbole o, et l'idée substantive particulière par le symbole o1, on peut écrire :

Idée substantive générale (ou abstraite)	o = atomes radicaux : *ens*, (*entité*), *ce* (qui est).
	= atomes suffixes : *ité, esse, eur, ment, tion, ture*, etc.
	= suffixe dissocié : *le, l'*, (*être*).
Idée substantive particulière (ou concrète)	o_1 = suffixe diss. : *un*.

La distinction entre l'idée générale o et l'idée particulière o_1, ne signifie pas qu'il y a deux sortes d'idée substantive, mais simplement que tout substantif peut être pris, soit dans le sens abstrait, soit dans le sens concret. À part cela, tous ces atomes sont interchangeables entre eux ; les suffixes «ité»,

reality). (see below for the analysis of the word *entité* 'entity').

Lastly, there are a number of suffixes that represent the general nominal idea: thus, the suffixes *ité* (in *égalité* 'equality'), *esse* (in *richesse* 'richness, wealth'), *eur* (in *grandeur* 'greatness, size', *ment* (in *abonnement* 'subscription'), *ture* (in *écriture* 'writing'), *tion* (in *abdication* 'abdication'), etc. are basic atoms, because they are simple nominalizers of adjectives or verbs.

If we then represent the general nominal idea by the symbol o and the specific nominal idea by the symbol o_1, we can write:

General (or abstract) nominal idea	o = root atoms: *ens*, (*entité*), *ce* (qui est).
	= suffix atoms: *ité, esse, eur, ment, tion, ture*, etc.
	= dissociated suffix: *le, l'*, (être).
Specific (or concrete) nominal idea	o_1 = dissociated suffix: *un*.

The distinction between the general idea o and the specific idea o_1 does not mean that there are two kinds of noun, but only that every noun can be taken either in the abstract or in the concrete sense. Apart from that, all of these atoms are interchangeable with one another; the suffixes *ité*,

«tion», par exemple, sont interchangeables avec l'atome «le», «l'être», «l'(être abstrait)»; en effet, les adjectifs et les verbes ne représentent pas des êtres, mais des attributs, des manières d'être ou l'agir d'un être; les suffixes «ité», «tion», etc., qui servent à substantifier soit un adjectif, soit un verbe, font bien de ces derniers un être, mais comme cette substantification n'est qu'un simple procédé de langage qui n'apporte aucune réalité nouvelle, l'être ainsi obtenu ne peut être qu'un être idéel, abstrait de nature, puisqu'on l'a abstrait de la réalité adjective ou verbale pour en faire un être. On a donc *beau-té* = *le beau* (l'être abstrait «beau»), de même que *bois-son* = *le boire*. Mais ce qu'il faut remarquer, c'est que dans les molécules «le beau» et «beau-té», l'atome «beau» reste toujours adjectif (principe de l'invariabilité des atomes). Il ne faut pas mettre dans les suffixes «ité», «esse», etc., une idée de «qualité», car on ne peut pas avoir *ité* = *qual-ité*; les atomes «ité», «tion», sont l'expression la plus pure de l'idée substantive générale o, c'est-à-dire de l'idée «l'être (en général)», «l'être abstrait». Et, en effet, nous avons vu que tout adjectif, comme «beau», contient en lui-même l'idée adjective «qual»; donc si «beau-té» exprime une «qual-ité», ce n'est pas parce que le suffixe «ité» exprime la qualité, mais *parce que l'atome adjectif «beau» contient implicitement en lui-même l'idée*

tion, for example, are interchangeable with the atom *le, l'être, l'(être abstrait)* 'the (abstract) (entity)'. Indeed, adjectives and verbs do not represent entities, but attributes, manners of being or acting of an entity. The suffixes *ité, tion*, etc. which serve to nominalize an adjective or a verb do make an entity from these items, but as this nominalization is only a simple linguistic process which brings in no new reality, the entity thereby obtained can only be something ideal, abstracted from nature, since one has abstracted from the adjectival or verbal reality to make an entity out of it. We thus have *beau-té* 'beauty' = *le beau* 'the beautiful' (the abstract entity *beau* 'beautiful'), just as *bois-son* 'drink (n)' = *le boire* 'the drink (v)'. But what has to be noted is that in the molecules *le beau* and *beau-té*, the atom *beau* still remains an adjective (principle of the invariability of atoms). It is necessary not to find in the suffixes *ité, esse*, etc. an idea of 'quality', because we cannot have *ité* = *qual-ité*. The atoms *ité, tion*, are the purest expression of the general nominal idea, that is, the idea 'entity (in general)', 'abstract entity'. And indeed we have seen that every adjective, like *beau*, contains in itself the adjectival idea 'qual'. Thus, if *beau-té* expresses a 'qual-ity', this is not because the suffix *ité* expresses the quality, but *because the adjectival atom <u>beau</u> implicitly contains in itself the idea*

general adjectival [idea]. We will come back to this in connection with the analysis of molecules, and we will see then what distinction can be made between *le beau* 'the beautiful' and *beau-té* 'beauty', *le boire* 'the drink (v)' and *boisson* 'drink (n)'. For the moment it suffices to note that atoms such as *ité, tion*, etc. contain only the general nominal idea. The atom *ité* can no more be equal to the molecule *qualité* 'quality' than the atom *tion* can be equal to the molecule *action* 'action', because a general nominal atom (like *ité* or *tion*) cannot contain at the same time the adjectival idea or the verbal idea, since these three basic ideas are fundamentally independent of one another.[1]

3. *Basic verbal atoms.* — There are two general verbal ideas: the dynamic idea 'perform an act' or 'an action' (corresponding to active verbs) and the static idea 'be in a state' or 'position' (corresponding to neutral verbs).

The static idea is however only a special case of the dynamic idea. The latter implies forces in activity: if the forces are not in equilibrium, we have the proper dynamic idea (action), which is the general case; if the forces

---

[1] Although we cannot write *ité* = *qual-ité* 'quality', we can in contrast write *ité* = *ent-ité* 'entity', because the root *ens* does nothing but repeat the nominal idea *l'être* or *un être* 'entity'.

viennent à se faire équilibre on a l'idée statique[1] (état). Et en effet dès que l'état change on retombe dans l'action (faite ou subie).

Mais comme les idées fondamentales (ou grammaticales) doivent toutes être exprimées par des atomes simples, il est à présumer que les expressions «faire une action» et «être dans une station » sont réductibles à une forme plus simple, de même que l'idée adjective «de qualité» est réductible au simple atome «qual».

Remarquons d'abord que l'idée verbale générale, que nous représenterons par le symbole i, peut être exprimée par une simple finale verbale, telle que la finale «er» (dans «couronn-er», «clou-er», «sci-er», «entour-er», «rag-er», etc.), car les atomes «couronne», «clou», «entour», «scie», etc., étant des atomes non verbaux, et conservant toujours ce caractère, d'après le principe de l'invariabilité des atomes, le mot «couronn-er» signifie «faire l'action (caractérisée par) l'objet couronne», «entour-er» signifie «faire l'action autour», etc. Les finales «er», «ir», etc., ne sont donc pas seulement des désinences destinées à indiquer les différents temps et personnes de la conjugaison d'un

---

[1] Du reste en mécanique, la statique (état d'équilibre des forces) n'est qu'un chapitre de la dynamique (mouvement et forces en activité); de sorte qu'on peut dire que les sciences mécaniques sont les sciences du verbe.

are in equilibrium, we have the static idea[1] (state). And indeed as soon as the state changes, we fall back into action (performed or undergone).

But since the basic (or grammatical) ideas must all be expressed by simple atoms, it is to be presumed that the expressions "perform an action" and "be in a state" are reducible to a simpler form, just as the adjectival idea "of quality" is reducible to the simple atom 'qual'.

Let us note initially that the general verbal idea, which we represent by the symbol i, can be expressed by a simple verbal ending, such as the ending er (in couronn-er 'to crown', clou-er 'to nail (down)', sci-er 'to saw', entour-er 'to surround', rag-er 'to rage, be in a rage', etc.). Since the atoms *couronne* 'crown', *clou* 'nail', *entour* 'surrounding', *scie* 'saw', etc. are non-verbal atoms, and always preserve that character according to the principle of the invariability of atoms, the word *couronn-er* means "to perform the action (characterized by) the object 'crown' " *entour-er* means "to perform the action 'around' ", etc. The endings *er, ir*, etc. are thus not only desinences indicating different tenses and persons in the conjugation of a

---

[1] Besides, in mechanics the static (state of equilibrium of forces) is only a part of the dynamic (movement and forces in action), so that we can say that the mechanical sciences are the sciences of the verb.

verbe, mais ce sont de véritables suffixes au point de vue logique, des atomes contenant en eux-mêmes l'idée verbale générale, puisque les molécules «couronn-er», «rag-er», etc., sont des verbes, tandis que les atomes «couronne», «rage», etc., sont de purs substantifs qui ne contiennent, en fait d'idées grammaticales, que l'idée d'un être (concret ou abstrait).

Voyons maintenant quels sont les atomes-radicaux qui permettent d'exprimer par un simple atome l'idée verbale générale «faire un actc, unc action», ou «être dans un état, une station». Tout d'abord, «faire une action» se réduit à «faire», car quand on «fait», on fait toujours «une action»; de même «être dans un état» se réduit à «être» (au sens statique, sens que nous avons représenté par le radical «sta»), car quand on «est» (au sens statique), on «est» toujours «dans un état». On peut donc considérer que dans les expressions «faire (une action)» ou «être (dans un état)», les parties entre parenthèses ne sont qu'explicatives; ainsi la parenthèse «dans un état» a pour but d'indiquer que le verbe «être» est pris ici au sens statique (*stare*) et non dans le sens d'«exister». Par conséquent, on peut représenter les deux idées verbales par les deux atomes-radicaux «fai(re)» (verbe dynamique) et «sta(re)[»](verbe statique).

Mais on peut procéder aussi autrement en remar-[quant]

verb, but they are true suffixes from the point of view of logic, atoms containing in themselves the general verbal idea, since the molecules *couronn-er* 'to crown', *rag-er* 'to (be in a) rage', etc. are verbs, while *couronne* 'crown', *rage* 'rage', etc. are pure nouns that only contain, as far as grammatical ideas are concerned, the idea of an entity (concrete or abstract).

Let us see now which root-atoms make it possible to express in a simple atom the general verbal idea "to perform an act, an action" or "to be in a state, a position". To begin with, "to do, perform an action" reduces to "to do", because when one "does" one always performs "an action"; similarly "to be in a state" reduces to "to be" (in the static sense, the sense which we have represented by the root *sta* 'be'), because when one "is" (in the static sense), one "is" always "in a state". We can thus consider that in the expressions "to do, perform (an action)" or "to be (in a state)", the parts in parentheses are only explicative; thus the parenthesized "in a state" serves to indicate that the verb "to be" is taken here in the static sense (*stare*) and not in the sense "to exist". Consequently we can represent the two verbal ideas by the two root-atoms "do" (dynamic verb) and "be" (static verb).

But we can also proceed differently in no[ting]

[remar]quant que *la dissociation d'une molécule condensée (ou la condensation d'une molécule dissociée) renverse l'ordre des atomes* : ainsi *beau-té = le beau, hum-ain = d'homme, différ-ent = qui diffère*, etc. Donc une molécule bi-atomique dissociée *(x)–(y)* est égale à la molécule condensée *(y–x)*. La molécule dissociée *(faire)–(action)* sera donc équivalente à la molécule condensée *(actionn-er)*, puisque les atomes «faire» et «er» expriment tous deux l'idée verbale générale i. Et de même que la molécule «de qualité» se réduit à l'atome «qual», de même la molécule «actionner» se réduit à l'atome «ac», parce que la dérivation qui mène du verbe «ac» (ou «ag»)[1] au substantif «action» est exactement inverse de celle qui mène du substantif «action» au verbe «actionner». On démontrerait de même que la molécule dissociée «être dans un état», ou mieux «être dans une station», est équivalente à la molécule condensée «stationner», laquelle est réductible au simple atome «sta», de sorte que les deux idées verbales générales peuvent être représentées aussi

[no]ting that *the dissociation of a condensed molecule (or the condensation of a dissociated molecule) reverses the order of the atoms*: thus *beau-té* 'beauty' = *le beau* 'the beautiful', *hum-ain* 'human' = *d'homme* 'of man', *différ-ent* 'different' = *qui diffère* 'which differs', etc. Therefore a dissociated bi-atomic molecule *(x)–(y)* is equal to the condensed molecule *(y–x)*. The dissociated molecule *(do)–(action)* will therefore be equivalent to the condensed molecule *(action-INFINITIVE)* 'to activate', since the atoms "to do" and "[INFINITIVE]" both express the general verbal idea i. And just as the molecule "of quality" is reducible to the atom 'qual', so the molecule "activate" is reducible to the atom 'ac', because the derivation which leads from the verb "ac" (or "ag")[1] to the noun *action* is exactly the inverse of that which leads from the noun *action* to the verb "to activate". We would similarly show that the dissociated molecule "to be in a state" or better "to be in a position" is equivalent to the condensed molecule *stationner* "to remain in a position", which is reducible to to the simple atom "sta", such that the two general verbal ideas can also be represented

---

[1] L'atome "ac" ou *act* du mot *action* est le même que l'atome *ag* du mot *agir*. Du reste, en anglais, la forme *ag* n'existe pas et l'on a les deux formes régulières (*to act* et *action*) pour le verbe et son substantif. On peut se demander aussi s'il est plus logique de diviser le mot «action» en «action» ou en «act-ion» ; mais comme le résultat de l'analyse logique est le même dans les deux cas, je choisirai la coupure «ac-tion», afin de rapprocher «ac» de «ag».

[1] The atom "ac" or "act" in the word *action* is the same as the atom "ag" in the word *agir* 'to act'. Besides, in English, the form "ag" does not exist and we have the two regular forms (*to act* and *action*) for the verb and its noun. We can also ask whether it is more logical to divide the word *action* as *ac-tion* or as *act-ion*; but since the result of the logical analysis is the same in the two cases, I will choose the division *ac-tion* in order to bring together "ac" and "ag".

by the two root-atoms: "ag" (for active verbs[1]) and "sta" (for neutral or static verbs[2]).

In English, we can again represent the verbal idea i by the dissociated suffix "to", for example: *(to)-(crown)* = *(couronn-er)* 'crown-INFINITIVE', *(to)-(nail)* = *(clou-er)* 'nail-INFINITIVE', etc. This suffix is placed before the noun (*crown, nail,* etc.) to which it is related, according to the law of reversal of atoms in dissociated molecules. In summary, we can write:

Verbal idea i = atoms: roots
    *ag, (to) do; sta,
    (to) be.*
= " (infin.) suffixes
    er, ir, re, etc.
= " dissociated suffix
    to (in English).

These atoms are interchangeable: consider, for example, the series *couronne* 'crown', *couronn-er* 'to crown', *couronn-e-ment* 'coronation'; we see that the verbal atom *er* in *couronner* is reduced to a simple *e* in *couronn-e-ment*, but this *e* is very important, because it represents by itself the verbal idea "ag" or "ac" in the word *couronnement* 'coronation'; we can

---

[1] The word *ac-tive* is a molecule which means "of quality *ac*" and since the atom "ac" is the same as "ag", the expression *active verb* means exactly "verb that contains the idea *ag*".

[2] The word "stat-ic" means "of quality *stat*", the expression *static verb* means exactly "verb that contains the idea "stat" (or "be" in the static sense).

therefore replace the verbal atom *e* with the equivalent atom "ag" or "ac", and since the nominal atom *ment* in *couronnement* 'coronation' is interchangeable with the atom *tion* of *ac-tion*, we can write:

couronn-e-ment = couronn-ac-tion

or symbolically[1]:

kron-i-o = kron-ag-o

as we wrote:

hum-an-ité = hom-qual-ité

Therefore it is not the atoms *ment*, *tion*, etc. that express the action, because these atoms are simple nominalizers, like the atoms *ité*, *esse* (*couronne-ment* 'coronation' = *le couronner* 'the to-crown'). The verbal idea "ac" is contained in the verbal atom which immediately precedes the nominal atoms *ment, tion* etc. This verbal atom is sometimes much reduced and barely recognizable, but its presence is signaled by the fact that the atoms *ment, tion* are only used after verbal atoms, just as the atoms *ité, esse* are only used after adjective atoms.[2]

---

[1] For the symbolic representation it is preferable to make use of the most international phonetic transcription; therefore *couronne* 'crown' will be written **kron** because of German *Krone* and English *crown*.

[2] Prof. Ch. Bally, who was so good as to reread the ma[nuscript]

Remarque. — Les suffixes verbaux «er», «ir», etc., s'accollent, non pas seulement à des atomes radicaux substantifs (comme «couronne», «clou», etc.) ou adjectifs (comme «grand», «gros», etc.), mais aussi à des atomes verbaux (comme «écri», «ouvr», «abdic»), puisque l'on dit : «écri-re», «ouvr-ir», «abdiqu-er», aussi bien que «couronner», «clou-er», «grand-ir», etc. Au point de vue logique, il y a évidemment un pléonasme dans le mot «écrire», car le radical «écri» contient déjà implicitement en lui-même l'idée dynamique «ag», par le seul fait qu'il est verbal ; comme l'atome suffixe «re» est lui-même équivalent à «ag», on voit que l'idée verbale «ag» ou i est exprimée deux fois dans le mot «écri-re», ainsi que dans tous les verbes dont le radical est verbal, comme «ag-ir»,

---

nuscrit de cet essai avant sa publication, fait ici une remarque très intéressante : «Si, dit-il, on se place au point de vue psychologique, on observe qu'un mot composé tend toujours à être conçu peu à peu comme un mot simple : l'idée adjective, qui n'est tout d'abord contenue que dans le radical «beau» du mot «beauté», finit par infecter et pénétrer le suffixe «té», de sorte que ce dernier (psychologiquement, sinon logiquement) participe de l'idée adjective et de l'idée substantive. Inversement, dans le mot «couronner», le radical «couronn» est contaminé par l'idée verbale contenue daus le suffixe «er».[»] — La remarque de M. Bally me semble très juste ; néanmoins, pour le but que je me suis proposé, et ainsi que l'indique le titre même de cette brochure, le point de vue logique est le seul qui doive être pris ici en considération.

Remark. — The [infinitive] verbal suffixes *er*, *ir*, etc. attach not only to root noun atoms (like *couronne* 'crown', *clou* 'nail', etc.) or adjectives (like *grand* 'big, tall', *gros* 'large, fat' etc.) but also to verbal atoms (such as *écri* 'write', *ouvr* 'open', *abdic* 'renounce'), since one says: *écri-re* '(to) write', *ouvr-ir* '(to) open', *abdiqu-er* '(to) abdicate, renounce', etc. From a logical point of view, there is a pleonasm in the word *écrire* '(to) write', since the root *écri* already contains in itself the dynamic idea "ag", from the very fact that it is verbal; as the suffix atom *re* is itself equivalent to "ag", we see that the verbal idea "ag" or i is expressed twice in the word *écri-re*, as well as in all verbs whose root is verbal, such as *ag-ir* 'to act',

---

[ma]nuscript of this essay before its publication, makes a very interesting remark here: "If, he says, we take the psychological point of view, we observe that a compound word always tends little by little to be conceived as a simple word: the adjective idea, which is initially contained only in the root *beau* 'beautiful' of the word *beauté* 'beauty' ends up by infecting and penetrating the suffix *té* such that the latter draws (psychologically, if not logically) on the adjective idea and the nominal idea. Conversely, in the word *couronner*, the root *couronn* is contaminated by the verbal idea contained in the suffix *er*." – Prof. Bally's remark seems to me quite accurate; nevertheless, for my ends, and also as the very title of this booklet indicates, the logical point of view is the only only one that should be taken into consideration here.

«abdiqu-er», etc. On peut même dire que *ag-ir* = *ag-ag* = **i-i**, puisque l'atome «ir» est interchangeable avec l'atome «ag», ou l'atome symbolique **i**.

Au point de vue purement logique, de tels pléonasmes sont contraires à l'un des principes qui gouvernent la formation des mots, comme nous le verrons en parlant de la synthèse des mots composés. Un suffixe doit toujours introduire dans un mot une idée qui n'y était pas encore contenue, c'est-à-dire que l'on ne doit pas répéter inutilement la même idée une ou plusieurs fois dans le même mot. Mais comme un même atome peut contenir en même temps une idée générale et une idée particulière, il y a des cas où l'on est obligé de répéter une idée générale déjà exprimée, afin d'introduire l'idée particulière non encore exprimée. Dans ces cas, le pléonasme est inévitable ; lorsque l'on dit «frappez», l'idée verbale exprimée par l'atome suffixe «ez» est déjà exprimée par l'atome radical «frap», mais cette répétition est permise parce que l'atome «ez» apporte dans le mot, outre l'idée générale «ag», les trois idées particulières de présent, d'impératif et de deuxième personne du pluriel. Du reste, ces pléonasmes n'ont aucun inconvénient ; ils ne changent pas le sens du mot, car «écrire» est la même chose que «faire l'action écrire», de même que «beau» = « qui est beau » ou «de qualité beau», parce que l'atome «qui» et la molécule «de qua-

abdiqu-er 'abdic-ate', etc. We could even say that *ag-ir* '(to) act' = *ag-ag* = **i-i**, since the atom *ir* is interchangeable with the atom "ag", or the symbolic atom **i**.

From a purely logical point of view, such pleonasms are contrary to one of the principles that govern the formation of words, as we will see in discussing the synthesis of compound words. A suffix should always introduce into a word an idea that is not already contained within it, that is, one should not repeat uselessly the same idea one or several times within the same word. But as the same atom can contain at the same time a general idea and a particular idea, there are cases where one is obliged to repeat a general idea that has already been expressed, in order to introduce the particular idea that has not yet been expressed. In those cases, the pleonasm is inevitable; when we say *frapp-ez* 'strike [2PL IMPERATIVE]', the verbal idea expressed by the suffix *ez* '2PL' is already expressed by the root atom *frap* 'strike', but this repetition is permitted because the atom *ez* brings to the word, besides the general idea "ag", the three particular ideas of present, imperative, and second person plural. Besides, these pleonasms are not disadvantageous: *they do not change the sense of the word*, since *écrire* '(to) write' is the same as "perform the action *écrire*", just as *beau* 'beautiful' = "which is beautiful" or "of beautiful quality", since the atom *qui* 'which' and the molecule "of qua[lity]"

[qua]lity" are equivalent to the adjectival idea a, which is already contained in *beau* 'beautiful'.

Having thus achieved the enumeration of the basic atoms[1] (adjectival, nominal or verbal), that is, the atoms that contain nothing other than the basic ideas a, o, or i, we can now proceed to the classification of all of the specific atoms, that is, of the roots and affixes that contain a particular idea in addition to the corresponding basic idea. We thus obtain a vocabulary organized as follows:

1. Basic atoms.

Adjectives	Nouns	Verbs
a	o	i
qual	ens (entity)	ag (or sta)
propre (à)	le (or un)	fai
de	ce	to (in English)
qui	-ité (suffix)	er (suffix)
-ain (suffix)	-esse (")	re (")
-ique (")	-eur (")	ir (")
-eux (")	-tion (")	etc., etc.
-el (")	-ment(")	
etc., etc.	-ture (")	
	etc., etc.	

---

[1]When I say enumeration, I do not mean complete enumeration, because even speaking only of the French language, there exist other basic suffixes than those

2. ATOMES PARTICULIERS.

Adjectifs	Substantifs	Verbes.
grand	homme	écrire)
beau	cheval	frapp(er)
fort	table	abdiqu(er)
riche	âme	tend(re)
bon	éspace	coud(re)
lourd	science	dorm(ir)
etc., etc.	théorie	souffr(ir)
	etc., etc.	etc., etc.
		ifi (suffixe)
-*able*	-*iste* (suffixe)	*is* (»)
(suffixe)	-*eur*¹ (»)	etc., etc.
	-*oir*² (»)	
	-*ie*³ (»)	
	-*ard*⁴ (»)	
etc., etc.	etc., etc.	

---

que j'ai cités. Ainsi le suffixe *ise* (dans *gourmandise*), est le même atome que *ité* (daus *égalité*), c'est-à-dire que ce suffixe *ise*, et d'autres encore, est égal à l'idée substantive **o**. Le but de cette étude est de proposer une méthode d'analyse, non d'appliquer cette méthode d'une manière complète à une langue particulière.

¹Dans *bross-eur*.
²Dans *abreuv-oir*.
³Dans *brosser-ie*.
⁴Dans *vieill-ard*.

2. PARTICULAR ATOMS.

Adjectives	Nouns	Verbs.
tall	man	(to) write
beautiful	horse	(to) strike
strong	table	(to) abdicate
rich	soul	(to) stretch
good	space	(to) sew
heavy	science	(to) sleep
etc., etc.	theory	(to) suffer
	etc., etc.	etc., etc.
		ifi (suffix)⁵
-*able*	-*iste* (suffixe)	*is* (")⁶
(suffix)	-*eur*¹(")	etc., etc.
	-*oir*²(")	
	-*ie*³(")	
	-*ard*⁴(")	
etc., etc.	etc., etc.	

that I have cited. Thus the suffix *ise* (in *gourmandise* 'gluttony' is the same atom as *ité* (in *égalité* 'equality'), that is, this suffix *ise* among others is equal to the nominal idea **o**. The goal of this study is to propose a method of analysis, not to apply that method in a complete fashion to a specific language.

¹In *b[r]oss-eur* 'hard worker'; cf. *bosser* 'to work hard'.
²In *abreuv-oir* 'drinking trough'; cf. *abreuver* 'to water (an animal)'.
³In *brosser-ie* 'brushery'; cf. *brosser* 'to brush'.
⁴In *vieill-ard* 'old man'; cf. *vieux, vieil* 'old'.
⁵In *sign-ifi-er* 'to signify'
⁶In *signal-is-er* 'to signalize'

§ 2. — Etude des molécules.

Tout mot composé de plusieurs atomes (radicaux ou affixes) est une *molécule*. Ainsi le mot «hum-an-ité» est une molécule contenant trois atomes : l'atome substantif «hom» (atome particulier), l'atome adjectif «an» (atome général) et l'atome substantif «ité» (atome général). Nous avons vu, en outre, que certaines expressions composées de plusieurs mots, comme «d'homme», «le beau», etc., doivent être considérées comme des molécules à l'état dissocié.

CLASSEMENT DES MOLÉCULES. — On peut classer les mots composés en trois classes principales, comme les atomes. Du reste, le classement des molécules est immédiatement déterminé par celui des atomes, car on constate facilement que *la classe d'une molécule est celle de son dernier atome*. Cette règle est très importante ; elle montre qu'à ce point de vue il n'y a pas de différence entre les mots composés d'atomes-radicaux (comme «Schlafzimmer» en allemand) et les mots dits dérivés, c'est-à-dire composés de radicaux et d'affixes : ainsi, de même que le mot «Schlafzimmer» est un substantif, parce que son dernier atome «Zimmer» en est un ; de même le mot «humanité» est substantif parce que son dernier atome «ité» est un atome substantif ; le

§ 2. — The study of molecules.

Every word composed of several atoms (roots or affixes) is a *molecule*. Thus, the word *hum-an-ité* 'humanity' is a molecule containing three atoms: the noun atom *hom* (particular atom), the adjective atom *an* (general atom), and the noun atom *ité* (general atom). We have seen in addition that certain expressions like *d'homme* 'of man', *le beau* 'the beautiful', etc. must be considered as molecules in the dissociated state.

CLASSIFICATION OF MOLECULES. — We can categorize compound words into three main classes, like atoms. In addition, the classification of molecules is immediately determined by that of atoms, because we can observe easily that *the class of a molecule is that of its final atom*. This rule is very important: it shows that from this point of view there is no difference between words compounded of root atoms (like *Schlafzimmer* 'bedroom' in German) and words said to be derived, that is, composed of roots and affixes: thus just as the word *Schlafzimmer* is a noun, because its final atom *Zimmer* 'room' is one; similarly, the word *human-ité* is a noun because its final atom *ité* is a nominal atom; the

mot «humain» est un adjectif parce que «ain» est un atome adjectif; le mot «clouer» est un verbe parce que «er» est un atome verbal, et ainsi de suite.

Toutefois, dans les molécules dissociées, c'est-à-dire dans les expressions «le beau», «un vieux», «le boire», «to crown», etc., ainsi que dans les mots composés comme «bateau à vapeur», «machine à coudre», «un porte-plume», etc., l'ordre des atomes est renversé, c'est-à-dire que c'est le premier atome, et non le dernier, qui détermine le classement de la molécule dissociée. En effet, «*le* beau» «beau-*té*», «*un* (homme) vieux» = «vieill-*ard*», «*le* boire» = «bois-*son*», «*to* crown = cou-ronn-*er* », «*chambre* à coucher» = «Schlaf-*Zimmer*», «*machine* à coudre» = «sewing-*machine*», «*un* (objet) porte-plume» = «Federhalt-*er*», «*un* (objet) porte-chandelle» = «chandel-*ier*», «*(argent)* pour boire» = «Trink-*geld*», etc., etc. Il faut donc compléter la règle de classement des molécules, en disant : *La classe d'une molécule est celle de son dernier atome, à moins que la molécule ne soit dissociée; dans ce cas, la classe est celle du premier atome*, à cause du renversement atomique qui est produit par la dissociation.

Au fond, l'ordre des atomes dans les molécules dissociées est l'ordre analytique, explicatif, et c'est la condensation, la synthèse de la molécule en un

the word *humain* 'human' is an adjective because *ain* is an adjective atom; the word *clouer* 'to nail' is a verb because *er* is a verbal atom, and so on.

However, in dissociated molecules, that is in the expressions *le beau* 'the beautiful', *un vieux* 'an old (man)', *le boire* 'the drink', *to crown*, etc., as well as in compound words like *bateau à vapeur* 'boat of steam: steamboat', *machine à coudre* 'machine to sew: sewing machine', *un porte-plume* 'a carry-pen: a penholder', etc., the order of atoms is reversed; that is, it is the first atom and not the last that determines the classification of the dissociated molecule. Actually, "*le* beau" [=] "beau-*té*", "*un* (homme) vieux" = "vieill-*ard*", "*le* boire" = "bois-*son*", "*to* crown" = "couronn-*er*", "*chambre* à coucher" 'room to sleep' = "Schlaf-*zimmer*", "*machine* à coudre" = "sewing *machine*", "*un* (objet) porte-plume" = "Federhalt-*er*", "*un* (object) porte-chandelle" 'an (object) carry-candle' = "chandel-*ier*" 'candlestick', "*(argent)* pour boire" '(money) for drink' = "Trink-*geld*" 'drink-money: tip', etc. etc. We must thus supplement the classification rule for molecules by saying: *The class of a molecule is that of its final atom, unless the molecule is dissociated: in that case, the class is that of its first atom*, because of the reversal of atoms that is produced by dissociation.

Basically, the order of atoms in dissociated molecules is the *analytic, explanatory* order, and it is condensation, the synthesis of a molecule into a

seul mot, qui renverse l'ordre des atomes et produit l'ordre synthétique. La soudure entre les atomes est donc l'effet provoqué par le renversement de leur ordre naturel. Mais, quel que soit l'ordre logique des atomes, la seule chose qui nous intéresse ici, c'est que dans la molécule dissociée l'ordre est inverse de ce qu'il est dans la molécule condensée.

Pour analyser une molécule, il faut tenir compte de tout ce qu'elle contient, c'est-à-dire de tout ce que contient chacun des atomes qui la composent.

Or, nous avons vu qu'en général un atome exprime non seulement une idée particulière, mais qu'il contient implicitement une ou plusieurs idées plus générales (et en particulier une idée grammaticale), qui accompagnent toujours cet atome et dont il faut tenir compte si l'on veut faire une analyse complète de la molécule.

Cependant, nous savons qu'il existe un certain nombre d'atomes qui ne contiennent qu'une idée générale (a, o ou i) et aucune idée particulière : ce sont les atomes fondamentaux. Ces atomes ont une constitution plus simple que les atomes particuliers ; ils montrent à nu tout leur contenu et ne cachent rien dans leur intérieur. Par conséquent, si un mot composé ne contient que des atomes fondamentaux, son analyse sera toute simple, parce que le sens total du mot résultera immédiatement de la

single word, which reverses the order of the atoms and produces the synthetic order. The fusion of the atoms is thus the effect provoked by the reversal of their natural order. But whatever the logical order of the atoms may be, the only thing that interests us here is that in the dissociated molecule the order is the opposite of what it is in the condensed molecule.

To analyze a molecule, it is necessary to take account of everything that it contains, that is of all that is contained in each of the atoms that make it up.

Now we have seen that in general, an atom expresses not only a specific idea, but that it implicitly contains one or several more general ideas (and in particular, a grammatical idea) which always go along with this atom and of which it is necessary to take account if we wish to make a complete analysis of the molecule.

However, we know that there exist a certain number of atoms that contain only a general idea (a, o, or i), and no specific idea: these are the fundamental atoms. These atoms have a simpler composition than the specific atoms: they show their content openly and hide nothing in their interior. Consequently, if a compound word contains only fundamental atoms, its analysis will be quite simple, since the complete sense of the word results immediately from the

juxtaposition des idées contenues dans les différents atomes, à raison d'une seule idée par atome.

A). Molécules fondamentales.

Il est donc naturel, avant d'aborder l'analyse d'un mot quelconque, d'étudier d'abord toutes les molécules que l'on peut obtenir en combinant entre eux les atomes fondamentaux. Ces molécules seront appelées *fondamentales* ou *mots fondamentaux* ; en effet, puisque les atomes fondamentaux ne contiennent que les idées les plus générales (idées grammaticales), ces atomes expriment les idées fondamentales du langage, c'est-à-dire les idées abstraites qui servent de modèle, de chef de file aux idées particulières ; il est donc à présumer que tous les mots composés uniquement d'atomes fondamentaux exprimeront aussi des idées fondamentales, des idées abstraites servant de modèle, de chef de file à des séries correspondantes d'idées particulières, celles-ci étant exprimées par des mots composés, de même type, mais contenant des atomes particuliers. Il en est en effet ainsi, et puisque nous connaissons déjà les atomes fondamentaux a, o, i, nous pouvons passer à l'étude des molécules fondamentales composées de deux atomes, c'est-à-dire des molécules :

(a-o), (i-o) ; (o-a), (o-i) ; (a-i), (i-a).

juxtaposition of the ideas contained in the different atoms, at the rate of one single idea per atom.

A). Fundamental Molecules.

It is thus natural, before undertaking the analysis of any word, to first study all of the molecules that we can obtain by combining the fundamental atoms with one another. These molecules will be called *fundamental*, or *fundamental words*: indeed, since the fundamental atoms contain only the most general ideas (grammatical ideas), these atoms express the fundamental ideas of the language, that is, the abstract ideas that serve as the model, as the leaders of the corresponding series of specific ideas; it is thus to be assumed that all words composed exclusively of fundamental atoms will also express fundamental ideas, abstract ideas that serve as the model, the leaders of the corresponding series of specific ideas, with these being expressed by compound words of the same type but containing specific atoms. This is the way things are, and since we already know the fundamental atoms a, o, i, we can move on to the study of fundamental molecules composed of two atoms, that is, the molecules:

(a-o), (i-o); (o-a), (o-i); (a-i), (i-a).

Molécules fondamentales biatomiques.

1. Molécule (a-o). — Pour trouver l'équivalent en français de la molécule (a-o), il suffit de remplacer les atomes fondamentaux **a** et **o** par un de leurs synonymes français choisis dans le tableau de la page 40. On doit seulement remarquer que dans la molécule (a-o), l'atome **o** est la finale du mot et l'atome **a** en est le radical ; il faut donc choisir le synonyme de **a** sous forme d'atome radical et celui de **o** sous forme d'atome-suffixe. Or, l'atome général adjectif **a** est exprimable par l'atome-radical «qual» ou par l'atome-radical «propre (à)» ; on a donc symboliquement : molécule (a-o) = *qual*-o ou *propr*-o.

L'atome **o** représente l'idée substantive générale «ce (qui est)», «l'être en général», «l'être abstrait», laquelle est exprimée en français par les suffixes synonymes «ité», «eur», «esse», etc., lorsque cette idée suit un atome adjectif, comme «qual», par conséquent (a-o) = *qual*-o = *qual-ité*.

Le mot «qualité» est donc un mot fondamental de la langue française, un mot exprimant une idée essentiellement abstraite, car il ne contient que des atomes généraux fondamentaux ; c'est *l'adjectivo-substantif* type, puisqu'on a :

$$qual\text{-}ité = (a\text{-}o)$$

Biatomic fundamental Molecules.

1. Molecule (a-o). — To find the equivalent in French of the the molecule (a-o), it suffices to replace the fundamental atoms **a** and **o** by one of their French synonyms found in the table on page 40. We must only observe that in the molecule (a-o), the atom **o** is final in the word and the atom **a** is the root; it is thus necessary to choose the synonym of **a** in the form of a root atom and that of **o** in the form of a suffix atom. Now the general adjective atom **a** can be expressed by the root atom "qual" or by the root atom *propre (à)*; we thus have symbolically: molecule (a-o) = *qual*-o or *propr*-o.

The atom **o** represents the general nominal idea "that (which is)", "existence in general", "abstract existence", which is expressed in French by the synonymous suffixes *ité, eur, esse*, etc. Since this idea follows an adjective idea such as "qual", it follows that (a-o) = *qual*-o = *qual-ité*.

The word *qualité* is thus a fundamental word of the French language, a word expressing an essentially abstract idea, because it only contains general fundamental atoms: it is the protoypical example of an *adjectivo-nominal*, since we have:

$$qual\text{-}ité = (a\text{-}o)$$

et ce mot servira de modèle à tous les adjectivo-substantifs particuliers (tels que «égal-ité», «bon-té», «grand-eur», «rich-esse», etc.). Tous ces mots sont des molécules biatomiques irréductibles à un seul atome ; ils expriment tous des «qualités», car ils se composent tous d'un radical adjectif particulier suivi de l'atome substantif général.

On peut aussi écrire *propr-o* = *propri-été*, donc aussi :

propri-été = (**a-o**)

ou en allemand :

Eigen-schaft = (**a-o**)

car nous avons vu qu'il n'y a guère de différence entre l'idée «qual» et l'idée «propre (à)» ou, en allemand, «eigen» ; ce qui justifie le terme «Eigenschaftswort» qui, en allemand, sert à désigner l'adjectif.

Quant au sens de la molécule (**a-o**), c'est-à-dire du mot «qualité», il résulte immédiatement de la juxtaposition des sens de ses atomes constituants, puisque ces atomes sont tous deux fondamentaux et ne contiennent rien de sous-entendu ; l'atome **o** exprime l'idée générale substantive «ce», «ce (qui est)», et l'atome **a** l'idée générale adjective «qual», «(qui est) qual», ou «propre (à)», «(qui est) propre (à)». Donc les mots «qualité», «propriété» signifient «*ce* qui est qual», ou «ce qui est propre à».

and this word will serve as a model for all specific adjectivo-nominals (such as *egal-ité* 'equality', *bon-té* 'goodness', *grand-eur* 'size', *rich-esse* 'riches', etc.).

All these words are biatomic molecules that cannot be reduced to a single atom; they all express "qualities", because they are all composed of a specific root adjective followed by the general nominal atom.

We can thus also write *propr-o* = *propri-été*, and therefore also:

propri-été = (**a-o**)

or in German:

Eigen-schaft = (**a-o**)

because we have seen that there is no real difference between the idea "qual" and the idea "proper (to)" or, in German, *eigen* 'own, characteristic'; which is what justifies the term *Eigenschaftswort* that, in German, serves to designate the adjective.

As for the sense of the molecule (**a-o**), that is, of the word *qualité* 'quality', this results immediately from the juxtaposition of the senses of its constituent atoms, since these atoms are both fundamental and do not contain anything understood: the atom **o** expresses the general nominal idea "this, that", "that (which exists)", and the atom **a** the general adjectival idea "qual", "(which is) qual", or "proper (to)", "(which is) proper (to)". Thus, the words *qualité*, *propriété* 'property' mean "(*that*) which is qual" or "(*that*) which is proper to".

Ainsi, par exemple, la phrase : *La qualité de cette étoffe est mauvaise*, signifie : *ce qui est «qual»*, (on pourrait même dire *ce qui est de caractère adjectif*) *dans cette étoffe est mauvais*.

De même l'expression : *Les propriétés d'un corps* signifie «*ce qui est propre à ce corps*», «*ce qui, dans ce corps, est de caractère adjectif*». Par exemple, l'étoffe ou le corps dont nous venons de parler est «lisse» ou «rugueux», «rouge» ou «noir», «lourd» ou «léger», etc.; autant d'adjectifs pour exprimer les qualités ou les propriétés d'un corps.

Remarquons que la soudure entre deux atomes fondamentaux est bien une simple juxtaposition : puisque l'atome «ité» = «ce» et que «qual» = «qui est qual», la molécule *qual-ité*= «*ce* (qui est) *qual*». Les deux membres de cette égalité sont identiques; l'ordre des atomes est seulement renversé, mais cela doit être, car on peut considérer l'expression «ce—qui est qual» comme une molécule biatomique à l'état dissocié, et nous savons que la condensation, la synthèse de la molécule, provoque le renversement de l'ordre de ses atomes.

2. Molécule (i-o). — Pour trouver l'équivalent, en français, de la molécule fondamentale (i-o), il suffit de remplacer les atomes i et o par un de leurs synonymes français donnés dans le tableau de la page 40, en ayant soin de prendre le synonyme de i sous la

Thus, for example, the sentence *La qualité de cette étoffe est mauvaise* 'The quality of this fabric is bad' means *that which is "qual"* (we could even say *that which is of adjective character*) *in this fabric is bad*.

Similarly the expression: *Les propriétés d'un corps* 'the properties of a body' means "*that which is proper to this body*", "*that which, in this body, is of adjective character*". For example, the fabric or the body that we were just speaking of is *lisse* 'smooth' or *rugueux* 'rough', *rouge* 'red' or *noir* 'black' *lourd* 'heavy' or *léger* 'light', etc.; as many adjectives as describe the qualities or properties of a body.

We note that the juncture between two fundamental atoms is just a simple juxtaposition: since the atom *ité* = "that" and "qual" = "which is qual", the molecule *qual-ité* = "*that* (which is) *qual*". The two sides of this equation are identical: only the order of atoms is reversed, but that must be the case, because we consider the molecule "that — which is qual" to be a biatomic molecule in the dissociated state, and we know that the condensation or synthesis of a molecule results in the reversal of the order of its atoms.

2. Molecule (i-o). To find the equivalent in French of the basic molecule (i-o), it suffices to replace the atoms i and o with one of their French synonyms in the table on page 40, taking care to choose the synonym of i in the

forme d'un atome radical, et celui de o sous la forme d'une finale, c'est-à-dire d'un atome-suffixe.

Or, le tableau montre que l'idée verbale générale **i** est synonyme, en français, des atomes-radicaux «ag» (agir, faire un acte, une «action») ou «êt», dans le sens «stat», (être, être dans un état, une «station»); on a donc d'abord **(i-o)** = *ag*-o ou *stat*-o. L'atome **o**, c'est-à-dire l'idée générale substantive «ce (qui est)», «ce (qui existe)», est représenté, en français, par les suffixes synonymes «tion», «ture», «ment», etc., lorsque cette idée suit un atome verbal comme «ag» ou «stat». On a donc finalement :

(i-o) = *ag*-o = *ag-tion* = *ac-tion*

Ou bien :

(i-o) = *stat*-o = *sta-tion*.

Ainsi, tout comme les mots «qualité», «propriété», les mots «action» et «station» (ou «état») sont des mots fondamentaux de la langue française, car ils ne contiennent que des atomes fondamentaux. De même que «qualité», «propriété», sont les types de l'adjectivo-substantif, de même les mots «action», «station», sont les types du verbo-substantif. Ces mots désignent des êtres abstraits, qui serviront de modèle à tous les verbo-substantifs particuliers (comme «abdica-tion», «écriture», «abonne-ment», etc.). Toutes ces idées particulières contiennent l'idée d'«action» (ou de «sta-

form of a root atom, and that of **o** in the form of a final, that is, of a suffix atom.

Now the table shows that the general verbal idea **i** is synonymous, in French, with the root atoms "ag" (to act, to perform an act, an *action*) or *êt* in the sense "stat" (to be, to be in a state, a "position"); we therefore have, first, **(i-o)** = *ag*-o or *stat*-o. The atom **o**, that is the general nominal idea "that (which is)", "that (which exists)" is represented in French by the synonymous suffixes *tion*, *ture*, *ment* etc. when this idea follows a verbal atom like "ag" or "stat". Thus we have finally:

(i-o) = *ag*-o = *ag-tion* = *ac-tion*

or else:

(i-o) = *stat*-o = *sta-tion*.

Therefore, just like the words *qualité* 'quality', *propriété* 'property', the words *action* and *station* (or *état* 'state') are fundamental words of the French language, because they contain only fundamental atoms. Just as *qualité*, *propriété* are prototypes of the adjectivo-nominal, so the words *action*, *station* are prototypes of the verbo-nominal. These words designate abstract entities which serve as models for all specific verbo-nominals (such as *abdica-tion* 'abdication', *écri-ture* 'writing', *abonne-ment* 'subscription, etc.). All of these specific ideas contain the diea of "action" (or of "sta[te]"

tion ») et se composent d'un radical verbal particulier suivi de l'atome substantif général ; ce sont des molécules biatomiques irréductibles à un simple atome.

Quant au sens de la molécule (**i-o**), c'est-à-dire des mots « action » et « station », il résulte immédiatement de la juxtaposition des sens de leurs atomes constituants, puisque ces atomes sont tous fondamentaux : l'atome **o** exprime l'idée substantive générale « ce (qui est) », et l'atome **i** l'idée verbale générale « ag » (agir) ou « sta » (stare). Donc la molécule (**i-o**) signifie « ce qui est *ag* », « ce qui est *agir* » ou bien « ce qui est *sta* », « ce qui est *stare* ». Ainsi, par exemple, la phrase : *L'action de cette machine est régulière*, signifie : *ce qui est «ag», ce qui est «agir»* (on pourrait même dire : *ce qui est de caractère verbal*) *dans cette machine est régulier* ; de même la phrase : *L'état de ces travaux est satisfaisant* signifie : *ce qui est «sta», ce qui est «stare»* (ou *ce qui est verbal*, dans le sens statique) *dans ces travaux est satisfaisant*.

Et de même que tout ce qui est qualité ou propriété d'un corps s'exprime par des adjectifs, de même tout ce qui est action ou état (station) s'exprime par des verbes. Ainsi la machine dont nous venons de parler « comprime », « concasse », « lamine », « coud », [«]rabote », etc. De même l'état des travaux sera exprimé par des verbes neutres : « les travaux dorment, languissent, progressent », etc. De même l'état des travaux sera exprimé par des verbes neutres : « les travaux dorment, languissent, progressent », etc.

[sta]te") and are composed of a specific verbal root followed by the general nominal atom; they are biatomic molecules not reducible to a simple atom.

As for the sense of the molecule (**i-o**), that is of the words *action* and *station* 'state', this follows immediately from the juxtaposition of the senses of their constituent atoms, since these atoms are all basic: the atom **o** expresses the general nominal idea "that (which is)" and the atom **i** the general verbal idea "ag" (*agir* 'to act') or "sta" (*stare* 'to be in a state'). Thus, the molecule (**i-o**) means "that which is *ag*", "that which is *agir*" or else "that which is *sta*", "that which is *stare*". Thus, for example, the sentence *L'action de cette machine est reguliére* 'the action of this machine is regular' means *that which is "ag", that which is* agir (we could even say *that which is verbal in character*) *in this machine is regular*; similarly, in the sentence *L'état de ces travaux est satisfaisant* 'the state of this job is satisfactory' means *that which is "sta", that which is* stare (or *that which is verbal*, in the static sense) *in this job is satisfactory*.

And just as everything that is a quality or property of of a body is expressed by adjectives, similarly everything that is an action or a state is expressed by verbs. Thus, the machine we were just speaking of *comprime* 'compresses', *concasse* 'crushes', *lamine* 'rolls', *coud* 'sews', *rabote* 'planes, scrapes', etc. Similarly the state of the job will be expressed by neutral verbs: *les travaux dorment, languissent, progressent* 'the job is dormant, languishes, progresses' etc.

Il faut bien distinguer la «qualité» de l'«état». Cependant, il n'y a pas de limite fixe et précise entre ces deux notions; on peut, en effet, passer de la «qualité» à l'«état» d'une manière continue, comme on passe de la notion de froid à celle de chaud. Les qualités d'un corps sont «ce qui est propre» à ce corps, car on ne peut les séparer du corps sans altérer profondément la nature de celui-ci. La «qualité» (**a-o**) est adjective, donc indépendante du temps. Au contraire, l'«état» (**i-o**) est verbal, donc passager, temporel, et il n'affecte pas la nature même du corps, de l'être qui subit cet état, cette «station». Ainsi, la «dureté» est une qualité, le «sommeil», c'est-à-dire «le dormir», est un état, une «station»; en effet, c'est le substantif d'un verbe neutre, tandis que «dureté» est le substantif d'un adjectif.[1]

Traduction en allemand de la molécule (**i-o**).

En allemand, le verbe est désigné par le vocable «Tätigkeitswort», c'est-à-dire «mot impliquant une action».

Cependant, la traduction ordinaire du mot «action» en allemand est «Handlung» et non pas «Tätigkeit», car la série «Tat», «tätig», «Tätigkeit» correspond à notre série «acte», «actif», «activité». Or, il est facile de voir que le mot «Handlung» est bien l'équivalent du mot français «action», c'est-à-dire l'équivalent allemand de la molécule fondamentale (**i-o**).

---

[1] Voir encore, à ce sujet, le dernier chapitre.

It is quite necessary to distinguish the "quality" from the "state". However, there is no fixed and precise boundary between these two notions: we can, indeed, pass from the "quality" to the "state" in a continuous fashion, as we pass from the notion of cold to that of hot. The qualities of a body are "that which is proper" to that body, for one cannot separate them from the body without profoundly altering its nature. The "quality" (**a-o**) is adjectival, thus independent of time. On the other hand, the "state" (**i-o**) is verbal, and thus passing, temporal, and it does not affect the very nature of the body, of the entity that goes through this state, this "position." Thus, "hardness" is a quality, "sleep", that is "sleeping" is a state, a "position"; indeed, it is the noun from a neutral verb, while "hardness" is the noun from an adjective.[1]

Translation in German of the molecule (**i-o**).

In German, the verb is designated by the word *Tätigkeitswort*, that is, "word implying an action."

However, the usual translation of the word *action* in German is *Handlung* and not *Tätigkeit*, since the series *Tat, tätig, Tätigkeit* corresponds to our series "act", "active", "activity". Now it is easy to see that the word *Handlung* is the equivalent of the French word *action*, that is, the German equivalent of the basic molecule (**i-o**).

---

[1] See also, on this subject, the final chapter.

Pour comprendre le mot «Handlung», il faut considérer la série «Hand», «handeln», «Handlung», qui, traduite *littéralement* en français, donne : *Hand* = main, *hand-eln* = *mani-er*, *Hand-l-ung* = *mani-e-ment*.

On voit que le suffixe «eln», en allemand, ou «er», en français, est l'atome verbal général **i**; donc «handeln», ou «manier», signifie littéralement «faire (une action) avec la main». Mais en allemand l'idée «main» est ici prise au sens figuré; l'organe humain de l'action symbolise l'organe de l'action en général; c'est pourquoi l'on peut mettre l'idée spéciale «Hand» entre parenthèses. Les molécules «(hand)eln» et «(Hand)lung» deviennent alors des molécules fondamentales, car elles ne contiennent plus d'idées particulières. On a en effet :

atome allemand *eln* = atome français *er* = atome verbal **i**;
atome allemand *ung* = atome français *ment* = atome substantif **o**.

Or, dans le mot «Hand-l-ung», la lettre *l* est ce qui reste de l'atome verbal *eln*; de même, dans le mot «mani-e-ment[»], la lettre *e* est tout ce qui reste de l'atome verbal *er*. On a donc finalement :

(hand)-eln = *(mani)-er* = **(man)-i**
(Hand)-l-ung = *(mani)-e-ment* = **(man)-i-o**

Donc, à part l'idée particulière symbolique «Hand», le mot «Handlung» est bien égal au mot français «action», puisque :

l-ung = **i-o** = *ag-o* = *ac-tion*.

Les mots «Eigenschaft» et «Handlung» sont donc les mots fondamentaux allemands qui correspondent aux mots français (ou anglais) «qualité» et «action», c'est-à-dire aux molécules fondamentales **(a-o)** et **(i-o)**.

To understand the word *Handlung* it is necessary to consider the series *Hand*, *handeln*, *Handlung* which, translated *literally* into French, gives *Hand* = *main* 'hand', *hand-eln* = *man-ier* '(to) handle', *Hand-l-ung* = *mani-e-ment* 'manipulation, handling'.

We see that the suffix *eln* in German, or *er* in French, is the general verbal atom **i**; thus, *handeln* or *manier* means literally "carry out (an action) with the hand." But in German the idea "hand" is here taken in a figurative sense: the human organ of action symbolizes the organ of action in general, which is why we can put the specific idea "hand" in parentheses. The molecules *(hand)eln* and *(Hand)lung* thus become basic molecules, since they no longer contain specific ideas. We thus actually have:

German atom *eln* = French atom *er* = verbal atom **i**;
German atom *ung* = French atom *ment* = nominal atom **o**.

Now in the word *Hand-l-ung*, the letter *l* is what remains of the verbal atom *eln*; similarly, in the word *mani-e-ment* the letter *e* is all that remains of the verbal atom *er*. We thus have finally:

(hand)-eln = *(mani)-er* = **(man)-i**
(Hand)-l-ung = *(mani)-e-ment* = **(man)-i-o**

Thus, other than the specific symbolic idea *Hand*, the word *Handlung* is quite equal to the French word *action*, since:

l-ung = **i-o** = *ag-o* = *ac-tion*.

The words *Eigenschaft* and *Handlung* are thus basic German words which correspond to the French (or English) words *qualité* 'quality' and *action*, that is to the basic molecules **(a-o)** et **(i-o)**.

En résumé, nous avons trouvé jusqu'ici comme mots fondamentaux :

a) Les atomes **o** = «l'(être)» ou «ce (qui est)», **a** = *qual* et **i** = *ag*.

b) Les molécules biatomiques **(a-o)** = *qual-ité* et **(i-o)** = *ac-tion*. Etudions maintenant les molécules inverses **(o-a)** et **(o-i)**, qui sont aussi fondamentales.

3° Molécule **(o-a)**. — Cette molécule représente *l'idée substantif adjectivée* ou l'adjectif de «l'(être)». En donnant à «l'être» le sens d'«essence», on peut traduire la molécule **(o-a)** par le mot français *essentiel*, ou encore par les mots *personn-el, ré-el,* en prenant l'idée substantive sous la forme concrète (personne ou chose). Cette molécule sert donc de type à tous les adjectifs dérivés de substantifs (comme «hum-ain», «industri-el», «pério-dique», etc.). Elle a un rôle important ; d'ailleurs, outre le mot français «essentiel», traduction sous forme condensée de la molécule **(o-a)**, il existe des expressions permettant de traduire cette molécule sous la forme dissociée **(a)-(o)**.

Dans les molécules dissociées, chaque partie entre parenthèses représente un mot à part ; on doit donc traduire ici les atomes **a** et **o**, non par des suffixes, mais par des radicaux : l'idée adjective **a** par «propre (à)» et l'idée substantive **o** par «l'(être)», donc **(a)-(o)** = «propre à l'être». Et, en effet, les mots «personn-el», «ré-el», «hum-ain», «industri-

In summary, to this point we have found as basic words:

a) the atoms **o** = "the (entity)" or "that (which is)", **a** = *qual,* and **i** = *ag*.

b) the biatomic molecules **(a-o)** = *qual-ité* and **(i-o)** = *ac-tion*. Let us now study the inverse molecules **(o-a)** and **(o-i)**, which are also basic.

3. Molecule **(o-a)**. — This molecule represents *the adjectivized nominal idea* or the adjective of "the (entity)". In giving to "the entity" the sense of "the essence", we can translate the molecule **(o-a)** with the French word *essentiel,* or also by the words *personn-el* 'personal', *ré-el* 'real', taking the nominal idea in the concrete form (person or thing). The molecule thus serves as the type for all adjectives derived from nouns (such as *hum-ain, industri-el* 'industrial', *périod-ique* 'periodic', etc.). It has an important role; moreover, besides the French word *essentiel,* translation in condensed form of the molecule **(o-a)**, there are also expressions allowing this molecule to be translated by the dissociated form **(a)-(o)**.

In disssociated molecules, each part in parentheses represents a separate word; we thus translate here the atoms **a** and **o** not by suffixes but by roots: the adjectival idea **a** by "proper (to)" and the nominal idea **o** by "the (entity)", thus **(a)-(o)** = "proper to the entity". And indeed, the words *personn-el, ré-el, industri-[el]*

el», etc., signifient «propre à la personne», «propre à la chose», «propre à l'homme», «propre à l'industrie», etc.

Naturellement, on pourrait traduire aussi l'atome adjectif **a** par un des suffixes dissociés équivalents «de», «qui (est)», c'est-à-dire que, suivant les cas, on pourra traduire la molécule dissociée **(a)-(o)** par «propre à l'être», ou par «de l'être», ou encore par «qui (est) l'être». Ainsi «hum-ain» peut signifier, suivant les cas, «propre à l'homme», ou «d'un homme», ou encore «qui est un homme»; par exemple, «un acte humain» (propre à l'homme), «une main humaine» (d'homme), «un être humain» (qui est un homme), etc.

4° MOLÉCULE **(o-i)**. — Cette molécule fondamentale n'existe pas à l'état condensé en français. Elle représente *l'idée substantive verbifiée*. Cette molécule servira donc de type à tous les verbes dérivés de substantifs (comme «couronn-er», «clou-er», «sci-er», «pein-er», «rag-er». etc.). D'ailleurs, on peut traduire cette molécule en français sous la forme dissociée. La forme condensée **(o-i)** est égale à la forme dissociée **(i)-(o)**; les atomes **i** et **o** devant être traduits par des radicaux, puisqu'ils représentent des mots séparés dans la molécule dissociée, on a : **i** = *ag* ou *sta*, et **o** = *un* (être) . Or, *ag* équivaut à «agir» ou «faire une action», et *sta* équivaut à «être dans un état» (station). La molécule dissociée

[industri-]el etc. mean "proper to the person", "proper to the thing", "proper to man", "proper to industry", etc.

Naturally, we can also translate the adjective atom **a** by one of the equivalent dissociated suffixes "of", "which (is)", that is, depending on the case, we can translate the dissociated molecule **(a)-(o)** by "proper to the entity" or "of the entity" or again by "which (is) the entity". Thus, *hum-ain* 'human' can mean, depending on the case, "proper to man" or "of a man" or again "which is a man"; for example, "a human act" (proper to man), "a human hand" (of a man), "a human being" (which is a man), etc.

4. MOLECULE **(o-i)**. — This basic molecule does not exist in the condensed state in French. It represents *the nominal idea verbalized*. This molecule will serve as the type of all verbs derived from nouns (like *couronn-er*, *clou-er* 'to nail', *sci-er* 'to saw', *pein-er* 'to pain (someone)', *rag-er* 'to rage', etc.). Moreover, we can translate this molecule in French by the dissociated form. The condensed form **(o-i)** is equivalent to the dissociated form **(i)-(o)**; the atoms **i** and **o** needing to be translated by roots, since they represent separate words in the dissociated molecule, we have **i** = *ag* or *sta*, and **o** = *a(n)* (entity). Now *ag* is equivalent to "to act" or "to perform an action", and *sta* is equivalent to "to be in a state" (position). The dissociated molecule

(i)-(o) signifie donc «faire l'action (caractérisée par) un être» ou bien «être dans l'état (caractérisé par) un être» (réel ou idéel). Ainsi «couronn-er» signifie «faire l'action caractérisée par l'être-réel (l'objet) *couronne*», «rag-er» signifie «être dans l'état caractérisé par l'être-idéel (le sentiment) *rage*», etc.

5° Molécule (i-a). — L'atome i sous la forme d'un radical est traduit par «agir» ou «stare» ou, en supprimant la terminaison infinitive, par «ag» ou «sta» (quelquefois «stat»); donc on a :

$$(\text{i-a}) = ag\text{-}a = ac\text{-}tif$$

ou bien :

$$(\text{i-a}) = stat\text{-}a = stat\text{-}ique.$$

Les mots «actif» et «statique» sont donc aussi des mots fondamentaux de la langue française; ils représentent *l'idée verbale adjectivée*. «Actif» signifie «de qualité *ag*», et «statique», «de qualité *stat*». Ces mots servent donc de chef de file à tous les adjectifs dérivés de verbes, tels que : «pallia-tif», «préservatif», «purga-tif», «différ-ent», etc.

On peut aussi traduire «ac-tif» par «qui ag», «qui agit», «pallia-tif» par «qui pallie», etc., puisque «qui» exprime l'idée adjective. Mais il faut soigneusement distinguer les adjectifs verbaux («actif», «préservatif», etc.), qui contiennent une idée qualitative, et les participes («agissant», «préservant», etc.), qui sont des formes purement verbales n'im-

(i)-(o) thus means "to perform the action (characterized by) an entity", or else "to be in the state (characterized by) an entity" (real or ideal). Thus, *couronn-er* means "to perform the action characterized by the real entity (the object) *crown*", *rag-er* means "to be in the state characterized by the ideal entity (the feeling) *rage*", etc.

5. Molecule (i-a). — The atom i in the form of a root is translated by *agir* or *stare*, or in suppressing the infinitive ending, by "ag" or "sta" (sometimes "stat"); thus we have:

$$(\text{i-a}) = ag\text{-}a = ac\text{-}tive$$

or else:

$$(\text{i-a}) = stat\text{-}a = stat\text{-}ic.$$

The words *actif* 'active' and *statique* 'static' are thus also basic words of the French language; they represent *the verbal idea adjectivized*. *Actif* means "of quality *ag*" and *statique* "of quality *stat*". These words serve as leading examples for all adjectives derived from verbs, such as *palliatif* 'palliate-ive', *préserva-tif* 'preservative', *purga-tif* 'purge-ative', *différ-ent* 'differ-ent', etc.

We can thus translate *ac-tif* as "who acts", *pallia-tif* by "which palliates", etc., since "who, which" translates the adjective idea. But it is necessary to carefully distinguish the verbal adjectives (*actif*, *préservatif*, etc.) which contain a qualitative idea from the participes *agissant* 'acting', *préservant* 'preserving', etc.) which are purely verbal forms im[plying]

pliquant qu'une idée d'action ou d'état. Nous avons dit, en effet, qu'il ne faut pas confondre la «qualité» (idée adjective) avec l'état ou l'action (idée verbale). Ainsi le «comité actif» d'une société peut n'être pas du tout «agissant». Il faut d'autant plus éviter cette confusion qu'en français le participe et l'adjectif ont souvent des formes très voisines (ex : «différ-ant» et «différ-ent», et même des formes identiques qui ne se distinguent plus que par l'accord de l'adjectif avec le substantif (ex. : «une fille aimant son père» et une «nature aimante»).

Nous reviendrons, du reste, dans le dernier chapitre, sur les rapports qui existent entre le participe et l'adjectif.

6° MOLÉCULE (a-i). — L'atome a est traduit sous la forme d'un radical par «qual» ou «propre», mais on ne peut pas verbifier directement ces radicaux, car les verbes «qual-er», «propri-er» n'existent pas. Par contre, on peut dire «qual-ifi-er» et «ap-propri-er». Ces mots servent de modèle à toute une série de verbes obtenus en remplaçant l'adjectif général «qual» ou «propre» par des adjectifs particuliers : ainsi «qual-ifi-er» sert de modèle aux mots tels que «béat-ifi-er», «pur-ifi-er», etc., ou encore «modern-is-er», etc., car on voit immédiatement que le suffixe «is» dans «moderniser» est le même que le suffixe «ifi» dans «béatifier». De même «ap-propri-er» sert de chef de file aux mots

[im]plying only an idea of action or state. We have said, indeed, that it is necessary not to confuse the "quality" (adjectival idea) with the state or action (verbal idea). Thus, the "active committee" of a society can be not at all "acting". It is all the more necessary to avoid this confusion since in French the participle and the adjective often have very similar forms (e.g. *différ-ant* 'differ-ing' and *différ-ent* 'different'[)], and even identical forms which are only distinguished by the agreement of the adjective with the noun (e.g. "une fille *aimant* son père" 'a daughter *loving* her father' and a "nature *aimant*" loving nature').

We will return in the final chapter, in addition, to the relations that exist between the participle and the adjective.

6. MOLECULE (a-i). — The atom a is translated as a root by "qual" or "proper (to)", but we cannot make these roots directly into verbs, because the verbs *qual-er* 'to qual', *propri-er* 'to proper' do not exist. On the other hand, we can say *qual-ifi-er* 'to characterize' and *ap-propri-er* 'to adapt'. These words serve as models for a whole series of verbs obtained by replacing the general adjective "qual" or "proper" by specific adjectives; thus, *qual-ifi-er* serves as the model for words such as *béat-ifi-er* 'to beatify', *pur-ifi-er* 'to purify', etc., or also *modern-is-er* 'to modernize' etc., because we see immediately that the suffix *is* in *moderniser* is the same as the suffix *ifi* in *béatifier*. Similarly, *ap-propri-er* serves as the leading example for words

61

tels que «a-grand-ir», etc. Le mot «béatifier» signifie «rendre béat», le mot «purifier» signifie «rendre pur», «moderniser» signifie «rendre moderne», «agrandir» signifie «rendre grand», etc. Les affixes «ifi», «is», «a», etc., sont donc des atomes verbaux qui ne contiennent rien d'autre que *l'idée verbale active*; ils ne contiennent pas d'idée particulière; cependant l'idée qu'ils contiennent n'est pas non plus tout à fait générale, ce n'est pas simplement l'idée verbale, c'est l'idée verbale *active* («faire» ou «rendre»), par opposition à l'idée verbale *neutre* («devenir»), qui peut être exprimée soit par la molécule dissociée «devenir qual» (par exemple «devenir grand»), soit par une fausse forme réfléchie de la forme active : «se qual-ifi-er», «s'ap-propri-er»; (par exemple : «s'a-grand-ir» signifie aussi «devenir grand», «se modern-is-er» signifie aussi «devenir moderne»; ainsi la phrase : «les rois *se moderni-is-ent*» équivaut à «les rois *deviennent modernes*»).

Donc, malgré les apparences d'irrégularité et la diversité des formes, le passage de l'adjectif au verbe ne présente que deux formes (forme active et forme neutre); ces deux formes sont symétriques quant à leur sens, mais elles ne sont pas exprimées par des formes symétriques, en français tout au moins, parce qu'il manque un suffixe neutre correspondant aux suffixes actifs «ifi», «is»,

such as *a-grand-ir* 'to enlarge' etc. The word *béatifier* means "to render beatific", the word *purifier* means "to make pure", *moderniser* means "to make modern", *agrandir* means "to make large", etc. The affixes *ifi*, *is*, *a*, etc. are thus verbal atoms which contain nothing but *the active verbal idea*; they contain no specific idea; however, the idea they contain is not completely general, it is not simply the verbal idea, it is the *active* verbal idea ("to cause" or "to make"), as opposed to the *neutral* verbal idea ("to become"), which can be expressed either by the dissociated molecule "to become qual" (for example "to become large"), or by a false reflexive form of the active form: *se qual-ifi-er* "to qualify oneself", *s'ap-propri-er* "to adapt oneself" (for example: *s'a-grand-ir* means also "to become large", *se modern-is-er* means also "to become modern"; thus the sentence "les rois *se modern-is-ent*" 'the kings modernize themselves' is equivalent to "the kings become modern").

Thus, despite the appearance of irregularity and diversity of form, the passage from adjective to verb involves only two forms (active form and neutral form); these two forms are symmetric with respect to their sense, but they are not expressed by symmetric forms, at least in French, because a neutral suffix is lacking corresponding to the active suffixes *ifi*, *is*,

etc. Also, just as we have represented the grammatical ideas by the conventional symbols **a**, **o**, **i**, we can similarly adopt new symbols to represent separately and symmetrically the active and neutral forms of the general verbal idea **i**: for example, the atom **ig**[1] will represent the active idea "to make", and the atom **ij** the neutral idea "to become", so that we can write: **ig-i** = *rend-re* 'make-INFINITIVE' and **ij-i** = *deven-ir* 'become-INFINITIVE'. Thus:

active verbal idea: **ig** = root-atoms: *fai, rend.*
　　　　　　　　　　suffix- " : *ifi, is,* etc.
　　　　　　　　　　préfix- " : *a-, em-, é-,* etc.
neutral　　　　"　　": **ij** = root-atom: *deven,*
　　　　　　　　　　double suffix ": *se-ifi, se-is,* etc., *s'a, s'em,* etc.

We thus reduce all of these different forms to two symmetric types which show that the basic molecule **(a-i)**, which we are studying, only has a precise sense when we break it down into two others: the molecule **(a-ig-i)**, which means "to make qual", "to make proper to" or *qual-ifi-er, ap-propri-er*, and the molecule **(a-ij-i)** which means "to become qual", "to become proper to", or "qualify oneself (as)", "adapt oneself (as)". We would thus have, for example,

rend-re pur = *pur-ifi-er* = **pur-ig-i**.
deven-ir grand = *s'a-grand-ir* = **grand-ij-i**.

---

[1]In the symbolic and phonetic transcription, the letter **g** always has the hard sound.

Les formes ci-dessus sont les formes régulières et complètes pour passer de l'adjectif au verbe. Cependant, il arrive quelquefois que l'on verbifie directement l'adjectif; par exemple, on dit *grossir, grandir*; dans ces cas, c'est le contexte qui montre si la verbification a lieu dans le sens actif ou dans le sens neutre; ainsi, «il a grossi» signifie «il est devenu gros»; au contraire, «il a grossi les faits» signifie «il a rendu les faits (plus) gros»; mais au point de vue logique, ces formes sont incomplètes.

Je termine ici l'étude des molécules fondamentales bi-atomiques, car nous avons examiné tous les types possibles : **(a-o)**, **(i-o)**; **(o-a)**, **(o-i)**; **(a-i)** et **(i-a)**.

Il est vrai que l'on peut encore considérer les molécules de la forme **(a-a)**, **(o-o)** et **(i-i)**. Ces molécules n'offrent pas beaucoup d'intérêt; elles représentent de simples pléonasmes. Or, nous savons qu'un pléonasme, introduit dans un mot, ne modifie pas le sens de celui-ci. Si le pléonasme est volontaire, il sert simplement à renforcer une idée déjà exprimée; s'il n'est pas volontaire, il n'apporte aucune modification au sens du mot. Par conséquent, les molécules telles que **(a-a)** sont réductibles à l'atome **a**. Les pléonasmes de cette sorte, très rares chez les adjectifs et les substantifs, se rencontrent constamment chez les verbes.

The forms above are the regular and complete forms for passing from adjective to verb. However, it sometimes happens that we make a verb directly from the adjective: for example, we say *grossir* 'to grow, get larger', *grandir* 'to grow, increase'; in these cases, it is the context that shows whether the verbalizing is in the active or the neutral sense: thus, "il a grossi" means "he has become large"; in contrast, "il a grossi les faits" means "he has made the facts large(r)", but from the logical point of view these forms are incomplete.

I conclude the study of basic bi-atomic molecules here, since we have examined all of the possible types: **(a-o)**, **(i-o)**; **(o-a)**, **(o-i)**; **(a-i)** et **(i-a)**.

It is true that we can also consider molecules of the form **(a-a)**, **(o-o)** and **(i-i)**. These molecules do not offer much of interest: they represent simple pleonasms. Now we know that a pleonasm, introduced into a word, does not modify its sense. If the pleonasm is deliberate, it serves simply to reinforce an idea already expressed; if it is not deliberate, it does not make any modification of the word's sense. Consequently, molecules such as **(a-a)** are reducible to the atom **a**. Pleonasms of this type, quite rare in the case of adjectives and nouns, are constantly found in verbs.

1. Molécule (i-i). — Puisque **i** est l'idée verbale «*ag*» ou «*sta*», on a :

(i-i) = *ag-ir* ou *sta-re*.

Nous avons déjà constaté précédemment que le mot «*ag-ir*» contient un pléonasme, puisque soit le radical «ag», soit le suffixe «**ir**», expriment la même idée verbale **i**, et comme la molécule (i-i) est une molécule fondamentale, le pléonasme qui se trouve dans le mot «agir» se retrouvera dans tous les verbes dont le radical est verbal, comme «écri-re», «abdiqu-er», etc. En effet, tous ces verbes sont des cas particuliers du verbe «agir», c'est-à-dire que les radicaux «écri», «abdiqu» contiennent implicitement l'idée «ag» (ou «sta»), qui est exprimée une seconde fois par la finale verbale «re» ou «er». Ce pléonasme est inévitable, c'est-à-dire qu'on ne peut pas supprimer les finales «ir» ou «er», même si le radical lui-même est verbal, parce que ces finales ne servent pas seulement à exprimer l'idée verbale générale **i**, mais aussi les différents temps et personnes de la conjugaison.

2. Molécule (a-a). — Si l'on traduit l'atome **a** par le radical «qual» et par le suffixe «eux», on obtient (a-a) — «qual-eux», mot qui n'existe pas. On trouve cependant de rares exemples d'adjectifs particuliers construits sur ce type, par exemple le mot allemand «süss-lich», dans lequel le suffixe «lich» égale le

1. Molecule (i-i). — Since **i** is the verbal idea "*ag*" or "*sta*", we have:

(i-i) = *ag-ir* ou *sta-re*.

We have already noted previously that the word *ag-ir* 'to act' contains a pleonasm, since both the root "ag" and the suffix *ir* express the same verbal idea **i**, and as the molecule (i-i) is a basic molecule, the pleonasm to be found in the word *agir* is to be found in all verbs whose root is verbal such as *écri-re* 'to write', *abdiqu-er* 'to abdicate', etc. Actually, all of these verbs are special cases of the verb *agir*, that is, the roots *écri*, *abdiqu* implicitly contain the idea "ag" (or "sta"), which is expressed a second time by the verbal ending *re* or *er*. This pleonasm is inevitable, that is, the endings *re* or *er* cannot be suppressed, even if the root itself is verbal, because these endings serve to express not only the general verbal idea **i**, but also the different tenses and persons of the conjugation.

2. Molecule (a-a). — If we translate the atom **a** by the root "qual" and by the suffix *eux*, we get (a-a) — *qual-eux*, a word that does not exist. We do however find rare examples of specific adjectives constructed according to that type, for example the German word *süss-lich*, in which the suffix *lich* equals the

suffixe français «eux», c'est-à-dire l'atome symbolique a, quoique le radical «süss» soit déjà lui-même adjectif, c'est-à-dire contienne déjà implicitement l'idée a ou «qual». Le mot «süss-lich» rentre donc dans le type «qual-eux». Il est évident qu'au point de vue purement logique «süss-lich» est un simple pléonasme réductible à «süss» ; nous savons, en effet, que le suffixe «lich» ou «eux» est équivalent au suffixe dissocié «qui», «qui est», c'est-à-dire que «süss-lich» signifie «qui est doux», ou simplement «doux», car l'atome «qui (est)» ne fait que répéter l'idée adjective déjà contenue dans «doux». En français, nous avons aussi les deux mots «doux» et «doucereux», qui sont aussi équivalents au point de vue logique, mais pour une autre raison ; la série «doux», «douc-eur», «douc-er-eux», est en effet analogue à la série «beau», «beau-té», «beau-ti-ful» (en anglais) ; on a donc *doucereux = doux* pour la même raison que *beau-tiful = beau*. La somme (*ti + ful*), en anglais, ou *eur + eux*, en français, est nulle, parce que cette somme représente l'adjectivation d'un substantif tiré lui-même d'un adjectif, opération double, dont la seconde est l'inverse de la première.

Bien entendu, si l'on emploie, en français, les deux formes «doux», «doucereux», et en allemand les deux formes «süss», «süsslich», c'est pour les distinguer l'une de l'autre, pour exprimer deux

French suffix *eux*, that is, the symbolic atom a, while the root *süss* is already itself an adjective, that is it already implicitly contains the idea a or "qual". The word *süss-lich* is thus of the type *qual-eux*. It is obvious that from the purely logical point of view *süss-lich* is a simple pleonasm reducible to *süss*; we know, indeed, that the suffix *lich* or *eux* is equivalent to the dissociated suffix "which", "which is" — that is, that *süss-lich* means "which is sweet", or simply "sweet", since the atom "which (is)" does nothing but repeat the adjectival idea already contained in "sweet". In French, we also have the two words *doux* 'sweet' and *doucereux* 'smooth, unctuous', which are also equivalent from the logical point of view, but for another reason: the series *doux, douc-eur, douc-er-eux* is actually equivalent to the series *beau, beau-té, "beau-ti-ful"* (in English); we thus have *doucereux = doux* for the same reason that *beau-tiful= beau*. The sum (*ti + ful*) in English, or *eur + eux* in French, is null, since that sum represents the adjectivization of a noun which is itself derived from an adjective, a double operation in which the second is the inverse of the first.

Of course, if we use the two forms *doux* and *doucereux* in French, and in German the two forms *süss* and *süsslich*, it is to distinguish the one from the other, to express two

different nuances of the same idea. Natural languages thus have recourse to an artifice to give two slightly different senses to the same idea: they construct two molecules, equivalent to one another from the point of view of logic, but with different forms[1]. Also these two forms are not both irreducible: the one contains superfluous atoms, and in suppressing these, we recover the other form, the one that is irreducible.

3. MOLECULE (o-o). — This molecule is interesting, because its French translation exists. Indeed, the nominal idea o can be translated by the Latin root *ens* ("the entity" or "an entity") and by the suffix *ité* ("the entity"); we thus have:

$$(o\text{-}o) = ens\text{-}ité = ent\text{-}ité:$$

If we take the root *ens* in the abstract sense ("the entity"), this root has exactly the same sense as the suffix *ité* and we then have:

$$ité = ent\text{-}ité = (o\text{-}o).$$

This is a simple pleonasm, but that pleonasm provides a body for the suffix *ité*, which cannot alone form a complete word.

---

[1] It is by an analogous artifice that in French, we give two different senses to the logically equivalent expressions *un homme grand* 'a tall man' and *un grand homme* 'a great man'.

If we take the root *ens* in the concrete sense (o_1 = "an entity"), then the molecule takes the form (o_1-o) which is no longer a pleonasm, since the second o is the abstract nominal idea, while the first is the concrete nominal idea; we then have:

ent-ité = (o_1-o) = "an — abstract entity".
= = "un-it".
= = "a un-it".

since the article *un* 'a(n)' can also represent the concrete nominal idea.

Having thus concluded the examination of the basic bi-atomic molecules, we can pass on to the tri-atomic molecules.

Basic tri-atomic molecules[1].

There are many tri-atomic words, but these are, for the most part, specific words, formed at least in part of specific atoms. Thus *hum-an-ité* is a tri-atomic word, but it contains the atom "**hom**", which expresses a specific idea.

In comparison to the number of possible combinations, there are very few basic tri-atomic molecules: for example, (i-o-i) can be translated by *ac-tionn-er* 'to activate' or *sta-tionn-er* 'to station', (i-a-o) by *ac-tiv-ité* 'activity', but nearly all of the other types have no correspondent in French; actually, *every poly-atomic molecule* (condensed or

---

[1]On a first reading, one can without problem skip over everything that is in small type.

dissociée) *est réductible en fin de compte aux molécules bi-atomiques*, de sorte que tous les types fondamentaux sont ou mono- ou bi-atomiques.

Prenons, par exemple, la molécule tri-atomique «hum-an-ité»; cette molécule représente le substantif dérivé de l'adjectif «humain», exactement comme «beau-té» représente le substantif dérivé de l'adjectif «beau»; la seule différence est que «beau» est un adjectif primitif, tandis que «humain» est un adjectif dérivé. On a donc : «humanité» = «human-ité», et non pas «hum-anité» (qui signifierait «la qualité homme», puisque le suffixe «an» = «qual»). Le mot «human-ité» ne contient donc que deux éléments dissociables : «humain» et «ité». A son tour, le mot «humain» en contient deux : «hum» et «ain»; la molécule «humanité» doit donc être représentée par le schéma :

$$[(\text{hum-an})\text{-ité}] \text{ ou } [(\textbf{hom-a})\text{-o}]$$

schéma qui montre que ce mot ne contient pas trois atomes indépendants, mais un atome et une molécule bi-atomique.

On peut aller plus loin et constater que «humanitaire» = «humanit-aire» et «humanitarisme[»]» = «humanitar-isme», de sorte que le schéma moléculaire de ce dernier mot est :

$$(\{[(\text{hum-an})\text{-it}]\text{-ar}\}\text{-isme}) \text{ ou }$$
$$(\{[(\textbf{hom-a})\text{-o}]\text{-a}\}\text{-o})$$

schéma qui montre que tout mot composé est réductible de proche en proche à des types bi-atomiques. Nous pourrions donc nous dispenser complètement de l'étude des types fondamentaux tri-atomiques; cependant, j'en examinerai quelques-uns qui sont plus particulièrement intéressants.

1. Molécule **(a-o-a)**. — Cette molécule est réductible au simple atome **(a)** ou «qual», parce que la dérivation **o-a** est exactement inverse de la dérivation **a-o** (par exemple le

dissociated) *is reducible in the end to bi-atomic molecules,* such that all of the basic types are either mono- or bi-atomic.

Take, for example, the tri-atomic molecule *hum-an-ité*; this molecule represents the noun derived from the adjective *humain*, exactly as *beau-té* represents the noun derived from the adjective *beau*; the only difference is that *beau* is a basic adjective, while *humain* is a derived adjective. We thus have *humanité* = *human-ité* and not *hum-anité* (which would mean "the quality man", since the suffix *an* = "qual"). The word *human-ité* thus contains only two dissociable elements: *humain* and *ité*. In its turn, the word *humain* contains two: *hum* and *ain*; the molecule *humanité* must thus be represented by the schema:

$$[(\text{hum-an})\text{-ité}] \text{ or } [(\textbf{hom-a})\text{-o}]$$

a schema which shows that this word does not contain three independent atoms, but one atom and a bi-atomic molecule.

We can go further and note that *humanitaire* = *humanit-aire* and *humanitarisme* = *humanitair-isme*, such that the molecular schema of this last word is:

$$(\{[(\text{hum-an})\text{-it}]\text{-ar}\}\text{-isme}) \text{ or }$$
$$(\{[(\textbf{hom-a})\text{-o}]\text{-a}\}\text{-o})$$

a schema which shows that every compound word is reducible gradually to bi-atomic types. We could thus dispense completely with the study of basic tri-atomic types; however, I will examine some which are particularly interesting.

1. Molecule **(a-o-a)**. — This molecule is reducible to the simple atom **(a)** or "qual", because the derivation **o-a** is exactly the inverse of the derivation **a-o** (for example, the

couple « joie », « joyeux » est inverse du couple « gai », « gaîté »). On peut d'ailleurs s'en rendre compte par des opérations symboliques, en remarquant que la molécule (a-o-a) ne peut désigner que l'adjectif de la molécule (a-o). On a donc, en dissociant :

$$(a\text{-}o\text{-}a) = [(a\text{-}o)\text{-}a] = (a) - (a\text{-}o) = \text{« de-qualité »}$$

et nous savons que la molécule « de qualité » se réduit à l'atome « qual » (« hom-qual » = « de qualité homme »[)]. Comme exemple particulier de molécule (a-o-a) réductible à (a), nous avons cité le mot anglais « beau-ti-ful[»] , qui est en effet équivalent au mot français mono-atomique « beau ».

Mais pour qu'une molécule tri-atomique du type (x-y-x) soit réductible à l'atome x, il faut que le premier atome x soit exactement le même que le dernier. Or, pour différentes raisons, cela n'a pas toujours lieu. Il peut arriver, par exemple, que dans la molécule (a-o-a), l'idée adjective exprimée par l'atome final a ne soit pas la même que l'idée adjective exprimée par l'atome a initial, car il y a dans l'idée adjective plusieurs nuances : l'idée « qual » (ou « de qualité ») et l'idée « propre (à) » (qui signifie plutôt « relatif à », « appartenant à »).

Ainsi, dans la série « sain », « san-té », « san-it-aire », le mot « sanitaire » rentre dans le type (a-o-a), mais la molécule « sanitaire » n'est pas réductible à l'atome « sain », parce que l'idée adjective contenue dans « sain » est purement qualitative : « un homme sain » signifie « un homme de qualité *santé* » ou « san-té-qual », car « san-té-qual » se réduit à « sain », puisque cette molécule est du type (a-o-a), où le dernier a a la même valeur que le premier. Au contraire, « san-it-aire » signifie « propre (à la) san-té » [(a) − (a-o)]; ainsi « un appareil sanitaire » est un appareil « propre à la santé », « relatif à la santé », et non pas « un appareil de qualité santé », car ce n'est pas l'appareil lui-même qui est « sain » ;

pair *joie* 'joy', *joyeux* 'joyous' is the inverse of the pair *gai* 'gay', *gaîté* 'gaiety'). We could, however, take account of this by symbolic operations, noting that the molecule (a-o-a) can only designate the adjective in the molecule (a-o). We thus have, by dissociating:

$$(a\text{-}o\text{-}a) = [(a\text{-}o)\text{-}a] = (a) - (a\text{-}o) = \text{"of-quality"}$$

and we know that the molecule "of-quality" reduces to the atom "qual" ("hom-qual" = "of quality man"). As a specific example of the molecule (a-o-a) reducible to (a), we have cited the English word "beau-ti-ful", which is actually equivalent to the mono-atomic French word *beau*.

But in order for a tri-atomic molecule of the type (x-y-x) to be reducible to the atom x, it is necessary that the first atom x should be exactly the same as the last. Now for various reasons, that is not always the case. It can happen, for example, that in the molecule (a-o-a) the adjectival idea expressed by the final a atom is not the same as the adjectival idea expressed by the initial a atom, because there are a number of nuances in the adjectival idea: the idea "qual" (or "of quality") and the idea "proper (to)" (which means rather "relative to", "belonging to").

Thus, in the series *sain* 'healthy', *san-té* 'health', *san-it-aire* 'sanitary', the word *sanitaire* belongs to the type (a-o-a), but the molecule *sanitaire* is not reducible to the atom *sain* because the adjectival idea contained in *sain* is purely qualitative: *un homme sain* 'a healthy man' means "a man of quality *health*" or *san-té-qual*, because *san-té-qual* is reducible to *sain* since that molecule is of the type (a-o-a) where the last a has the same value as the first. On the other hand, *san-it-aire* means "proper (to) health" [(a) − (a-o)]; thus *un appareil sanitaire* 'a sanitary appliance' is an appliance "proper to health", "relative to health", and not "an appliance of quality health", because it is not the appliance itself that is "healthy";

le mot «san-it-aire» est donc du type **(a-o-a)**, le second **a** signifiant «propre à», tandis que le premier (qui est contenu dans le radical «san») signifie «qual»; nous sommes dans le cas où la molécule est irréductible.

2. Molécule **(i-o-i)**. — Nous avons aussi déjà rencontré cette molécule fondamentale, dont la traduction en français (sous forme synthétique) est «ac-tion-ner». Cette molécule se réduit à l'atome «ac» ou «ag», parce que le dernier atome **i** a la même valeur que le premier; en effet, les finales verbales «er», «ir», etc., sont équivalentes à l'atome «ag» et signifient «faire une action», ou simplement «faire», car «faire» est synonyme de «agir». On peut démontrer, du reste, toutes ces équivalences par la méthode symbolique, en se rappelant que la condensation ou la dissociation d'une molécule produit le renversement de l'ordre de ses atomes :

i = «ag» = finales verbales «er», «ir», «re».
(i-i) = «ag-ir» = «fai-re».
(i-o) = «ac-tion».
(i-i) — **(i-o)** = «(fai-re) — (ac-tion)».

Comme **(i-i)** est un simple pléonasme qui se réduit à **i**, on a : «(fai-re) — (act-ion)» = **(i)** — **(i-o)** = **(i-o-i)** = «(ac-tionn-er)».

Or, la molécule **(i-o-i)** se réduit à l'atome **i**, on a donc bien : **i** = «faire une action». Cet exemple suffit pour montrer comment on peut opérer sur les symboles **a, o, i**, et retrouver toujours les mots ou les expressions logiquement équivalentes, malgré la diversité des formes apparentes. Ainsi l'atome verbal **i**, ayant aussi le sens neutre ou statique «sta», est aussi équivalent à l'expression «être dans une station (un état)».

3. Molécule **(o-a-o)**. — Cette molécule sera réductible à l'atome **o** ou, au contraire, irréductible, suivant que le dernier **o** aura ou non la même valeur que le premier. Donc, si chacun des deux **o** représentait l'idée substantive dans toute

the word *san-it-aire* is thus of type **(a-o-a)**, the second **a** signifying "proper to" while the first (which is contained in the root *san*) means "qual"; we thus have a case where the molecule is irreducible.

2. Molecule **(i-o-i)**. — We have also already encountered this basic molecule, whose translation in French (in synthetic form) is *ac-tion-ner* 'to activate'. This molecule reduces to the atom "ac" or "ag", because the final atom **i** has the same value as the first; indeed, the verbal endings *er*, *ir*, etc. are equivalent to the atom "ag" and mean "to carry out an action" or simply "to do", since "to do" is synonymous with *agir* 'to act'. We can, besides, demonstrate all of these equivalences by the symbolic method, recalling that the condensation or dissociation of a molecule results in the reversal of the order of its atoms:

i = "ag" = verbal endings *er*, *ir*, *re*
(i-i) = *ag-ir* = *fai-re*
(i-o) = *ac-tion*
(i-i) — **(i-o)** = "(fai-re) — (ac-tion)"

Since **(i-i)** is a simple pleonasm which reduces to the atom **i**, we have: "(fai-re) — (ac-tion)" = **(i)** — **(i-o)** = **(i-o-i)** = «(ac-tionn-er)».

Now the molecule **(i-o-i)** reduces to the atom **i**, and we have: **i** = "carry out an action". This example suffices to show how we can operate on the symbols **a, o, i** and always recover the logically equivalent words or expressions, in spite of the diversity of their apparent forms. Thus, the verbal atom **i**, having also the neutral or static sense "sta", is also equivalent to the expression "to be in a condition (a state)".

3. Molecule **(o-a-o)**. — This molecule will be reducible to the atom **o**, or alternatively irreducible, depending on whether the final **o** has or has not the same value as the first. Thus if each of the two **o**s represents the nominal idea in all

sa généralité, la molécule serait réductible. Mais, en réalité, dans la molécule (o-a-o), le second o remplace un suffixe substantificateur (comme «ité»), c'est-à-dire l'idée substantive générale de «l'être», «l'être abstrait» (o). Donc, si le premier o représente aussi un être abstrait, la molécule (o-a-o) sera réductible à l'atome o ; au contraire, si le premier o représente un être concret (o_1), la molécule sera irréductible, parce qu'elle sera du type (o_1-a-o), dans lequel le premier o n'a pas la même valeur que le dernier.

Il n'existe pas, en français, de mot unique pour traduire, sous forme synthétique, la molécule (o_1-a-o), parce qu'il n'existe pas d'autre atome que l'article «un» pour désigner «un être concret», et que cet article ne peut pas entrer dans la composition des mots, au moins dans ce sens[1]. Mais si l'on remarque qu'un être concret est une «personne» ou une «chose», on peut dire que la molécule (o_1-a-o) est équivalente à l'un des deux mots «personn-al-ité» ou «ré-al-ité», (puisque l'atome a = «qual» = suffixes «el», «eux», «ique», etc., et que l'atome «chose» prend la forme latine «res» quand il entre dans la composition des mots).

On a donc :

$$o_1 = \text{«un (être concret)»} = \begin{cases} \text{«personne»,} \\ \text{«chose» (res).} \end{cases}$$

$$(o_1\text{-a}) = \begin{cases} \text{«personn-el»,} \\ \text{«ré-el».} \end{cases}$$

$$o_1\text{-a-o} = \begin{cases} \text{«personn-al-ité,»,} \\ \text{«ré-al-ité».} \end{cases}$$

La molécule fondamentale (o_1-a-o) sert donc de chef de file à tous les mots, tels que «hum-an-ité», [«]nébul-os-ité»,

---

[1] En effet, le mot français «un-ic-ité» existe bien et pourrait servir à traduire la molécule en question, puisqu'on a : o_1 = «un», (o_1-a) = «unique», donc (o_1-a-o) = «un-ic-ité» ; mais le mot «un» n'a pas ici le sens de «un être» ; il représente l'idée «un» par opposition à «plusieurs».

---

its generality, the molecule will be reducible. But in reality, in the molecule (o-a-o), the second o replaces a nominalizing suffix (like *ité*), that is, the general nominal idea of "the entity", "the abstract entity" (o). Thus, if the first o also represents an abstract entity, the molecule (o-a-o) will be reducible to the atom o; on the other hand, if the first o represents a concrete entity (o_1), the molecule will be irreducible, since it will be of the type (o_1-a-o), in which the first o does not have the same value as the last.

In French, there does not exist a unique word to translate in synthetic form the molecule (o_1-a-o), because there exists no other atom than the article *un* to designate "a concrete entity", and this article cannot enter into the composition of words, at least in this sense[1]. But if we note that a concrete entity is a "person" or a "thing", we can say that the molecule (o_1-a-o) is equivalent to one of the words *personn-al-ité* or *ré-al-ité* (since the atom a = "qual" = suffixes *el, eux, ique*, etc., and the atom *chose* 'thing' takes the Latin form *res* when it enters into the composition of words).

We thus have:

$$o_1 = \text{"a (concrete entity)"} = \begin{cases} \text{"person",} \\ \text{"thing" (res),} \end{cases}$$

$$(o_1\text{-a}) = \begin{cases} \text{"person-al",} \\ \text{"re-al".} \end{cases}$$

$$o_1\text{-a-o} = \begin{cases} \text{"person-al-ity,",} \\ \text{"re-al-ity".} \end{cases}$$

The basic molecule (o_1-a-o) thus serves as the leading form for all of the words like *hum-an-ité* 'humanity', *nébul-os-ité* 'cloudiness',

---

[1] Actually, the French word *un-ic-ité* 'uniqueness' does exist and could serve to translate the molecule in question, since we have: o_1 = *un*, (o_1-a) = *unique*, thus (o_1-a-o) = *un-ic-ité*; but the word *un* here does not have the sense of "an entity"; it represents the idea "one" as opposed to "several".

«électr-ic-ité», «caus-al-ité», etc., mots qui signifient tous «qual-ité d'une (personne ou chose)», «propri-été d'une (personne ou chose)», puisque tous les atomes adjectifs «an» («ain»). «os» («eux»), «ic» («ique»), «el» («al»), etc., sont, synonymes de l'atome «qual». Ainsi «hum-an-ité» = «hom-qual-ité», «nébul-os-ité» = «nuage-qual-ité» (l'atome «nuage» prenant la forme «nébul» en composition), «électr-ic-ité[»] = «ambre-propri-été» (l'atome «ambre» prenant la forme grecque spéciale «électr» en composition, pour indiquer qu'il ne s'agit pas d'une propriété quelconque, mais de la propriété spéciale qu'a l'ambre d'attirer les corps légers, lorsqu'on le frotte), etc. Dans tous ces mots, le premier atome représente un être concret, comme «nuage», «ambre», «homme», «personne», «chose». En effet, si dans la molécule (o_1-a-o) on prenait le substantif concret (o_1) au sens abstrait (o), la molécule deviendrait réductible au simple atome o, parce que l'opération a-o serait alors inverse de o-a. C'est pourquoi le mot «humanité» (ainsi que tous les autres mots analogues), peut prendre deux sens, suivant que l'on donne à l'atome «hom» le sens concret ou le sens abstrait. Si l'on dit «l'humanité de Jésus-Christ», cela signifie «la qualité humaine, la nature d'homme (concret) de Jésus-Christ»; de même «traiter quelqu'un avec humanité» signifie «traiter d'une manière humaine, propre à un homme (concret)», et dans ces deux cas, le mot «humanité» est tout différent de «homme»; l'un est une molécule du type (o_1-a-o), l'autre un atome du type o_1. Si, au contraire, on donne à l'atome «homme» le sens abstrait «homme en général», alors le mot «humanité», qui en dérive, change de sens et ne signifie rien de plus que l'«homme eu général»; c'est qu'en effet, en donnant au mot «homme» le sens d'un être abstrait, le mot «humanité» n'est plus une molécule du type (o_1-a-o) mais du type (o-a-o), lequel type se réduit à l atome o.

On pourrait aussi dire que ce second sens du mot «humanité» provient de ce qu'on étend la notion de «qual-ité» (ou «an-ité») à l'«abstrait en général», par le fait que la qualité est une notion abstraite. Cela revient à prendre la partie pour le tout, car tous les abstraits ne sont pas des «qualités». L'être abstrait général est représenté par le suffixe «ité» et non par la molécule «qual-ité»; il suffirait donc de dire «hom-ité» (au lieu de «hum-an-ité[»]) pour désigner l'homme en général, l'homme au sens abstrait. C'est ce qu'on fait en allemand, où l'on a les deux mots : «Mensch-lich-keit» = «hum-an-ité» = «hom-qual-ité» (o_1-a-o) et «Mensch-heit» = «hom-ité», type (o_1-o) qui signifie «l'être abstrait homme», «l'homme en général[1]».

Le second sens du mot «humanité» (Menschheit) n'a donc que l'apparence d'une molécule; en réalité, c'est un simple atome qui signifie «l'homme (en général)» et, par suite, «l'ensemble des hommes». Or, «l'ensemble des hommes» peut être considéré à son tour comme une nouvelle entité concrète (o_1) donnant naissance à une nouvelle série de mots :

«humanité», «humanit-aire», «humanit-ar-isme»,

série qui correspond exactement à la famille initiale :

«homme», «hum-ain», «hum-an-ité»,

ou symboliquement :

hom, hom-a, hom-a-o,

avec cette seule différence que dans cette dernière série le mot «hom» a le sens de «un homme», tandis que dans la première le mot «humanit» doit être traité comme un simple atome signifiant «l'ensemble des hommes», «les

---

[1] Le mot «Mensch-heit» ou «hom-ité» rentre dans le type «ent-ité» (o_1-o) analysé plus haut.

We could also say that this second sense of the word "humanity" comes from extending the notion of "qual-ity" (or "an-ity") to the "abstract in general", from the fact that quality is an abstract notion. This comes down to taking the part for the whole, because not all abstracts are "qualities". The general abstract entity is represented by the suffix *ité* 'ity' and not by the molecule "qual-ity"; it would then suffice to say *hom-ité* (instead of *hum-an-ité*) to designate man in general, man in the abstract sense. This is what we do in German, where we have the two words *Mensch-lich-keit* = "hum-an-ity" = "hom-qual-ity" (o_1-a-o) and *Mensch-heit* = "hom-ity", type (o_1-o), which means "the abstract entity man", "man in general[1]".

The second sense of the word "humanity" (Menschheit) only appears to be a molecule; in reality, it is a simple atom that means "man (in general)", and following that, "the set of men". Now "the set of men" can be considered in turn as a new concrete entity (o_1) giving rise to a new series of words:

"humanité", "humanit-aire", "humanit-ar-isme",

a series that corresponds exactly to the initial series:

"homme", "hum-ain", "hum-an-ité",

or symbolically:

hom, hom-a, hom-a-o,

with the sole difference that in this last series the word *hom* 'man' has the sense of "a man", while in the first the word *humanit* must be treated as a simple atom signifying "the set of men",

---

[1] The word *Mensch-heit* or "hom-ity" belongs to the type "ent-ity" (o_1-o) analyzed above.

hommes», cet ensemble étant considéré comme une nouvelle entité concrète, donnant par conséquent naissance à un nouveau substantif abstrait (humanit-ar-isme) du type $(o_1\text{-a-o})$.

Les mots français les plus généraux rentrant dans le type $(o_1\text{-a-o})$ sont les mots «personn-al-ité» et «ré-al-ité», puisque les suffixes «al» et «ité» sont des atomes généraux et que les radicaux «personne» et «chose» (*res*) sont, sinon des atomes généraux, du moins de simples subdivisions de l'idée substantive concrète o_1. On a «personn-al-ité» = «personn-propri-été» = «ce qui est — propre à — une personne», lorsqu'on prend «personne» au sens concret ; mais si l'on prend cet atome au sens abstrait, alors il n'y a plus de différence entre la molécule «personnalité» et l'atome «la personne en général». De même «réalité» signifie «la chose en général», parce que sous la forme latine *res*, le mot «chose» a plutôt le sens abstrait. De même, «causalité» n'est que «la cause en général», si l'on donne à l'atome «cause» le sens abstrait.

4. Molécule (o-i-o). — Comme la molécule précédente, la molécule (o-i-o) sera réductible ou non, suivant que les deux atomes o auront ou non la même valeur. Comme nous savons déjà que (i-o) = «ac-tion» ou «sta-tion» (état), l'atome final o a toujours le sens abstrait o exprimé par les suffixes «tion», «ment», «ture», etc., qui suivent toujours un atome verbal. La molécule sera donc irréductible si l'o initial est concret, car elle prend alors la forme $(o_1\text{-i-o})$; elle sera réductible si l'o initial est abstrait, car alors (o-i-o) = o.

On ne peut pas traduire en français la molécule $(o_1\text{-i-o})$ par une molécule condensée, mais comme on a, d'après la loi de renversement : $(o_1\text{-i-o})$ = (i-o) — (o_1), cette molécule signifie : «action (caractérisée par) un être concret» (o_1), tel que, par exemple, «couronne», «main», etc. La molécule $(o_1\text{-i-o})$ sert donc de chef de file aux mots tels que :

"men", this set being considered as a new concrete entity, therefore giving rise to a new abstract noun (*humanit-ar-isme*) of the type $(o_1\text{-a-o})$.

The most general French words belonging to the type $(o_1\text{-a-o})$ are the words *personn-al-ité* and *ré-al-ité*, since the suffixes *al* and *ité* are general atoms and the roots *personne* and *chose* (*res*) are, if not general atoms, at least simple subdivisions of the concrete nominal idea o_1. We have *personn-al-ité* = "person-proper-ty" = "that which is — proper to — a person", when we take "person" in the concrete sense; but if we take that atom in the abstract sense, then there is no longer a difference between the molecule "personality" and the atom "the person in general". Similarly, *réalité* means "things in general", because in its Latin form *res*, the word "thing" has rather the abstract sense. Similarly, *causalité* is only "cause in general" if one gives the atom "cause" the abstract sense.

4. Molecule (o-i-o). — Like the preceding molecule, the molecule (o-i-o) is reducible or not depending on whether the two o atoms have the same value or not. As we already know that (i-o) = *ac-tion* or *sta-tion* (state), the final atom o always has the abstract sense o expressed by the suffixes *tion*, *ment*, *ture*, etc., which always follow a verbal atom. The molecule will thus be irreducible if the initial o is concrete, since it then takes the form $(o_1\text{-i-o})$; it will be reducible if the initial o is abstract, since then (o-i-o) = o.

We cannot translate the molecule $(o_1\text{-i-o})$ in French by a condensed molecule, but since we have, by the law of reversal, $(o_1\text{-i-o})$ = (i-o) — (o_1), this molecule means "action (characterized by) a concrete entity" (o_1), such as, for example, "crown", "hand" etc. The molecule $(o_1\text{-i-o})$ thus serves as leading example for words such as:

«couronn-e-ment», «mani-e-ment», etc., puisque le suffixe «ment» est égal à «tion» et que l'atome «e» est ce qui reste de la finale verbale «er» du verbe «courron-er», laquelle finale contient l'idée générale i ou «ac».

Considérons encore la série «règle», «régl-er», «règl-e-ment» : si l'on donne au substantif «règle» le sens concret de «une règle», le mot «règlement» signifie «l'action (faite d'après) une règle», (l'action de régler), comme, par exemple, dans la phrase : «le règlement de cette question s'impose». Au contraire, si l'on donne au substantif «règle» le sens abstrait de «la règle en général», la différence entre «règlement» et «règle» disparait, parce que la molécule rentre alors dans le type (o-i-o) réductible à o ; ainsi, le «règlement d'une société» signifie «la règle en général», c'est-à-dire «l'ensemble des règles» de cette société, tout comme «humanité» signifie «l'homme en général», «l'ensemble des hommes», lorsqu'on donne à l'atome «hum» le sens abstrait o. Lorsqu'on prend le mot «règlement» dans ce dernier sens, on peut le considérer comme n'étant plus, à proprement parler, une molécule tri-atomique, mais un atome signifiant «la règle» au sens abstrait, «l'ensemble des règles». Or, «l'ensemble des règles» (comme «l'ensemble des hommes») peut être considéré comme une nouvelle entité concrète pouvant donner à son tour naissance à une nouvelle famille de mots : :

règlement, réglement-er, réglement-at-ion

tout à fait semblable à la famille initiale :

règle, régl-er, règl-e-ment

ou symboliquement :

regul, regul-i, **regul**-i-o.

La seule différence entre ces deux familles est que l'atome «règle», qui sert de point de départ à la famille

couronn-e-ment 'coron-at-ion', *mani-e-ment* 'man(ipul)-at-ion', etc., since the suffix *ment* is equal to *tion* and the atom *e* is what remains of the verbal ending *er* of the verb *couronn-er*, which ending contains the general idea i or "ac".

Let us consider again the series *règle* 'rule', *règl-er* 'regulate', *règl-e-ment* 'regulation': if we give to the noun *règle* the concrete sense of "a rule", the word *règlement* means "the action (done according to) a rule", (the action of regulating), as for example in the sentence *le règlement de cette question s'impose* 'the regulation of this matter is obvious'. On the other hand, if we give to the noun *règle* the abstract sense of "rule in general", the difference between *règlement* and *règle* disappears, because the molecule then belongs to the type (o-i-o) reducible to o; thus, the *règlement d'une société* 'regulation of a society' means "rule in general", that is "the set of rules" of that society, just as "humanity" means "man in general", "the set of men" when one give the atom "hum" the abstract sense o. Once we take the word *règlement* in this latter sense, we can consider it as not being, properly speaking, a tri-atomic molecule, but an atom meaning "rule" in the abstract sense, "the set of rules". Now "the set of rules", like "the set of men", can be considered a new concrete entity able to give rise in its turn to a new family of words: :

règlement, réglement-er, règlement-at-ion 'regulation', 'to control', 'rules, regulations'

entirely comparable to the initial family:

règle, régl-er, règl-e-ment

or symbolically:

regul, regul-i, **regul**-i-o.

The only difference between these two families is that the atom *règle* serves as the point of departure for the [first] family

first [family], in the sens of "a rule" (concrete entity) while the atom *règlement*, which serves as the point of departure for the other family means "a set of rules", for example "the set of rules" of such and such a society. This set, considered as concrete, can then engender a new abstract noun (*règlementation*) which bears the same relation to the word *règlement* (concrete) as the word *règlement* (abstract) bears to the word *règle* (concrete).

Indeed, just as the tri-atomic sense[1] of the word *règl-e-ment* is "action (done according to) a rule", the sense of the word *règlement-at-ion* is "action (done according to) the rules".

5. MOLECULE (a-i-i). — In studying the two senses of the biatomic molecule (a-i), we have represented the active sense by the molecule (a-ig-i) and the neutral sense by (a-ij-i). the atoms ig and ij are verbal atoms which are not strictly basic: they do not represent the verbal idea i in its full generality: they are *subdivisions* of the verbal idea i into "active" and "neutral", as o and o_1 are subdivisions of the nominal idea into "abstract" and "concrete". We can thus represent the "active" and "neutral" ideas by the symbols i and i_1 instead of ig and ij, and consider the molecules (a-i-i), (a-i_1-i) as basic molecules where we have simply given the first i a specially "active" or "neutral" sense[2].

We can translate the molecule (a-i-i) in several ways in French: 1. by the word *qual-ifi-er*, since a = "qual"

---

[1] We can distinguish the two senses of the words *règlement* and *humanité* by calling one the tri-atomic sense (règl-e-ment) and the other the mono-atomic sense (règlement = rules, in the general sense).

[2] I have employed the notations o and o_1 to designate the abstract and concrete forms of the nominal idea, because the nominal idea naturally has the abstract form. Similarly, we can employ the notion i and i_1 to designate the verbal idea, because the verbal idea naturally has the active form.

et **i** = **ig**= «ifi»; alors la molécule **(a-i-i)** sert de chef de file à tous les mots, tels que : «béat-ifi-er», «pur-ifi-er», «laïc-is-er», etc.; 2° par un trio de suffixes fondamentaux, comme, par exemple : «an-is-er», dans le mot «(hum)-an-is-er», «iqu-is-er», dans «(électr)-iqu^1-is-er», «é-ifi-er», dans «(class)-é-ifi-er». Tous ces assemblages de suffixes sont équivalents et interchangeables, car on a :

$$qual = ain = ique = eux = \text{etc.}$$
$$rend(\text{re}) = ifi = is = \text{etc.}$$

de sorte que, par exemple : (hum-an-is-er) = (hum-an-ifi-er) = (rend-re) — (hum-ain) — (rend-re) = (hom-qual), etc.

6. Molécule **(a-i-o)**. — En remplaçant le dernier atome verbal **i** par l'atome substantif **o**, on obtient la molécule fondamentale :

(a-i-o) = «qual-ifica-tion» = «an-isa-tion», molécule qui sert de chef de file à la série des mots tels que : «béat-ifica-tion», «pur-ifica-tion», «laïc-isa-tion», «(hum)-an-isa-tion», etc.

7. **Molécule (i-a-o)**. — Comme **i** = radicaux verbaux «ag» ou «ac», que **a** = suffixes adjectifs «ain», «if», etc., et que **o** = suffixes substantifs «ité», etc., ôn a :

i = «ac», **(i-a)** = «act-if», **(i-a-o)** = «act-iv-ité», la molécule **(i-a-o)** sert donc de chef de file aux mots tels que : «divis-ibil-ité», «collect-iv-ité», etc., etc., puisque «divis», «collect», etc., sont des cas particuliers de l'idée verbale «ac» ou **i**, et que le suffixe «ibl» est un cas particulier de l'idée adjective «if» ou a.

Je termine ici l'étude des molécules fondamentales, car il n'existe guère d'autres types intéres-

---

^{1}La forme régulière du mot «électriser» est «électr-iqu-is-er», car ce mot signifie «rend-re électr-ique» et l'on sait que «rend-re» = ig-i = «is-er». On devrait de même dire «class-é-ifi-er» (rend-re class-é) au lieu de «classifier»

and **i** = **ig** = *ifi*; so the molecule **(a-i-i)** serves as the leading example for all words such as *béat-ifi-er* 'to beatify', *pur-ifi-er* 'to purify', *laïc-is-er*" 'to secularize', etc. 2. by a trio of basic suffixes, such as for example: *an-is-er* in the word *(hum)-an-is-er*"to humanize', *ique-is-er* in *(électr)-iqu^1-is-er* 'to electrify', *é-ifi-er* in *(class)-é-ifi-er* 'to classify'. All these assemblages of suffixes are equivalent and interchangeable, since we have:

$$qual = ain = ique = eux = \text{etc.}$$
$$rend(\text{re}) = ifi = is = \text{etc.}$$

such that, for example, (*hum-an-is-er*) = (*hum-an-ifi-er*) = (*rend-re*) — (*hum-ain*) = (*rend-re*) — (*hom*-qual), etc.

6. Molecule **(a-i-o)**. — By replacing the final verbal atom **i** by the nominal atom **o**, we obtain the basic molecule:

(a-i-o) = *qual-ifica-tion* = *an-isa-tion*, the molecule that serves as the leading form for the series of words such as: *béat-ifica-tion, pur-ifica-tion, laïc-isa-tion, (hum)-an-isa-tion*, etc.

7. **Molecule (i-a-o)**. — As **i** = verbal root "ag" or "ac", **a** = adjectival suffixes *ain, if*, etc. and **o** = nominal suffixes *ité*, etc., we have:

i = "ac", **(i-a)** = *act-if*, **(i-a-o)** = *act-iv-ité*. The molecule **(i-a-o)** thus serves as the leading form for words such as *divis-ibil-ité, collect-iv-ité*, etc. etc., since *divis, collect*, etc. are specific cases of the verbal idea "ac" or **i**, and the suffix *ibl* is a specific case of the adjectival idea *if* or *a*.

I conclude here the study of the basic molecules, because there exist hardly any other interes[ting] types

---

^{1}The regular form of the word *électriciser* is *électr-iqu-is-er*, because this word means "to make electric" and we know that *rend-re* 'to make' = ig-i = *is-er*. We ought similarly to say *class-é-ifi-er* (*rendr-re class-é* 'to make classed') instead of *classifier* 'to classify'.

[interes]ting [types] among the tri-atomic or poly-atomic types, and the preceding examples are sufficient — all the more so since we can always reduce any poly-atomic type at all to bi-atomic types. We can now pass on to the analysis of *non* basic molecules, that is, molecules containing only specific atoms or a mixture of basic atoms and specific atoms. But first I will make a small digression concerning the symmetry of the three grammatical ideas.

DIGRESSION ON THE SYMMETRY OF THE VERB
AND THE ADJECTIVE
IN RELATION TO THE NOUN.

The *noun* [French *substantif*], as its name indicates, is the "substance", the "body" of language: "man", "table", etc. designate "entities" (*ens*); but it must not be forgotten that the word "substance" relates to the cosmos, while "noun" is related to language, so that the noun includes not only the words that designate beings in the cosmos (like "man", "table", etc.) but also "beings of reason" (*ens rationis*), that is

à-dire des «entités» créées par l'homme en vue du langage, comme «science», «théorie», etc.

D'autre part, le substantif tout seul ne peut pas plus fonctionner qu'un corps sans membres. Pour construire des phrases, et même pour construire des mots composés, des «molécules» représentant des idées complexes, le verbe et l'adjectif sont nécessaires. Je n'envisagerai la question qu'au point de vue de la formation des mots, celle des phrases étant en dehors de mon programme.

De l'étude sommaire que nous avons faite des différents types de molécule, il ressort, non pas seulement que le verbe et l'adjectif sont les membres qui permettent au substantif de fonctionner, mais encore que ces deux membres ont des rôles *symétriques* par rapport au substantif, de sorte que Verbe, Substantif et Adjectif forment une triade, un organisme dont le Substantif est le corps et dont le Verbe et l'Adjectif sont les deux ailes, les deux membres symétriques. Nous avons déjà vu, par exemple, que les trois atomes fondamentaux a, o, i donnent naissance aux deux molécules fondamentales (**a-o**) et (**i-o**), dans lesquelles l'adjectif a et le verbe i jouent des rôles symétriques par rapport au substantif o (tandis que a et o n'ont pas des rôles symétriques par rapport à i, ni i et o par rapport à a). Ces molécules (**a-o**) et (**i-o**) représentent d'ailleurs deux mots fondamentaux de la langue : «qual-ité»

[that is] "entities" created by man in language, like "science", "theory", etc.

On the other hand, the noun cannot function alone any more than a body without limbs. To construct sentences, and even to construct compound words, the "molecules" representing complex ideas, the verb and the adjective, are necessary. I will consider the question only from the point of view of the formation of words, that of sentences being beyond the scope of my program.

From the summary study which we have made of the different types of molecule, it emerges not only that the verb and the adjective are the limbs that allow the noun to function, but also that these two limbs have *symmetric* roles in relation to the noun, such that Verb, Noun and Adjective form a triad, an organism of which the Noun is the body and the Verb and the Adjective are the two wings, the two symmetric limbs. We have already seen, for example, that the three basic atoms a, o, i give rise to two basic molecules (**a-o**) and (**i-o**), in which the adjective a and the verb i play symmetrical roles in relation to the noun o (while a and o do not have symmetric roles in relation to i, nor i and o in relation to a). These molecules (**a-o**) and (**i-o**) represent moreover two fundamental words of the language: *qual-ité*

et «ac-tion», c'est-à-dire que la substantification d'un adjectif est le pendant de la substantification d'un verbe.

On peut vérifier ce fait de plusieurs manières différentes :

1° Les mots «grand-eur», «rich-esse», «bon-té», etc., font pendant aux mots : «abonne-ment», «abdica-tion», «écriture», etc.

2° Les expressions «le beau», «le laid», «le propre», etc., font pendant aux expressions «le boire», «le manger», «le rire», etc. (par exemple, suivant Rabelais «*le rire est le propre de l'homme*»).

3° Nous avons vu que si un mot contient un atome adjectif, l'idée exprimée par ce mot contient une idée «qualificative», et si un mot contient un atome verbal, l'idée exprimée par ce mot contient une idée d'«agir» (ou de «stare»); aussi lorsqu'un substantif (comme «homme» ou symboliquement **hom**) ne contient pas d'idée qualificative et veut s'en assimiler une, il va la chercher chez l'adjectif («hum-ain» ou **hom-a**) et la ramène dans un nouveau substantif («hum-an-ité» ou **hom-a-o**); de même, lorsqu'un substantif (comme «règle» ou **regul**) ne contient pas d'idée d'«agir» et veut s'en assimiler une, il va la chercher chez le verbe («régl-er» ou **regul-i**) et la ramène dans un nouveau substantif («règl-e-ment» ou **regul-i-o**); il y a symétrie parfaite eutre les deux séries :

and *ac-tion*. That is, the nominalization of an adjective is the counterpart of the nominalization of a verb.

We can verify this fact in several different ways:

1. The words *grand-eur*, *rich-esse*, *bon-té*, etc. are the counterparts of the words *abonne-ment* 'subscription', *abdica-tion*, *écri-ture* 'writing', etc.

2. The expressions *le beau* 'the beautiful', *le laid* 'the ugly', *le propre* 'what is specific' , etc. are counterparts of the expressions *le boire* 'the drink', *le manger* 'the food', *le rire* 'laughter' etc. (for example, according to Rabelais "*le rire est le propre de l'homme*" 'laughter is what is specific to man').

3. We have seen that if a word contains an adjectival atom, the idea expressed by this word contains a "qualifying" idea, and if a word contains a verbal atom, the idea expressed by this word contains an idea of "acting" (or "being in a state"); also, when a noun (like *homme* 'man' or symbolically **hom**) does not contain a qualifying idea and wishes to acquire one, it looks for this from an ajective (*hum-ain* or **hom-a**) and brings this to a new noun (*hum-an-ité* or **hom-a-o**); similarly, when a noun (like *règle* or **regul**) does not contain an idea of "to act" and wishes to incorporate one, it looks for this from a verb (*régl-er* or **regul-i**) and brings this to a new noun (*règl-e-ment* or **regul-i-o**). There is perfect symmetry between the two series:

homme, humain, humanité, humanitaire, humanitarisme;

règle, régler, règlement, réglementer, réglementation.

4. In terms of nouns, every basic adjective (like *grand*) only yields one directly (*grand-eur*), an abstract noun, while to every derived adjective (like *hum-ain*) there correspond two nouns (*homme* and *human-ité*) obtained in the one case by suppressing, and in the other by retaining the adjectival atom (*ain*); and as this atom is qualifying, abstracting, one of these nouns is concrete and the other abstract. Similarly, every basic verb (such as *écri*) only yields directly one noun (*écri-ture*) of an abstract sort, while to every derived verb (like *couronn-er*) there correspond two nouns (*couronne* and *couronnement*), obtained in the one case by suppressing and in the other by retaining the verbal atom (*er* or *e*). These nouns also are the one concrete, the other abstract, because every "action" is an idea abstracted from reality ("to act").

We can sum up the relations between the Verb, the Noun and the Adjective by the following table:

$$\text{NOUN } (\mathbf{o} = ens)$$
$$\text{ADJECTIVE } (\mathbf{a} = qual) \qquad \text{VERB } (\mathbf{i} = ag)$$

which shows that we have to do with a symmetrical triad of which the noun is the center.

B). Molecules in General.

Up to this point we have only studied basic molecules, since the specific molecules mentioned in preceding paragraphs have only been cited as examples.

It is now necessary to examine more closely the specific molecules, that is, those which contain specific atoms, in order to be in a position to analyse any word whatsoever.

In fact, there is no precise limit between general ideas and specific ideas. It is in subdividing the first that we obtain the second, but it is difficult to say at what point we pass from the one to the other. Thus, in subdividing the nominal idea into abstract (o) and concrete (o_1), we obtain ideas that we have still considered general; similarly, in subdividing concrete entities into "things" and "persons", we obtain ideas that are more specific, or if you wish, less general, and so on.

The analysis of specific molecules presents no difficulty, now that we are familiar with atoms and the basic molecules, and that

nous savons que chaque atome particulier contient, outre l'idée particulière qu'il exprime, une ou plusieurs idées générales qui sont implicitement contenues en lui. Ceci revient à considérer tout atome particulier comme un cas spécial d'un atome général qui lui sert de chef de file ; par exemple l'atome verbal particulier «abdiqu» est un cas spécial de de l'atome verbal général «ag» ; l'atome adjectif particulier «bon» est un cas spécial de l'atome adjectif général «qual».

Donc, *pour analyser un mot composé quelconque, il faut d'abord remplacer tous les atomes particuliers contenus dans ce mot par les atomes généraux correspondants ; on obtient ainsi le mot composé fondamental qui sert de chef de file au mot particulier que l'on étudie.*

Prenons, par exemple, les deux mots particuliers «abdication» et «bonté» ; ces mots sont tous deux bi-atomiques («abdica-tion», «bon-té») et ils contiennent tous deux un atome particulier (abdica, bon) et un atome général ou grammatical (tion, té). L'atome particulier «abdica» étant verbal a pour chef de file l'atome général «ag» ou «ac», et l'atome «bon» étant adjectif est un cas spécial de l'atome général «qual». Donc le mot «abdication» n'est qu'un cas spécial du mot fondamental «ac-tion» et le mot «bon-té» n'est qu'un cas spécial du mot fondamental «qual-ité».

we know that each specific atom contains, besides the specific idea that it expresses, one or more general ideas that are implicitly contained within it. This comes down to considering every specific atom as a special case of a general atom, which serves as its leading form. For example, the specific verbal atom *abdique* 'abdic(ate)' is a special case of the general verbal atom "ag"; the specific adjectival atom *bon* 'good' is a special case of the general adjectival atom "qual".

Thus, *to analyze an arbitrary compound word, it is necessary first to replace all of the specific atoms contained in the word by the corresponding general atoms; we obtain in that way the basic compound word which serves as the leading form for the specific word we are studying.*

Let us take, for example, the two specific words *abdication* and *bonté* 'goodness'. These words are both bi-atomic (*abdica-tion* and *bon-té*), and they each contain a specific atom (abdica, bon) and a general or grammatical atom (tion, té). The specific atom *abdica* being verbal, it has as its leading form the general atom "ag" or "ac", and the atom *bon* being an adjective, it is a special case of the general atom "qual". Thus, the word *abdica-tion* is only a special case of the basic word *action*, and the word *bon-té* is only a special case of the basic word *qual-ité*.

Pour bien montrer que les idées particulières «abdica», «bon», contiennent implicitement en elles-mêmes les idées générales «ac», «qual», on peut écrire ces dernières sous les premières et entre parenthèses :

abdica-tion   *bon-té*
(*ac*)   (*qual*)

Pour avoir maintenant le sens exact d'un mot particulier, il suffit de présenter ce mot comme un cas spécial du mot fondamental correspondant. On écrira donc :

abdica-tion = *ac-tion* (espèce particulière
(*ac*)   «*abdica*»)

et :

bon-té = *qual-ité* (espèce particulière *bon*)
(*qual*)

Cette méthode d'analyse est complète, car elle ne laisse plus aucun élément caché et elle permet de ramener l'analyse d'un mot quelconque à celle d'un petit nombre de mots fondamentaux. En effet, nous avons déjà étudié les mots généraux «action» et «qualité»; nous savons que dans ces mots la soudure est une simple juxtaposition (précisément parce que les atomes généraux ne contiennent rien de sous-entendu); donc, pour analyser le sens des mots «ac-tion» et «qual-ité», il suffit de dissocier

To demonstrate that the specific ideas *abdica* and *bon* implicitly contain in themselves the general ideas "ac", "qual", we can write these last under the first and in parentheses:

abdica-tion   *bon-té*
(*ac*)   (*qual*)

Now to obtain the exact sense of a specific word, it suffices to present that word as a special case of the corresponding basic word. We thus write:

abdica-tion = *ac-tion* (specific type
(*ac*)   *abdica*)

and:

bon-té = *qual-ité* (specific type *bon*)
(*qual*)

This method of analysis is complete, since it no longer leaves any element hidden and allows us to unite the analysis of an arbitrary word with that of a small number of basic words. Indeed, we have already studied the general words *action* and *qualité*: we know that in these words the juncture is a simple juxtaposition (precisely because the general atoms contain nothing understood). Thus, to analyze the sense of the words *ac-tion* and *qual-ité* it suffices to dissociate

ces molécules en appliquant la loi du renversement des atomes, et nous avons trouvé ainsi :

(ac-tion) = (ce qui est) — (ag)
(qual-ité) = (ce qui est) — (qual)

en nous rappelant que «ag» = «ag-ir» et «qual» = «de qualité». On ne peut aller plus loin dans l'analyse, car après avoir ramené les molécules particulières aux molécules générales, et après avoir dissocié celles-ci de manière à montrer leur sens, uniquement au moyen des atomes fondamentaux qu'elles contiennent et sans qu'il n'existe plus aucun lien, aucune soudure entre ces atomes (condition importante), on a fait le même travail que le chimiste qui, pour analyser une molécule particulière, la fait rentrer dans une famille, dans une molécule servant de type à toute une série, puis analyse le contenu de cette molécule-type en en séparant tous les atomes. L'analyse est alors terminée, car les atomes fondamentaux, c'est-à-dire les idées grammaticales (**a, i, o**) sont le résidu ultime de l'analyse, les derniers éléments irréductibles, nécessaires et suffisants pour définir le sens d'un mot fondamental et, par suite, d'un mot quelconque.

Ainsi, si l'on ne veut pas tomber dans un cercle vicieux en faisant l'analyse des mots, puisqu'un mot ne peut être défini que par d'autres mots, *il*

these molecules by applying the law of reversal of atoms, and we thus find:

(ac-tion) = (that which is) — (ag)
(qual-ité) = (that which is) — (qual)

while recalling that "ag" = *ag-ir* 'to act' and "qual" = "of quality". We cannot go further in the analysis, because after having brought the specific molecules back to general molecules, and after having dissociated these so as to show their sense, solely by means of the fundamental atoms that they contain and without which there would not exist any link, any juncture between these atoms (an important condition), we have done the same work as the chemist who, to analyze a specific molecule, puts it into a family, with a molecule that serves as the type for an entire series, and analyzes the content of that type-molecule by separating its atoms. The analysis stops there, since the fundamental atoms, that is the grammatical ideas (**a, i, o**) are the ultimate residue of the analysis, the last irreducible elements, necessary and sufficient to define the sense of a basic word and consequently of any arbitrary word.

Thus, if one does not wish to fall into a vicious circle in performing the analysis of words, since a word cannot be defined except by other words, *it*

is necessary to define the meaning of specific words by that of general words, then define those by dissociating the atoms of which they are composed and which, moreover, number only three (basic atoms a, o, i), for in spite of their diversity of forms, the basic atoms represent only the adjectival idea, the nominal idea or the verbal idea. These three ideas are the elements on which all the rest is built.

It would thus be an error, begging the question, to define the general words such as *action*, *qualité*, etc. (which are basic molecules) by other words which are often less general than those which one claims to be defining. This error is found in many writers and in the majority of dictionaries.

Let us see for example what the *Littré* says on the subject of the words *action* and *qualité*:

1. *Action* — On p. 72, we can read: "Action (gramm.) = *ce qu'exprime, ce que marque le verbe*." 'that which the verb expresses, marks'. This definition is perfect, because it is composed (like the word *action*) of two parts: *ce* 'that' and *qu'exprime le verbe* 'which the verb expresses'. Now we have seen that *ce* represents precisely the nominal idea, like the suffix *tion*, and to the question "what does the verb express?" we have answered "It expresses the idea represented by the atom "ac", an atom which contains only one ultimate [basic] idea

fondamentale que nous avons figurée par le symbole i[»] ; donc on a exactement :

(ce) – (qu'exprime le verbe) = (tion) – (ac)
= (ac-tion) = **(i-o)**.

Mais il ne faut pas oublier que c'est nous qui avons répondu à la question «qu'exprime le verbe ?» en disant qu'il exprime l'idée «ac» (ou «sta»). En réalité, Littré répond tout autrement, car si l'on cherche la définition du mot «verbe» (à la page 1256), on trouve : «verbe» = «*partie du discours qui exprime une action ou un état sous forme variable*» ! Cette définition ôte toute sa valeur à la première définition du mot «action» ; car après avoir défini le mot «action» par le mot «verbe», Littré définit à son tour le mot «verbe» par le mot «action». On ne saurait concevoir de cercle vicieux plus parfait, mais comme il y a environ 1200 pages de texte entre les deux définitions, on a eu le temps d'oublier la première quand on lit la seconde. En réalité, la première définition de Littré est la seule juste ; en disant que «ac-tion» est «ce—qu'exprime le verbe», il donne précisément la définition qui résulte de la dissociation des deux atomes «ac» et «tion», puisque «tion» est l'idée substantive «ce», et que, d'autre part, «qu'exprime le verbe ?» sinon l'idée verbale i = «ac» (ou «sta») ? La définition de Littré revient donc bien à dire que «action» =

basic [idea] which we have represented by the symbol **i**": thus, we have exactly:

(that) – (which the verb expresses)
= (tion) – (ac)
= (ac-tion) = **(i-o)**.

But it is necessary not to forget that it is we who have responded to the question "what does the verb express?" by saying that it expresses the idea "ac" (or "sta"). In reality, *Littré* responds quite differently, for if we seek the definition of the word "verb" (on page 1256), we find: *verbe* = "*part of speech which expresses an action or a state in variable form*"! This definition deprives the first definition of the word *action* of all its value, since after defining the word *action* by the word "verb", *Littré* defines in turn the word verb by the word "action". It would be hard to imagine a more perfect vicious circle, but since there are about 1200 pages of text between the two definitions, we have had time to forget the first when we read the second. In reality, the first definition of the *Littré* is the only legitimate one: in saying that *ac-tion* is "that — which the verb express" it gives precisely the definition which results from the dissociation of the two atoms "ac" and "tion", since "tion" is the nominal idea "that"; and what is it, on the other hand, "which the verb expresses?" except the idea **i** = "ac" (or "sta")? The *Littré* definition thus comes down to saying that *action* =

(i-o); the idea *action* is thus simply *the idea that results from the juxtaposition of the nominal idea with the verbal idea.* On the other hand, the definition of the word "verb" given by the *Littré* has no value, not only because it constitutes a vicious circle, but also because it claims to define a basic atom like i by means of the word "action" which is a molecule.

In summary, the only logical method is the *reduction to atoms*; it is the atom "verb" i that must define the word *action* and not the reverse, and one can write this definition in any of the following ways:

(*ac-tion*) = (*that*) – (which the *verb* expresses),
  = (*that* which is) – (*verbal* idea),
  = (*that* which is) – (*ac* or *ag* or *agir*[1]),
  = (*tion*) – (*ac*),
  = (*nominal idea*) joined to (*verbal idea*),
  =   (o)   –   (i),
  = molecule   (i-o).

and that is all.

2. *Quality.* — If we now look in the *Littré* for the definition of the word *qualité*, we find: *qualité* = "that which makes it that a thing is

---

[1] Because *ag-ir* 'to act' is a simple pleonasm equivalent to *ag*.

telle». Cette définition est bonne, mais peut être mise sous une forme plus symétrique. Tout d'abord, l'adjectif «tel» (*talis*) correspond à l'adjectif «quel» (*qualis*) ; l'un est seulement la réponse de l'autre ; quand on demande : «Quelle est cette chose ?» on répond : «Elle est telle». On peut donc considérer l'atome «tel» comme atome adjectif fondamental, au même titre que «qual» ; de sorte que l'on peut dire que «qual-ité» = «ce qui est — tel» ou «ce qui est — qual» dans une chose. Cette définition est la seule bonne, parce qu'elle explique le mot composé «qualité» au moyen des deux atomes qui le composent et sans utiliser autre chose.

Littré dit aussi : «qualité» = «ce qui constitue la manière d'être d'une chose». Cette définition est moins lumineuse ; néanmoins, on peut l'utiliser en la comparant à celle de l'adjectif qualificatif. Littré dit en effet : «adjectif» = «l'une des dix parties du discours, mot que l'on joint au substantif pour le qualifier,... mot qui sert à exprimer la manière d'être...». Comme nous avons vu que «qual-ifi-er» = «rendre qual», la définition de Littré signifie que l'adjectif sert à rendre «qual» le substantif (par exemple «hum-ain» = «hom-qual») ; il ajoute donc au substantif l'idée «qual», ce qui revient à dire tout simplement que l'idée adjective («ain») est l'idée «qual».

En outre, à la question : «qu'exprime l'adjectif ?»

such". This definition is good, but can be put into a more symmetric form. First of all, the adjective *tel* 'such' (*talis*) corresponds to the adjective *quel* 'what (kind)' (*qualis*): the one is simply the answer to the other. When we ask *Quelle est cette chose?* 'What kind of thing is that?', we answer *Elle est telle* 'It is such (a thing)'. We can thus consider the atom *tel* as a basic adjective, in the same capacity as "qual"; so that we can say that *qual-ité* = "that which is — such" or "that which is — qual" in a thing. This definition is the only good one, because it explains the compound word "quality" by means of the two atoms that compose it and without using anything else.

The *Littré* also says *qualité* = "that which constitutes the manner of being of a thing". This definition is less lucid; nevertheless, we can make use of it by comparing it to that of the qualifying adjective. *Littré* says indeed: *adjectif* = "one of the ten parts of speech, a word which one joins to a noun to qualify it, ... a word which serves to express the manner of being ...". As we have seen that *qual-ifi-er* 'to qualify' = "to make qual", the *Littré* definition means that the adjective serves to make the noun "qual" (for example *hum-ain* = "hom-qual"). It thus adds to the noun the idea "qual", which comes down to saying simply that the adjectival idea (*ain*) is the idea "qual".

In addition, to the question "what does the adjective express?"

Littré responds: "it expresses the manner of being", and since previously *Littré* defined the *qualité* as being "that which constitutes the manner of being of a thing", we immediately conclude, by combining these two definitions, that "quality" is "*that which the adjective expresses*", a form from which we derive a double advantage, because in combining the two definitions of the *Littré*, we have completely eliminated the troubling expression "manner of being" (as one eliminates a superfluous variable between two equations); and secondly, the definition of the word "quality" now corresponds to that of the word "action" which, according to the *Littré* itself, means "that which the verb expresses". We thus reduce the definition of these two words to the analysis of their atoms and consider the verbal and adjectival ideas as primary materials for the construction of words. It is the adjectival atom (**a**) which must define the word "quality", and not the reverse; also we will eliminate the last part of the *Littré* definition, which adds "the adjective serves to express the *quality* of things", for that part of the definition is simply a vicious circle[1] On the contrary, it is necessary to say that the "quality is *the idea that results from the juxtaposition of the nominal idea with the adjectival idea*".

---

[1] *Littré* also says "the state of things", but it is necessary not to confuse the "quality" with the "state". See the final chapter.

In summary, the definition of the word "quality" can take any one of the following forms, which are however completely symmetric with the forms that define the word "action":

(*qual-ité*) = (*that*) − (which the *adjective* expresses),
        = (*that* which is) − (*adjective idea*),
        = (*that* which is) − (*qual* or *tel*)
        =   (*ité*)   −   (*qual*),
        = (*nominal idea*) joined to (*adjectival idea*),
        =   (o)   −   (a),
        = molecule (a-o).

EXAMPLES OF ANALYSES OF WORDS. — We now have all of the elements necessary to to proceed to the logical analysis of an arbitrary specific word. Some examples will suffice.

1. *Analysis of the word* beauté. —We begin by indicating the atoms that compose the word in writing *beau-té*; we replace the atom *beau* by the corresponding general atom "qual", and since the atom *té* or *-ité* is already a basic atom, we conclude that *beau-té* is a specific case of *qual-ité* since *beau* is a specific case of "qual. Thus we write:

beau-té = "qual-ité *beau*".
(qual)

The analysis terminates, because the basic word *qualité* has already been analyzed, but the equation above shows us different things.

We have seen that in the basic molecules, the junction between atoms is a simple juxtaposition (apart from the reversal of the order of atoms resulting from the condensation of the molecule). Thus, we know that *ité* = "that (which is)", thus *qualité* = "that (which is) — qual". We thus have *beauté* = "that which is beautiful", providing we give the atom *ce* 'that' its full generality; this atom designates "being in general", "abstract being", and thus *beau-té* = "the abstraction beautiful" = "the beautiful". But the analysis is more precise and clearer, since one makes use of the understood general ideas that are present in specific atoms. We thus have *beauté* = "quality *beautiful*", a narrower sense than "abstraction *beautiful*", because even if all qualities are abstractions, not all abstractions are qualities. There is thus a nuance between *beauté* ("quality *beautiful*") and *le beau* ("abstraction *beautiful*")[1] This last sense is more general than the

---

[1] There is an analogous nuance between *boisson* 'drink(ing)' ("action *to drink*") and *le boire* ("abstraction *to drink*").

premier, puisque la «qualité» n'est qu'un cas de l'«abstraction».

Les idées générales sous-entendues sont donc très utiles dans l'analyse des mots. Ce ne sont, du reste, pas seulement les idées les plus générales (idées grammaticales) qui peuvent servir à cette analyse. Prenons, par exemple, le mot «Lyonnais»; ce mot contient deux atomes «Lyon» et «ais»; l'atome «Lyon» est un atome particulier substantif, mais, outre l'idée substantive («un être concret»), l'idée «Lyon» contient des idées moins générales, comme, par exemple, l'idée «France», si l'on se place au point de vue géographique. On peut donc écrire :

«Lyonn-ais» = «Franç-ais de *Lyon.*»
(France)

tout comme on a écrit[1] :

«beau-té» = «qual-ité *beau*».
(qual)

---

[1]Ces équations sont justes au sens mathématique, c'est-à-dire que les deux membres sont exactement équivalents, quoiqu'il semble possible de faire l'objection suivante : puisque l'atome «beau», dans le premier membre de l'équation, contient en lui-même l'idée «qual», ce même atome «beau», dans le second membre, doit aussi contenir l'idée «qual» en lui-même, et alors il n'y aurait qu'un atome «qual» dans le premier membre et deux dans le second ; donc les deux membres ne seraient pas équivalents ; en d'au-

first, since the "quality" is only one case of the "abstraction".

The understood general ideas are thus very useful in the analysis of words. Moreover, it is not only the most general ideas (grammatical ideas) that can be made use of in this analysis. Take for example the word *Lyonnais*: this word contains two atoms *Lyon* and *ais*. The atom *Lyon* is a specific nominal atom, but besides the nominal idea "*a* concrete entity"), the idea "Lyon" contains less general ideas, such as for example the idea "France", if one takes the point of view of geography. We can thus write:

Lyonn-ais = "Franç-ais from *Lyon.*"
(France)

just as we wrote[1]:

beau-té = " qual-ité *beau*".
(qual)

---

[1]These equations are correct in the mathematical sense, that is, the two sides are exactly equivalent, even though it is possible to make the following objection: since the atom *beau* in the first member of the equation contains in itself the idea "qual", this same atom *beau* in the second member must also contain in itself the idea "qual", and then there would be only one atom "qual" in the first member and two in the second, and thus the two members would not be equivalent. In [other]

Les idées générales sous-entendues servent donc à donner un sens précis aux mots composés, car c'est par elles que le sens général d'un mot est déterminé. Ainsi, dans le mot «beauté», les idées gé-

---

tres mots, si l'on relranche l'atome «beau» dans les deux membres, il reste «té» ou «ité» = «qual-ité», ce qui est faux.

Cette objection n'est pas bien fondée, car, en réalité, l'atome «beau», dans le second membre, n'est plus du tout le même que l'atome «beau» dans le premier membre. Le premier atome «beau» est un vrai adjectif qui a un pouvoir qualificateur et qui, par conséquent, contient en lui-même l'idée générale adjective «qual»; c'est un atome complet, un atome vivant. Tout autre est l'atome «beau» dans le second membre : il n'a plus de pouvoir qualificateur, il ne qualifie plus le substantif qui est à côté de lui, car la «qualité *beau*» n'est pas du tout la même chose qu'une «belle qualité»; l'atome «beau» du second membre n'exprime donc plus qu'une idée particulière et ne contient plus l'idée générale «qual» : cette idée «qual», qui constituait pour ainsi dire la vie, l'âme de l'atome «beau» dans le premier membre de l'équation, a été extirpée et mise en évidence dans le mot «qualité», où elle figure explicitement; l'atome «qual» du mot «qualité», dans le second membre, est donc bien le même que l'idée «qual» qui était contenue dans l'atome «beau» du premier membre; donc l'atome «beau» du second membre n'est plus qu'une sorte de cadavre, une coquille dont l'animal intérieur («qual») a été extirpé; ce n'est plus qu'un numéro; si l'on numérote tous les adjectifs du dictionnaire, la qualité «beau» sera, par exemple, la qualité N° 127; c est pourquoi, dans les équations ci-dessus, j'ai distingué les atomes vivants «beau», «Lyon» des mêmes atomes morts, en mettant ceux-ci en italiques.

The understood general ideas thus serve to give a precise sense to compound words, because it is through them that the general sense of a word is determined. Thus, in the word *beauté*, the ge[neral] ideas

---

other words, if we delete the atom *beau* on the two sides, what remains is *té* or *ité* = *qual-ité*, which is false.

This objection is not well founded, because in reality, the atom *beau* in the second member is not at all the same as the atom *beau* in the first member. The first atom *beau* is a true adjective which has qualifying power and which, as a result, contains in itself the general adjectival idea "qual": it is a complete atom, a living atom. The atom *beau* in the second member is quite different: it no longer has qualifying power, it does not qualify the noun beside it any more, for the "quality *beau*" is not at all the same thing as a "beautiful quality". The atom *beau* in the second member thus expresses nothing more than a specific idea and no longer contains the general idea "qual". This idea "qual", which constitutes as it were the life, the soul of the atom *beau* in the first member of the equation, has been rooted out and made obvious in the word *qual-ité*, where it figures explicitly. The atom "qual" of the word *qualité* in the second member is thus just the same as the idea "qual" which was contained in the atom *beau* of the first member. Thus the atom *beau* of the second member is no more than a sort of cadaver, a shell from which the animal inside ("qual") has been extracted; it is no more than a number; if one enumerated all of the adjectives in the dictionary, the quality *beau* would be, for example, #127. That is why, in the equations above, I have distinguished the living atoms *beau*, *Lyon*, from the same atoms in death, putting these in italics.

nérales sont **a** et **o**, et l'on peut écrire symboliquement :

bel-o = (a-o) espèce *bel*.
(a)

équation qui montre que le mot «beauté» rentre dans le type **(a-o)**, c'est-à-dire dans le type des adjectivo-substantifs (comme «richesse», «grandeur», etc.), dont le sens général est «qual-ité».

On peut dire que le mot «beau» est égal à l'atome général a coiffé de l'idée particulière *beau*, atome que l'on peut représenter symboliquement par â, l'accent circonflexe étant destiné à faire une distinction entre les atomes particuliers et les atomes généraux ; ainsi j'écrirai :

«beau» = â, «té» = o, d'où «beau-té» = â-o.

2. *Analyse du mot «violoniste»*. — Cette molécule est bi-atomique («violon-iste») et les deux atomes qui la composent sont tous deux substantifs. Elle rentre donc dans le type général **(o-o)**, qui contient par conséquent un pléonasme. Mais le pléonasme est ici à peine perceptible et ne joue qu'un rôle tout à fait secondaire, car ce qui importe dans le mot «violoniste», ce sont les idées particulières «violon» et «iste» ; or, le pléonasme ne se rapporte pas à ces idées particulières (ô), mais seulement à l'idée substantive générale (o).

general [ideas] are **a** and **o**, and one can write symbolically:

bel-o = (a-o) type *bel*.
(a)

an equation that shows that the word *beauté* belongs to the type **(a-o)**, that is, to the type of nominalized adjectives (like *richesse* 'rich-ness: wealth', *grandeur* 'large-ness: size', etc.), whose general sense is *qual-ité*.

We can thus say that the word *beau* is equal to the general atom a elaborated by the specific idea *beau*, an atom that we can represent symbolically by â, the circumflex accent intended to make a distinction between specific atoms and the general atoms. Thus, I will write:

beau = â, *té* = o, thus *beau-té* = â-o.

2. *Analysis of the word* violoniste. — This molecule is bi-atomic (*violon-iste*), and the two atoms that make it up are both nouns. It thus belongs to the general type **(o-o)**, which contains as a result a pleonasm. But the pleonasm is hardly perceptible here, and only plays a completely secondary role, because what matters in the word *violoniste* are the specific ideas *violon* and *iste* and pleonasm is not related to specific ideas (ô), but only to the general nominal idea (o).

Also, although the general molecules of the type (o-o) or (a-a) are quite rare, because they are simple pleonasms, the specifici molecules (ô-ô) or (â-â), etc. are very frequent and are not reducible, because the two atoms each express a different specific idea and have in common only the general nominal (or adjectival) idea. We take this into account by writing under each atom all of the more general ideas that are implicitly contained in that atom:

$$\begin{array}{ccc} violon & - & iste \\ (\text{object}) & & (\text{person}) \\ (\text{concrete entity}) & & (\text{concrete entity}) \\ (\text{an entity}) & & (\text{an entity}) \\ o & & o \end{array} = (\text{ô-ô})$$

Thus we have:

iste = a person-entity (type *professional*).
violon = an object-entity (type *violin*).

and following that, by dissociating and reversing the atoms, the meaning of the word *violoniste* is "a person-entity *professional* (characterized by) the object-entity *violin*"[1].

3. *Analysis of the word* mammifère. — The atom *mammi* 'teat' is a [specific] noun root

---

[1] Here the juncture between the two atoms of the word *violon-iste* is not a simple juxtaposition. We will come back to this in the second chapter.

particulier (ô); l'atome «fère» (qui porte) est un suffixe adjectif particulier (â).

Cette molécule ne contient aucun pléonasme et s'analyse immédiatement, comme suit :

$$mammi \quad - \quad fère = (ô\text{-}â)$$
$$(objet) \qquad\qquad a$$
$$(un\ être\ concret)$$
$$(un\ être)$$
$$o$$

Le mot «mammifère» est donc un adjectif, et signifie, sous forme dissociée : «(qui porte) — (l'être-objet *mammelle*)».

4. *Analyse du mot «chandelier»*. — L'atome «chandel» est un radical substantif particulier (ô); l'atome «ier» est un suffixe substantif particulier (ô) qui signifie «objet qui porte». On a donc :

$$chandel \quad - \quad ier \quad = (ô\text{-}ô)$$
$$(objet) \qquad\quad (objet)$$
$$(un\ être\ concret) \ (un\ être\ concret)$$
$$(un\ être) \qquad\quad (un\ être)$$
$$(o) \qquad\qquad\quad o$$

On voit que toutes les idées générales contenues dans «chandel» sont les mêmes que celles contenues dans «ier», et pourtant le mot «chandelier» ne peut pas être simplifié ; il est irréductible, parce que les deux atomes (ô) différent par les idées

specific [noun root] (ô); the atom *fère* (which bears) is a specific adjective suffix (â).

This molecule contains no pleonasm, and is immediately analyzed as follows:

$$mammi \quad - \quad fère = (ô\text{-}â)$$
$$(object) \qquad\qquad a$$
$$(concrete\ entity)$$
$$(an\ entity)$$
$$o$$

The word *mammifère* is thus an adjective, and means, in dissociated form, "(which bears) — (the object-entity *teat*)".

4. *Analysis of the word* chandelier *'candelabra'.—* The atom *chandel* 'candle' is a specific noun root (ô); the atom *ier* is a specific nominal suffix (ô) which means "object that holds". We thus have

$$chandel \quad - \quad ier \quad = (ô\text{-}ô)$$
$$(object) \qquad\quad (object)$$
$$(concrete\ entity) \ (concrete\ entity)$$
$$(an\ entity) \qquad\quad (an\ entity)$$
$$(o) \qquad\qquad\quad o$$

We see that all of the general ideas contained in *chandel* are the same as those contained in *ier*, but nonetheless the word *chandelier* cannot be simplified: it is irreducible, because the two (ô) atoms differ in terms of the [specific] ideas

particulières («chandelle», «ier») qu'ils représentent. En dissociant les atomes, on a : «chandelier» = (être-objet qui *porte*) — (l'être-objet *chandelle*).

5. *Analyse du mot «héroïne»*. Ce mot est aussi du type (ô-ô), comme le précédent. Les atomes (ô) représentent seulement des personnes au lieu d'objets. Le suffixe «ine» (dans héroïne) ou «esse» (dans «princesse»), désigne en effet une «personne du sexe féminin» :

```
    héro        —      ine      =(ô-ô)
 (personne)         (personne)
(un être concret) (un être concret)
   (un être)        (un être)
     (o)              (o)
```

D'où, en dissociant : «héroïne» = (personne du sexe *féminin*) — (du type *héros*).

Si, au lieu du mot «héroïne», nous prenons le mot «matronine», nous aurons l'analyse suivante :

```
    matron       —       ine       =(ô-ô)
(personne féminine)   (personne)
   (personne)      (un être concret)
(un être concret)     (un être)
    (un être)            (o)
      (o)
```

Cette analyse montre que non seulement toutes les idées générales sous-entendues dans le suffixe «ine» sont les mêmes que celles qui sont sous-entendues dans l'atome «matrone», mais encore que

specific [ideas] that they represent (*chandelle* 'candle', *ier*). By dissociating the atoms, we have *chandelier* = (object-entity which *holds*) — (object-entity candle).

5. *Analysis of the word* héroïne 'heroine'. — This word is also of the type (ô-ô), like the preceding one. The (ô) atoms merely represent persons instead of objects. The suffix *ine* (in héroïne) or *esse* (in *princesse*) actually designates a "person of the feminine sex":

```
    héro        —      ïne      =(ô-ô)
  (person)          (person)
(concrete entity) (concrete entity)
  (an entity)       (an entity)
     (o)              (o)
```

From which, by dissociating, *héroïne* = (person of sex *feminine*) — (of type *hero*).

If instead of the word "héroïne" we take the word *matronine*, we would have the following analysis:

```
    matron       —       ine       =(ô-ô)
(person feminine)     (person)
    (person)      (concrete entity)
(concrete entity)    (an entity)
  (an entity)           (o)
      (o)
```

This analysis shows that not only all of the general ideas assumed by the suffix *ine* are the same as those which are understood by the atom *matron*, but also that

the *specific* idea *ine* (person of sex *feminine*) is itself understood in the specific idea *matrone* 'matron'. Therefore the word *matronine* contains a useless pleonasm: the atom *ine* is already implicitly and totally contained in the atom *matrone*; we can thus eliminate it and reduce *matonine* to *matrone*. Moreover, the word *matronine* does not exist in French: indeed, the very usage of the language prevents the introduction of useless suffixes, and if a newly created word contained such a suffix, the principle of least effort would soon have made it disappear.

Apparently, *every suffix must introduce into the word to which it is attached an idea* (general or specific) *which was not already contained in it*. Thus, the suffix *eux*, necessary in *glorieux*, is useless in *grandiose*, since *ose* = eux^1 = adjectival idea **a**; thus:

glor-ieux = **glor-a** (irreducible),

while:

grand-iose[2] = *grand-eux* = **grand-a** = **grand**,

---

[1] We can establish that *ose* = *eux* in the words *nébul-eux* 'cloudy', *nébul-os-ité* 'cloudiness'.
[2] *Grandiose* is only equal to *grand* from the logical point of view. Actually, in *grandiose*, the suffix has a specific sense (augmentative), just as the suffix *lich* in *süsslich*, has a specific (diminutive) sense.

car l'idée adjective a n'est pas contenue dans le substantif «gloire», mais elle l'est déjà dans l'adjectif «grand».

Ces remarques nous amènent à étudier les lois de la *synthèse* des mots composés, problème inverse de celui que nous venons de traiter jusqu'ici. Ces lois de synthèse sont particulièrement utiles pour les savants et les techniciens, qui forgent souvent des mots nouveaux plus ou moins bien construits.

since the adjectival idea a is not contained in the noun *gloire* 'glory', but it is so in the adjective *grand*.

These remarks lead us to study the laws of *synthesis* in compound words, the inverse problem of that which we have just been treating up to this point. These laws of synthesis are quite useful for scientists and technicians, who often build new words that are more or less well constructed.

CHAPITRE II

SYNTHÈSE DES MOTS

Le problème à résoudre pour pouvoir effectuer la synthèse des mots est l'inverse de celui que nous avons étudié dans le chapitre premier. On peut l'énoncer comme suit :

Etant donnée une idée complexe, construire le mot composé qui représente cette idée, c'est-à-dire trouver la combinaison de radicaux et d'affixes qui évoquera cette idée.

Nous avons déjà dit que le tout étant l'ensemble de ses parties, l'idée totale évoquée par un mot composé est l'ensemble, ou, si l'on veut, la résultante des idées partielles évoquées par les différentes parties de ce mot. Donc, réciproquement, pour représenter par un mot composé une idée donnée, il faut introduire dans ce mot (au moyen de radicaux et d'affixes), toutes les idées partielles contenues dans l'idée totale à représenter.

CHAPTER II

SYNTHESIS OF WORDS

The problem that must be resolved in order to carry out the synthesis of words is the inverse of that which we have studied in the first chapter. We could formulate it as follows:

Given a complex idea, construct the compound word that represents that idea, that is, find the combination of roots and affixes that will evoke that idea.

We have already said that the whole being the sum of its parts, the total idea evoked by a compound word is the set, or if you wish the result of the partial ideas evoked by the different parts of this word. Thus, reciprocally, to represent a given idea by a compound word, it is necessary to introduce into the word (by means of roots and affixes) all of the partial ideas contained in the total idea to be represented.

Mais, énoncée sous cette forme, la solution du problème n'aurait aucune valeur pratique, car : 1° une idée complexe contient une quantité d'idées partielles que l'on ne peut pas toutes énumérer ; 2° quoique le nombre des mots simples soit considérable, le nombre des affixes est assez restreint, et l'on ne peut pas toujours exprimer exactement par un affixe l'idée partielle que l'on voudrait exprimer. Pour ces deux raisons, l'idée totale n'est pas toujours exprimable exactement au moyen de radicaux et d'affixes. Dans ce cas, il faut se contenter d'une solution approchée et enfermer l'idée à exprimer entre deux limites aussi rapprochées que possible de cette idée, à l'instar des mathématiciens qui, ne pouvant pas représenter exactement les quantités incommensurables par un nombre, enferment ces quantités entre deux limites commensurables aussi rapprochées que possible l'une de l'autre.

On est donc conduit, afin de prévoir tous les cas possibles, à poser les deux principes suivants qui s'opposent et se complètent mutuellement et qui forment la base logique de la synthèse des mots :

1. Principe de nécessité : *Dans la formation d'un mot composé, il faut introduire (au moyen de radicaux et d'affixes) tous les éléments nécessaires pour évoquer clairement et complètement l'idée que ce mot doit représenter.*

However, set out in that form, the solution to the problem would have no practical value, since 1. a complex idea contains so many partial ideas that one could not enumerate them all; 2. although the number of simple words is considerable, the number of affixes is rather limited, and one cannot always express through an affix exactly the partial idea that one would like to express. For these two reasons, the total idea is not always exactly expressible by means of roots and affixes. In that case, it is necessary to be content with an approximate solution, and to confine the idea to be expressed between two limits as close as possible to that idea, following the example of mathematicians who, not being able to represent irrational quantities exactly by a number, confine these quantities between two rational limits as close as possible to one another.

We are thus led, in order to anticipate all possible cases, to set down the two following opposed and complementary principles which form the logical basis of the synthesis of words:

1. Principle of necessity: *In the formation of a compound word, it is necessary to introduce (by means of roots and affixes) all elements necessary to evoke clearly and completely the the idea that this word should represent.*

2. Principe de suffisance : *Il ne faut pas répéter (sans nécessité) plusieurs fois la même idée dans le même mot, et il ne faut pas y introduire des idées étrangères non contenues dans l'idée totale à exprimer.*

Lorsqu'un mot composé est construit conformément à ces deux principes, on est sûr que : 1° chaque idée partielle, nécessaire pour évoquer l'idée totale, est contenue dans quelque partie du mot composé qui exprime cette idée totale (ainsi l'idée totale exprimée par le mot «humanité» contient une idée partielle qualificative, laquelle se trouve contenue dans l'atome adjectif «an») ; 2° toute idée contenue dans un élément du mot composé est une idée partielle nécessairement contenue dans l'idée totale représentée par ce mot (ainsi l'atome «hum» de «humanité» contenant, par exemple, l'idée de «personne», cette idée de personne se retrouve forcément aussi dans le mot «humanité») ; 3° aucune idée n'est exprimée (sans nécessité), plus d'une fois.

En résumé, *le sens d'un mot ne dépend que de son propre contenu et de tout son contenu*, et non pas de la manière dont on peut supposer ce mot dérivé d'un autre ; à condition, bien entendu, que l'on connaisse (par le classement des atomes de la page 40) la nature grammaticale de chacun des atomes dont ce mot est composé.

2. Principle of sufficiency: *It is necessary not to repeat (unnecessarily) the same idea multiple times in the same word, and it is necessary not to introduce alien ideas not contained in the total idea to be expressed.*

When a compound word is constructed in conformity with these two principles, we can be sure that 1. each partial idea, necessary to evoke the total idea, is contained in some part of the compound word which expresses that total idea (thus the total idea expressed by the word *humanité* contains a qualifying partial idea, which is found in the adjective atom *an*); 2. every idea contained in an element of the compound word is a partial idea that is necessarily contained in the total idea represented by the word (thus since the atom *hum* in *humanité*, contains for example the idea of "person", that idea of person is necessarily found also in the word *humanité*): 3. No idea is expressed (unnecessarily) more than once.

In sum, *the meaning of a word depends only on its own content, and on all of its content*, and not on the manner in which one supposes this word to be derived from another; on condition, of course, that we know (from the classification of atoms on page 40) the grammatical nature of each of the atoms of which the word is composed.

Pour construire le mot composé représentant une idée complexe donnée, le moyen le plus simple est d'exprimer d'abord cette idée complexe sous forme analytique, au moyen de plusieurs mots : si l'on considère alors cette définition analytique de l'idée comme une molécule dissociée, il suffit pour obtenir le mot cherché de condenser cette molécule en en expulsant (grâce au principe de suffisance) les pléonasmes qu'elle contient presque toujours, et en appliquant la loi du renversement des atomes.

Deux cas peuvent se présenter suivant que l'idée à représenter est, ou non, exprimable au moyen des radicaux et suffixes dont dispose la langue. Dans le premier cas, le problème a une solution exacte, dans le second cas la solution n'est qu'approchée.

EXEMPLES : 1. Prenons d'abord comme exemple l'idée complexe représentée analytiquement par le groupe de mots : *action « d'écrire »*. Si l'on remplace chaque atome par son équivalent symbolique («ac» = i, «tion» = o, «écri» = $î$, «re» = i) on voit que :

$$\text{«(ac-tion) d'(écrire)»} = (i\text{-}o) - (î\text{-}i)$$

L'idée complexe en question est ainsi mise sous forme d'une molécule dissociée à deux éléments dont chacun est bi-atomique ; mais cette molécule contient encore plusieurs pléonasmes inutiles : d'abord la molécule $(î\text{-}i)$ se réduit à l'atome $(î)$ ou

To construct the compound word representing a given complex idea, the simplest means is first to express this complex idea in analytic form, by means of several words: if one then considers this analytic definition of the idea as a dissociated molecule, it suffices to obtain the word sought by condensing this molecule while expelling from it (thanks to the principle of sufficiency) the pleonasms that it almost always contains, and applying the law of the reversal of atoms.

There can be two cases, depending on whether the idea to be represented is or is not expressible by means of the roots and suffixes that the language has. In the first case, the problem has an exact solution; in the second case, the solution can only be approximated.

EXAMPLES: 1. Let us first take as an example the complex idea represented by the group of words *action "d'écrire"* 'action "to write"'. If we replace each atom by its symbolic equivalent ("ac" = i, "tion" = o, *écri* = $î$, *re* = i), we see that:

$$\text{"(ac-tion) d'(écri-re)"} = (i\text{-}o) - (î\text{-}i)$$

The complex idea in question is thus put into the form of a dissociated molecule with two elements, each of which is bi-atomic. However this molecule also contains several unnecessary pleonasms: first, the molecule $(î\text{-}i)$ reduces to the atom $(î)$ or

«écri», car l'idée verbale générale i est déjà contenue dans l'idée verbale particulière «écri» (î); en d'autres mots le mot «écri-re» (î-i) contient, au point de vue logique, un pléonasme analogue à celui du mot «grand-iose» (â-a), et l'on a : «écrire» = «écri», comme «grandiose» = «grand». Si, maintenant, après avoir chassé ce premier pléonasme, on condense la molécule dissociée (en renversant l'ordre de ses éléments), on aura :

(ac-tion) d'(écri-re) = (i-o) − (i)
= (î-i-o) = (écri-ac-tion).

Sous cette forme condensée nous voyons qu'il reste encore un pléonasme, car l'idée verbale générale i (ou «ac») est contenue déjà dans l'atome précédent î (ou «écri»). On peut donc supprimer «ac» et il reste :

(action) d'(écrire) = (écri-tion) = (î-o)

ou en remplaçant l'atome «tion» par l'atome synonyme «ture» :

(action) d'(écrire) = (écri-ture) = (î-o).

2. Prenons encore comme exemple l'idée complexe représentée analytiquement par le groupe de mots : *la qualité «grand»*. Cette expression est aussi une molécule dissociée à deux éléments, dont

écri, because the general verbal idea i is already contained in the specific verbal idea *écri* (î): in other words, the word *écri-re* (î-i) contains, from the logical point of view, a pleonasm analogous to that of the word *grand-iose* (â-a), and we have *écrire* = *écri* like *grandiose* = *grand*. If now, having gotten rid of this first pleonasm, we condense the dissociated molecule (reversing the order of its elements), we will have:

(ac-tion) d'(écri-re) = (i-o) − (i)
= (î-i-o) = (écri-ac-tion).

In this condensed form, we see that another pleonasm remains, since the general verbal idea i (or "ac") is already contained in the preceding atom î (or *écri*). We can thus eliminate "ac", and what remains is:

(action) d'(écrire) = (écri-tion) = (î-o)

or replacing the atom *tion* by the synonymous atom *ture*:

(action) d'(écrire) = (écri-ture) = (î-o).

2. Let us take now as an example the complex idea represented analytically by the group of words *la qualité "grand"*. This expression is also a dissociated molecule with two elements, of which

one is a bi-atomic molecule and the other a simple atom. We have, indeed:

$$(\text{qual-ité}) - (\text{grand}) = (\textbf{a-o}) - (\textbf{â})$$

or by condensing and reversing the elements:

$$(\text{qual-ité}) - (\text{grand}) = (\textbf{â-a-o})$$
$$= (\text{grand-qual-ité})$$

but since the general idea **a** or «qual» is already contained in *grand* (**â**), we can eliminate it, and there remains:

$$(\text{qual-ité}) - (\text{grand}) = (\text{grand-ité}) = (\textbf{â-o}).$$

or, replacing the atom *ité* by its synonym *eur*:

$$(\text{qual-ité}) - (\text{grand}) = (\text{grand-eur})$$

or:

$$(\textbf{a-o}) - (\textbf{â}) = (\textbf{â-o}).$$

3. If instead of the idea "qualité *grand*" we take "*qualité humain*", we will have a dissociated molecule with two elements, each of which is a bi-atomic molecule. Because the atom "hom" designates a concrete entity (o_1), and the atom *ain* the adjectival idea (**a**), we have:

$$(\text{qual-ité}) - (\text{hum-ain}) = (\textbf{a-o}) - (\textbf{ô}_1\textbf{-a})$$
$$= (\textbf{ô}_1\textbf{-a-a-o})$$
$$= (\text{hum-an-qual-ité})$$

ou en supprimant le pléonasme causé par la présence de deux atomes **a** identiques :

(qual-ité) — (hum-ain)=(ô,-a-o)=(hum-an-ité)

4. Synthèse de l'idée complexe : «*objet fait pour porter une chandelle*». Cette synthèse est très simple, car il se trouve qu'il existe en français un suffixe qui exprime précisément l'idée «objet qui porte» : ce suffixe est le suffixe substantif «ier». On a donc :

(objet qui porte) - (chandelle)=(ier) - (chandelle)
=(ô) — (ô)

ou en condensant et renversant l'ordre des atomes :

(objet qui porte) - (chandelle) = (chandel-ier).

5. Synthèse de l'idée complexe : «*mettre une couronne sur la tête de* (quelqu'un)». Il n'existe pas de suffixe pour exprimer l'idée particulière : «prendre un objet et le fixer sur un autre objet». Nous nous trouvons donc dans le cas où le problème de la synthèse n'est pas susceptible d'une solution exacte ; dans ce cas il faut enfermer la solution entre deux autres aussi rapprochées que possible l'une de l'autre. L'une de ces solutions sera la solution par *défaut* et l'autre, la solution par *excès*, car la solution exacte étant comprise entre les deux solutions approchées, il faut nécessairement que l'une de celles-ci ne contienne pas toutes les idées exprimées par

or, eliminating the pleonasm produced by the presence of two identical atoms **a**:

(qual-ité) — (hum-ain)=(ô,-a-o)=(hum-an-ité)

4. Synthesis of the complex idea "*objet fait pour porter une chandelle*" 'object made to hold a candle'. This synthesis is very simple, because it happens that there exists in French a suffix which expresses precisely the idea "object that holds": this is the nominal suffix *ier*. Thus we have:

(objet qui porte) - (chandelle)=(ier) - (chandelle)
=(ô) — (ô)

or in condensing and reversing the order of atoms:

(objet qui porte) - (chandelle) = (chandel-ier).

5. Synthesis of the complex idea "*mettre une couronne sur la tête de* (quelqu'un)" '*to put a crown on the head of* (someone)'. There is no suffix that expresses the specific idea "to take an object and place it on another object". Thus we find ourselves in the situation where the problem of synthesis is not amenable to an exact solution; in that case it is necessary to confine the solution between two others as close as possible to one another. One of these solutions will be the solution by *rounding down*, and the other, the solution by *excess*. Since the exact solution is found between the two approximate solutions, one of these necessarily does not contain all of the ideas expressed by

the total idea, while the other, on the contrary, contains ideas in excess, that is, alien ideas not contained in the total idea to be expressed.

In the example above, the idea "to take an object and place it on another object" contains above all the idea "to perform an action", which is represented by the general verbal suffix *er*. We can thus translate in an approximate way the expression "to put a crown on the head of" by the word *couronn-er*, and this solution constitutes a solution by rounding down, since the atoms *couronn* and *er* do not contain in themselves all of the ideas which are supposed to be expressed: the word *couronn-er* only means, actually, "to perform an action relative to a *crown* (*couronne*), or characterized by a *crown*".

On the other hand, if one wants to specify the nature of the action performed on the object "crown", we must, in the absence of an appropriate suffix or root, be content with existing simple words, such as for example the verb *garnir* 'to decorate'. Then we get to representing the idea "to put a crown on the head of (someone)" by the compound word *couronn-garnir* if we allow the root word *garn* to be used as a suffix[1]; but this solution is

---

[1] We cannot use the suffix *ifi* here, because the word *couronn-ifi-er* would mean "to make (something) a crown", "to transform into a crown".

obviously an approximate solution by excess, because the idea *garnir* contains alien ideas that are not contained in the total idea to be expressed.

Does this mean that, in practice, all cases of this nature (and they are many) have two equally acceptable solutions? Certainly not, because a quick examination of the two solutions leads us to posit the following principle: *Between the solution by rounding down and that by excess, it is always necessary to choose the solution by rounding down.*

This principle is justified by that of least effort: actually, of the two solutions, by rounding down and by excess, the one by rounding down requires less effort, since it corresponds to an incomplete description of the idea to be expressed. We can compare it to a painting which is not completely finished. Furthermore, the principle of least effort is in agreement with the practice of all languages, and we say *couronn-er* as well in English (*to crown*) and in German (*krön-en*[1]).

On the other hand, no language allows solutions by excess, and that not only because this would require a greater effort, but also because it could give rise to errors of interpretation,

---

[1] In German, the umlaut indicates only the verbalization of the root *Kron*; this umlaut does double duty with the verbal final *en*.

due to the fact that every solution by excess necessarily contains ideas alien to the idea to be expressed; indeed, if it did not contain alien ideas, it would not be a solution by excess, it would be either an exact solution or else a solution by rounding down. Supposing for a moment that one said *couronn-garnir* instead of *couronn-er*, the noun derived from this verb would be *couronn-garni-ture* instead of *couronn-e-ment*, which would create confusion between the two distinct ideas "action of crowning" and "decoration of crowns".

6. — The same goes for representing the idea "*fixer un objet sur un autre au moyen de colle*" 'to attach an object to another by means of glue'. Since as we have just seen, there is no suffix that represents exactly the idea "to attach an object to another object", we will adopt here the solution by rounding down *coll-er*, a solution which literally means "to perform an action relative to *glue* (*colle*), characterized by *glue*", and we will reject the solution by excess (colle-garnir), because that would infringe the principle of least effort, and because the word *colle-garnir* contains alien ideas, given that "garnir de colle" 'to decorate with glue' (the dissociated form of *colle-garnir*) is not the same thing as "to attach by means of glue"; indeed, a postage stamp, for example, can be badly *collé* 'glued' to an envelope, while being quite well "garni, enduit de colle" 'decorated, coated with glue'.

7. — Synthesis of the idea "*personne dont l'occupation ou la profession est de jouer du violon*" 'person whose occupation or profession is to play the violin'. There exist several suffixes in French (*iste, ien, ier,* etc.) that designate "a person characterized by the idea contained in the root" to which these suffixes are attached. Thus, the word *violon-iste* (a bi-atomic molecule of the type **(ô-o)**) would be one approximate solution by rounding down for the synthesis in question. Actually, this solution evokes in a clear way the idea which is to be expressed; however, it does not explicitly contain the idea "to play", which is why this solution is only approximate. It slightly infringes the principle of necessity, and indeed, the word *violoniste* can also, if necessary, mean "a maker" or "a seller of violins". However, the goal of the violin being not to manufacture it, but to make use of it, the word *violoniste* is acceptable, and those persons who make or sell violins should be designated in a more explicit way, either by dissociated molecules like *fabricant des violons* 'maker of violins'[1], or by

---

[1] In French we use the word *luth-ier* to designate "makers of violins" as well as those of cellos, lutes, etc. We have thus specialized the logical sense of the word *luthier* so as to fill the role of the missing molecule 'maker of violins'.

des molécules condensées explicites, comme en allemand «Violinmacher», «Violinfabrikant[1]».

8. *Synthèse des mots composés de plusieurs radicaux.* — Jusqu'ici nous nous sommes occupés surtout des mots composés d'un seul radical et d'un ou de plusieurs affixes; c'est, qu'en effet, les mots composés de plusieurs radicaux ne se distinguent pas des mots composés d'un radical et d'affixes; ils rentrent seulement dans la catégorie des solutions approchées par défaut: la molécule «bateau à vapeur», ou en allemand «Dampf-Schiff» est construite d'une façon analogue aux molécules «couronn-er» ou «violon-iste». Dans l'expression «bateau à vapeur», la relation entre les deux radicaux n'est pas exprimée explicitement, car on ne dit pas «bateau mû par vapeur», pas plus que l'idée de «jouer» n'est exprimée dans le mot «violoniste». Le mot «Dampf-Schiff» est un tableau incomplet comme le mot «violoniste», mais ce tableau est suffisant, car, en général, les idées non énoncées ne feraient qu'alourdir le mot sans augmenter beaucoup sa clarté.

Il est donc inutile de faire une distinction entre

---

[1]Du reste en allemand on dit aussi «Violinspieler»; ce mot constitue une solution exacte de la synthèse proposée, car il n'enfreint plus le principe de nécessité comme le mot français «violoniste».

explicit condensed molecules, as in German *Violinmacher, Violinfabrikant*[1].

8. *Synthesis of words composed of several roots.* — Up to this point, we have been concerned especially with words composed of a single root and one or more affixes. Actually, words composed of several roots are not distinct from words composed of a root and affixes: they simply belong to the category of approximate solutions by rounding down. The molecule *bateau à vapeur* 'steam ship', or in German *Dampf-Schiff* is built in a way analogous to the molecules *couronner* or *violon-iste*. In the expression *bateau à vapeur*, the relation between the two roots is not explicitly expressed, since we do not say *bateau mû par vapeur* 'boat moved by steam' any more than the idea "to play" is expressed in the word *violoniste*. The word *Damp-Schiff* is an incomplete picture like the word *violoniste*, but this picture suffices, because in general the ideas that are not set out would do nothing but weigh down the word without adding greatly to its clarity.

It is thus useless to make a distinction between

---

[1]Furthermore, in German we also say *Violinspieler*; this word constitutes an exact solution to the proposed synthesis, becasuse it no longer infringes the principle of necessity as the French word *violoniste* does.

les mots composés à un seul radical et les mots composés à plusieurs radicaux. Beaucoup plus utile, au contraire, est la distinction entre les mots composés qui représentent une solution exacte (comme par exemple «qual-ité», «action», «princ-esse», «chandel-ier», «louable», «grand-eur», etc.) et ceux qui ne représentent qu'une solution approchée par défaut (comme par exemple «couronn-er», «vio-lon-iste», «Dampf-Schiff», «Schlaf-Zimmer», etc.). Dans le premier cas, la soudure entre les deux éléments de la molécule est une simple juxtaposition, ainsi «chandel-ier» = (objet qui porte) — (chandelle), «qual-ité» = (ce qui est) — (qual), etc. : les soudures de cette sorte sont des soudures rigides. Dans le second cas la soudure est élastique, c'est-à-dire que le second élément de la molécule est simplement caractérisé par l'idée contenue dans le premier élément, c'est pourquoi la solution n'est qu'approchée au point de vue logique, et le sens précis du mot n'est fixé d'une manière tout à fait nette que par l'usage ou par le contexte. Il suffit pour s'en rendre compte de comparer les deux mots allemands «Dampf-Schiff» et «Luft-Schiff», qui, quoique semblables, puisque la vapeur et l'air sont tous deux des gaz, correspondent à des notions très différentes.

Les exemples qui précèdent suffisent pour montrer comment il faut appliquer les principes de

compound words with a single root and words composed of several roots. Much more useful, on the other hand, is the distinction between compound words that represent an exact solution (like for example *qual-ité, ac-tion, princ-esse, chandel-ier, lou-able* 'commendable', *grand-eur*, etc.) and those that only represent an approximate solution by rounding down (like for example *couronn-er, violon-iste, Dampf-Schiff, Schlaf-Zimmer*, etc.). In the first case, the juncture between the two elements of the molecule is a simple juxtaposition, thus *chandel-ier* = (object that holds) — (candle), *qual-ité* = (that which is) — (qual), etc.: junctures of this kind are rigid junctures. In the second case, the juncture is elastic, that is, the second element of the molecule is simply characterized by the idea contained in the first element. That is why the solution is only approximate from the logical point of view, and the precise meaning of the word is fixed clearly only by usage or the context. To see this it suffices to compare the two German words *Damp-Schiff* and *Luft-Schiff* which, although similar since steam and air are both gases, correspond to very different notions.

The preceding examples will suffice to show how it is necessary to apply the principles of

nécessité et de suffisance pour opérer la synthèse d'une idée complexe et la représenter par un seul mot, c'est-à-dire, en somme, pour condenser une molécule dissociée. Ces principes peuvent être utiles aux techniciens qui ont à forger de nouveaux mots.

NOTES ADDITIONNELLES.

1. *Des atomes synonymes.* — Les atomes synonymes sont les atomes qui expriment la même idée ; ce sont des atomes identiques de sens, mais différents par la forme : ils sont donc interchangeables entre eux ; ainsi, par exemple l'atome «ité» dans «probité» est synonyme de l'atome «esse» dans «richesse», ou «eur» dans «grandeur». Au point de vue logique, un seul atome suffirait pour exprimer l idée substantive générale **o**, et si les langues naturelles en emploient plusieurs, c'est surtout pour des raisons d'euphonie. Ainsi le suffixe «ien» dans «pharmacien», ou «ier» dans «bottier» est aussi synonyme de «iste» dans «violoniste», ou «eur» dans «vendeur».

Mais la diversité de formes d'un même atome est aussi due à d'autres causes : *cette diversité peut servir à indiquer le caractère grammatical de l'atome immédiatement précédent.* Ainsi nous avons vu par exemple que les suffixes «ment», «tion», «ture», «age», etc., sont synonymes des suffixes «ité», «esse», «eur». etc., mais il y a cette différence que les premiers suivent toujours un atome verbal («écriture», «abonne-ment», «abatt-age», etc.), tandis que les seconds viennent toujours après un atome adjectif («prob-ité >», «rich-esse», etc.). Cette distinction est très utile, car il arrive souvent que le dit atome adjectif ou verbal a été à tel point réduit par l'usure du langage qu'il ne serait plus reconnaissable si sa présence n'était pas signa-

necessity and sufficiency to carry out the synthesis of a complex idea and to represent it by a single word; that is, in sum, to condense a dissociated molecule. These principles can be useful to technicians who have to construct new words.

SUPPLEMENTARY NOTES

1. *Synonymous atoms.* Synonymous atoms are atoms that express the same idea. These are atoms identical in sense, but different in form: thus, for example, the atom *ité* in *probité* 'integrity" is synonymous with the atom *esse* in *richesse* 'richness, wealth' or *eur* in *grandeur*. From the point of view of logic, a single atom would suffice to express the general nominal idea **o**, and if natural languages make use of several, it is especially for reasons of euphony. Thus, the suffix *ien* in *pharmacien* 'pharmacist' or *ier* in *bottier* 'bootmaker' is also a synonym of *iste* in *violoniste* or *eur* in *vendeur* 'seller, salesperson'.

But the diversity of form of the same atom is also due to other causes: *this diversity can serve to indicate the grammatical nature of the immediately preceding atom.* Thus we have seen for example that the suffixes *ment, tion, ture, age,* etc. are synonymous with the suffixes *ité, esse, eur,* etc., but there is this difference, that the first ones always follow a verbal atom (*écriture, abonne-ment, abatt-age* 'slaughter', etc.) while the second set always come after an adjectival atom (*prob-ité, rich-esse,* etc.). This distinction is quite useful, because it often happens that the adjectival or verbal atom in question has been reduced to such a point by the erosion of language that it would no longer be recognizable if its presence were not indica[ted]

115

lée par la forme extérieure de l'atome suivant. C'est ainsi que dans le mot «couronn-e-ment», le caractère verbal de l'atome «e» n'est reconnu que grâce à l'emploi du suffixe «ment», qui suit toujours un atome verbal.

2. *Importance des idées générales sous-entendues pour fixer le sens des mots composés.* — Lorsqu'on dérive d'un même radical une famille de mots, le sens des dérivés dépend du caractère grammatical de ce radical, c'est-à-dire de l'idée générale (substantive, adjective ou verbale) contenue implicitement dans ledit atome-radical.

Prenons par exemple l'atome-radical «brosse» (ou symboliquement **bros**), et dérivons en le mot «bross-ier» en ajoutant l'atome «ier», synonyme de «iste». On pourra écrire indifféremment «bross-ier» ou **bros-ist** (symboliquement). Or, le sens de ce mot varie suivant l'idée générale contenue dans l'atome **bros**. En francais, le mot «brosse» est substantif, puisque la série «brosse», «bross-er», «bross-e-ment», est tout à fait analogue a «couronne». «couronn-er», «couronn-e-ment»; donc l'idée générale sous-entendue dans l'atome **bros** est celle d'un «être concret», d'un «objet»; donc : (*bross-ier*) = (*une personne*) caractérisée par (*l'objet-brosse*), par exemple «un fabricant de brosses» ou «un vendeur de brosses».

Si, au contraire, on voulait parler d'une personne dont l'occupation actuelle est de brosser, il faudrait d'abord verbifier l'atome substantif «brosse», ce qui donne la molécule «bross-er», ou symboliquement **bros-i** (type **ô-i**); cette molécule ne désigne alors plus un objet, mais l'agir relatif à cet objet; et de même que de «bross-er» (**bros-i**) nous avons déjà dérivé le substantif «bross-e-ment» (**bros-i-o** ou *bross-ac-tion*), de même on peut dériver aussi de «bross-er» (**bros-i**) le substantif «bross-e-eur» (**bros-i-ist**) qui signifiera «personne caractérisée par l'action de «brosser» [»], parce que l'atome «eur» est synonyme de «ier» : et si l'on choisit «eur» au lieu de «ier», c'est que ce

[indica]ted by the external form of the following atom. It is thus that in the word *couronne-ment*, the verbal character of the atom *e* is only recognizable thanks to the use of the suffix *ment* which always follows a verbal atom.

2. *Importance of understood general ideas to establish the sense of compound words.* — When we derive a family of words from the same root, the sense of the derived words depends on the grammatical character of this root, that is, the general (nominal, adjectival or verbal) idea implicitly contained in the root atom in question.

Let us take, for example, the root atom *brosse* 'brush' (or symbolically **bros**), and derive from it the word *bross-ier* by adding the atom *ier*, a synonym of *iste*. We could write equally *bross-ier* or **bros-ist** (symbolically). Now the meaning of this word varies according to the general idea contained in the atom **bros**. In French, the word *brosse* is a noun, since the series *brosse, bross-er, bross-e-ment* is completely analogous to *couronne, couronn-er, couronn-e-ment*; thus, the general idea understood in the atom **bros** is that of a "concrete entity", of an "object": thus: (*bross-ier*) = (*a person*) characterized by (*object-brush*), for example "a maker of brushes", or "a seller of brushes".

If, on the other hand, we wanted to speak of a person whose current occupation is to brush, it would first be necessary to verbalize the nominal atom *brosse*, which would yield the molecule *bross-er* or symbolically **bros-i** (of type **ô-i**); this molecule no longer designates an object, but an action relative to that object; and just as from *bross-er* (**bros-i**) we have already derived the noun *bross-e-ment* (**bros-i-o** or *bross-ac-tion*), we can also derive from *bross-er* (**bros-i**) the noun *bross-e-eur* (**bros-i-ist**) which would mean "person characterized by the the action of brushing", since *eur* is a synonym of *ier*, and if we choose *eur* instead of *ier*, it is because this

suffix always comes after a verbal atom (e.g. *achet-eur* 'buy-er', *vend-eur*, etc.), such that even if this verbal atom *e* completely disappears, the word *bross-eur* will nonetheless preserve its meaning, since the suffix *eur*, though itself nominal, has an external form that bears witness to the verbalization of the root **bros**. Thus the word "bross-(e)-eur" is really a triatomic molecule of the type (ô-i-o), while *bross-ier* is a biatomic molecule of the type (ô-ô). The first molecule contains the verbal idea "ag", which the second does not.

3. *Partial ideas contained in the total idea.* — Following the principles of necessity and sufficiency, every partial idea contained in the total idea to be expressed must be contained in one part of the compound word that serves to express this total idea. This applies not only to the atoms that compose the molecule, but also to the different sub-molecules that may be contained within the total molecule.

Thus for example the idea *couronn-e-ment* (**kron**-i-o) contains a verbal atom because it contains the idea of acting (*ag*). But in addition a *couronnement* is an "action" (i-o); the molecule *couronnement* must thus contain not only the verbal atom i, but the molecule (i-o), which is indeed the case. Similarly, since the word *écri-ture* represents an action, it must contain the molecule (i-o), and it indeed does, because the atom *écri* is a specific verbal atom î, that is, it implicitly contains in itself the general verbal idea i, and so the specific molecule *écri-ture* or (î-o) contains the general molecule (i-o). Etc. etc.

4. *On the juncture between atoms.* — We have said that there are two sorts of juncture between the atoms of a molecule: 1. *rigid juncture*, which is a simple juxtaposition of the ideas contained in the different atoms (with reversal of the order of the atoms): for example *qual-ité* =

(ce qui est) − (qual); cette soudure se rencontre toutes les fois que le mot composé représente exactement et complètement l'idée qu'il s'agissait d'exprimer; 2° la *soudure élastique*, qui est équivalente à l'expression «caractérisé par»; par exemple «Dampfschiff» − (Schiff) caractérisé par (Dampf); cette soudure se rencontre toutes les fois que le mot composé ne représente l'idée totale que d'une manière approximative (solution approchée par défaut).

Mais, quelle que soit la nature de la soudure entre deux atomes, il est intéressant de remarquer que ces atomes peuvent être soudés *soit directement, soit par l'intermédiaire des idées générales* implicitement contenues dans ces atomes. Dans l'exemple «qual-ité» = (ce qui est) − (qual), il n'y a qu'une manière d'opérer la soudure, parce que les atomes «qual» et «ité» représentent tous deux des idées grammaticales, donc ils ne contiennent pas d'idées plus générales sous entendues, puisqu'il n'y a pas d'idées plus générales que les idées grammaticales. Par contre, dans l'exemple «beau-té», l'atome «beau» contient l'idée plus générale «qual», de sorte que l'on peut souder l'atome «ité» soit à l'atome «beau», ce qui donne :

«beau-té»=(ce qui est) − (beau)=(le) − (beau),

soit à l'atome «qual» contenu dans «beau», ce qui donne :

«beau-té» = (ce qui est) − (qual) [espèce *beau*]
(qual) = «qual-ité *beau*».

Cette deuxième manière est préférable, parce qu'elle fournit une analyse plus complète.

Si un atome contient plusieurs idées générales sous-entendues, on peut effectuer la soudure au moyen de l'une quelconque d'entre elles. Ainsi le mot «cheval-in», adjectif

(that which is) − (qual); this juncture is found every time the compound word represents exactly and completely the idea which is to be represented; 2. *elastic juncture*, which is equivalent to the expression "characterized by": for example *Dampschiff* = (ship) characterized by (steam). This juncture is found every time the compound word represents the total idea only approximately (solution by rounding down).

But whatever the nature of the juncture between two atoms, it is interesting to note that these atoms can be joined *either directly, or through the intermediary of the general ideas* implicitly contained in those atoms. In the example *qual-ité* = (that which is) − (qual), there is only one way of carrying out the juncture, since the atoms "qual" and *ité* both represent grammatical ideas and therefore do not contain any more general ideas that are understood, because there are no ideas that are more general than the grammatical ideas. On the other hand, in the example *beau-té*, the atom *beau* contains the more general idea "qual", so that one can join the atom *ité* either to the atom *beau*, giving:

«beau-té»=(that which is) − (beautiful) = (the) − (beautiful),

or to the atom "qual" contained in *beau*, giving:

«beau-té» = (that which is) − (qual)
  [type *beautiful*]
(qual) = "qual-ity *beautiful*".

This second way is to be preferred, since it yields a more complete analysis.

If an atom contains several understood general ideas, we can carry out the juncture by means of any one of them. Thus, the word *cheval-in* 'equine', adjective

from the word *cheval* 'horse' (**cheval-a**), means "horse-qual" or "(proper) to a (horse)", and as the atom *cheval* implicitly contains the more and more general ideas "mammalian animal", "vertebrate animal", "animal", "concrete entity", etc., we can join the adjectival atom *in* or *a* to any one of these understood ideas, which gives the following progressively more complete analyses:

cheval-in = (proper) to (horse)
cheval-in = (proper) to (animal *mammal, horse*)
(a. mamm.)

cheval-in = (proper) to (animal *vertebrate, mammal, horse*)
(a. mamm.)
(a. vert.)

and so on.

For the same reason, since the idea "Lyon" contains the more general ideas "France", "Europe", etc., the derived word *Lyonn-ais* will contain the more general ideas "French-man", "Europe-an", etc., because the suffix *en* is a synonym of *ais*. Thus:

Lyonn-ais = "French-man from *Lyon*"
(France)

or also:
Lyonn-ais = "Europe-an from *France*, from *Lyon*"
(France)
(Europe)

5. *Superfluous words and missing words.* — Natural languages contain many superfluous words. The issue here is not that of synonyms that serve to express different nuances of the same idea, such as for example *sommeiller* 'to doze' and *dormir* 'to sleep', but that of simple words, like

«jument», qui pourraient être traduits aussi exactement par une molécule biatomique, n'impliquant que des atomes déjà connus ; en effet :

«jument» = «cheval-femelle»
= «cheval-esse» ou «cheval-ine[1]»

puisque les suffixes «esse» dans «princesse», ou «ine» dans «héroïne» désignent la femelle.

De même le mot «chêne» est superflu, car ou pourrait aussi bien dire «gland-ier» (arbre qui porte des glands), comme on dit «poir-ier» (qui porte des poires) ou «chandel-ier» (qui porte des chandelles).

Au contraire, lorsque le mot régulièrement dérivé n'existe pas, on le remplace par un synonyme qui a à peu près le même sens. Ainsi, par exemple, pour exprimer l'«action de dormir» ou «dorm-ir-ac-tion» (î-i-i-o) on pourrait dire, en supprimant les pléonasmes : «dormi-tion» (î-o) ; mais ce mot n'existant pas en français, on le remplace par le mol «sommeil», qui n'est pas une molécule du type (î-o), mais un simple atome substantif (ô)- Le mot «sommeil» n'est donc qu'une traduction approchée de l'expression «action de dormir», d'abord parce que les radicaux «sommeil» et «dorm» ne sont pas tout à fait synonymes, l'idée «sommeil» impliquant une idée de lassitude qui ne se trouve pas dans le radical «dorm», ensuite parce que la molécule «dormi-tion» (î-o) contient un atome verbal (î) qui ne se trouve pas dans l'atome «sommeil» (ô) ; cependant l'atome «sommeil» rentrant, en tant que substantif primitif, dans la catégorie des «êtres idéels» (abstraits de nature) est très voisin du mot «dormition», qui, en tant que substantif dérivé de verbe, rentre aussi dans la catégorie des «êtres

---
[1] Il ne faut pas confondre ce suffixe *ine*, qui désigne ici la femelle, avec le suffixe adjectif *in* du mot français «chevalin», qui est le même suffixe que *ain* dans «humain».

jument 'mare' which could also be translated exactly as a bi-atomic molecule, involving nothing but known atoms; actually:

jument = "horse-female"
= *cheval-esse* or *cheval-ine*[1]

since the suffixes *esse* in *princesse* and *ine* in *héroïne* designate the female.

Similarly, the word *chêne* 'oak (tree)' is superfluous, since we could just as well say *gland-ier* (tree that bears *glands* 'acorns'), as we say *poir-ier* (that bears *poires* 'pears') or *chandel-ier* (that holds candles).

On the other hand, when the regularly derived word does not exist, we replace it by a synonym that has almost the same meaning. Thus, for example, to express "the action of sleeping" or *dorm-ir-ac-tion* (î-i-i-o) we could say, while suppressing the pleonasms, *dormi-tion* (î-o), but this word does not exist in French, and we replace it with the word *sommeil* 'sleep (n)' which is not a molecule of the type (î-o) but rather a simple nominal atom (ô). The word *sommeil* is thus only an approximate translation of the expression "action of sleeping", first because the roots *sommeil* and *dorm* are not completely synonymous, and then because the molecule *dormi-tion* (î-o) contains a verbal atom (î) which is not found in the atom *sommeil* (ô). However, the atom *sommeil*, belonging as a basic noun to the category of "ideal entities" (natural abstractions), is quite close to the word *dormition*, which as a noun derived from a verb, also belongs to the category of "[ideal] entities["]

---
[1] It is necessary not to confuse this suffix *ine*, which here means the female, with the adjectival suffix *in* of the French word *chevalin* 'equine', which is the same suffix as *ain* in *humain*.

idéels»; nous avons vu en effet qu'il n'y a qu'une nuance entre «dormi-tion» et «le dormir», c'est-à-dire «l'être abstrait, l'idée abstraite *dorm*»; «dormi-tion» exprime plus spécialement l'action ou l'état, et «le dormir» plus spécialement l'idée abstraite.

Les caprices des langues naturelles, qui tantôt créent des mots superflus, tantôt se privent des mots régulièrement construits, proviennent surtout des exigences de l'euphonie, mais ces accidents n'infirment en rien les lois de la formation normale des mots.

6. *Des atomes à double sens.* — D'après le principe de l'invariabilité des atomes, chaque atome ne devrait avoir qu'un sens, et réciproquement à chaque idée ne devrait correspondre qu'un seul atome. En réalité, il existe souvent plusieurs atomes synonymes, comme «eur» (grandeur), «esse» (richesse), «ité» (probité), et réciproquement un même atome peut avoir deux sens totalement différents; ainsi «esse» dans «richesse» n'a aucun rapport avec «esse» dans «princesse»

Ces coïncidences n'ont rien à voir avec l'analyse logique; elles sont encore dues aux exigences de l'euphonie et dans l'analyse logique, on peut éviter ces coïncidences en employant l'écriture symbolique; ainsi on peut par exemple représenter tout être femelle par le suffixe symbolique[1] **in**; on voit alors qu'il n'y a aucune parenté entre «richesse» et «princesse», puisqu'on aura phonétiquement :

rich-esse = **rich-o** et *princ-esse* = **princ-in**.

7. *Des adverbes* : Dans le tableau de la classification des atomes (p. 40), nous n'avons considéré que trois classes (substantifs, adjectifs et verbes). Ces trois classes ne comprennent pas tous les atomes, puisqu'il existe encore des

---

[1]Prononcez phonétiquement «inne».

["]ideal [entities]". We have seen actually that there is only a nuance between *dormi-tion* and *le dormir* 'sleep', that is "the abstract entity or idea *dorm*". *Dormi-tion* expresses more particularly the action or the state, and *le dormir* more particularly the abstract idea.

The vagaries of natural languages, which sometimes create superfluous words and sometimes deprive themselves of regularly constructed words, come especially from the requirements of euphony, but these accidents do not in any way weaken the laws for the normal formation of words.

6. *Atomes with two senses.* — According to the principle of the invariability of atoms, every atom should not have more than one sense, and reciprocally, only a single atom should correspond to each idea. In reality, there are often several synonymous atoms, such as *eur* (grandeur). *esse* (richesse), *ité* (probité); and reciprocally the same atom can have two totally different senses: thus *esse* in *richesse* has nothing to do with *esse* in *princesse*.

These coincidences have nothing to do with the logical analysis; they are due to the requirements of euphony and in the logical analysis we can avoid these coincidences by making use of the symbolic transcription. Thus we can for example represent any female entity with the symbolic suffix[1] **in**. We can then see that there is no relation between *richesse* and *princesse*, since we will have phonetically

rich-esse = **rich-o** and *princ-esse* = **princ-in**.

7. *Adverbs.* — In the table of classification of atoms (p. 40), we have only considered three classes (nouns, adjectives and verbs). These three classes do not include all atoms, since there are also

---

[1]Pronounced phonetically *inne* (IPA [in] — eds.)

atomes-adverbes, des atomes-prépositions, etc., qui eux aussi peuvent entrer dans la formation de mots composés ; cependant il n'y a pas lieu de classer ces atomes, car ils ne contiennent pas en eux-mêmes d'idée générale permettant de faire un classement ; on pourrait bien par exemple classer les adverbes, en adverbes contenant l'idée de *temps*, adverbes contenant l'idée de *lieu*, etc., mais ces idées de *temps, lieu,* etc. sont encore des idées particulières, et ce classement n'aiderait pas à fixer le sens des mots composés. En effet, le classement des atomes n'est utile que si un même atome peut être transféré d'une classe dans une autre : ainsi l'atome «bros» pourrait aussi bien être un atome verbal qu'un atome substantif, et le sens des mots dérivés de «bros» dépend du classement adopté pour ce radical ; au contraire les atomes-adverbes, prépositions, etc., ne sont pas susceptibles de contenir deux idées générales différentes ; leur classement est donc inutile. Ainsi le mot «pré-dire» par exemple ne peut pas avoir plusieurs sens, car l'adverbe «pré» signifiant «d'avance», contient forcément l'idée de temps et n'en peut pas contenir d'autres.

On peut toutefois mettre à part les adverbes de «manière», car cette catégorie comprend non seulement des adverbes primitifs, comme «ainsi», «comment», etc., mais tous les adverbes dérivés d'adjectifs, comme «agréable-ment», «facile-ment», etc., de sorte que cette classe d'adverbes sera aussi grande que la classe des adjectifs. Cette classe comprend aussi des molécules dissociées comme «en aimant», «en abondance», «à pied», «à cheval», «par écrit», etc., etc , en effet :

«en abondance» = «abondam-ment»
 = «(d'une manière) – (abondante)»,
«à pied» = «pédestre-ment»
 = «(à la manière) – (pédestre)», etc.

adverb atoms, preposition atoms, etc. which can also enter into the formation of compound words. This is not, however, the place to classify these items, since they do not contain in themselves general ideas that would allow us to make a classification. We could, for example, classify adverbs into adverbs containing the idea of *time*, adverbs containing the idea of *place*, etc., but these ideas of *time, place* etc. are still specific ideas, and this classification would not help in fixing the meaning of compound words. Indeed, the classification of atoms is only useful if the same atom can be transferred from one class to another: thus, the atom *bros* can just as well be a verbal atom as a nominal atom, and the sense of words derived from *bros* depends on the classification adopted by that root. On the contrary, adverb atoms, prepositions, etc. are not able to contain two different general ideas; their classification is thus pointless. Thus the word *pré-dire* 'to predict' cannot have multiple senses: since the adverb *pré* means "in advance", it necessarily contains the idea of time and cannot contain any others.

We can, however, treat separately adverbs of "manner", since this category includes not only basic adverbs like *ainsi* 'thus', *comment* 'how', etc., but also all adverbs derived from adjectives, like *agréable-ment* 'pleasant-ly', *facile-ment* 'easi-ly', etc., so that this class of adverbs is as large as the class of adjectives. This class also included dissociated molecules like *en aimant* 'in loving', *en abondance* 'in abundance', *à pied* 'on foot', *à cheval* 'on horseback', *par écrit* 'in writing', etc. etc. Actually:

en abondance = *abondam-ment*
 = (in a fashion) – (abundant),
à pied = *pédestre-ment*
 = (in a way) – (pedestrian), etc.

Si donc on représente par **e** l'idée adverbiale générale «à la manière», «d'une manière», on aura :

idée adverbiale **e** = *à la manière, d'une manière,*
                = suffixe *ment,*
                = suff. dissociés *à, en, par,* etc.

Il faut seulement remarquer que les suffixes dissociés comme «à», dans la molécule dissociée «(à) − (pied)», signifient bien «à la manière», mais *à condition de prendre le second atome sous la forme adjective*; autrement dit, la molécule «à-picd» n'est pas une simple molécule biatomique du type (**e**) − (**ô**); c'est une molécule triatomique du type (**e**) − (**ô-a**). On a, en effet :

(*à*) − (*pied*) = (*à la manière*) − (*péd-estre*) = (**e**) − (**pied-a**)

ou en condensant la molécule :

(**e**) − (**pied-a**) = (**pied-a-e**) = *péd-estre-ment.*

Ainsi l'atome **e** doit toujours être précédé d'un atome adjectif; si cet atome manque, il faut le rétablir avant de faire l'analyse logique. Dans le mot «agréable-ment» ou symboliquement **agrabl-e**, l idée adjective **a** est contenue implicitement dans le radical adjectif **agrabl**; en effet, cette molécule est du type (**â-e**) ainsi que tous les adverbes dérivés d'adjectifs par le suffixe «ment».

8. *Des préfixes.* − Les préfixes sont en général des prépositions; ce sont donc des atomes qui ne contiennent pas en eux-mêmes d'idée générale ; cependant les préfixes offrent ceci de particulier qu'ils jouent le rôle d'un adverbe dans la formation des mots composés. Ainsi «avant-poste» = «(poste) − (en avant)», «prédire» = «(dire) −(d'avance)»,

If we thus represent by **e** the general adverbial idea "in the way", "in a manner", we will have:

adverbial idea **e** = *in a way, in the manner,*
                = suffix *ment,*
                = dissociated suff. *à, en, par,* etc.

It is only necessary to note that the dissociated suffixes like *à* in the dissociated molecule "(à) − (pied)" do mean "in the manner" but *only if we take the second atom in adjectival form*: in other words, the molecule *à pied* is not a simple bi-atomic molecule of the type (**e**) − (**ô**); it is a tri-atomic molecule of the type (**e**) − (**ô-a**). We actually havet:

(*à*) − (*pied*) = (*in the manner*) − (*ped-estrian*) = (**e**) − (**pied-a**)

or by condensing the molecule:

(**e**) − (**pied-a**) = (**pied-a-e**) = *ped-estrian-ly.*

Thus the atom **e** must always be preceded by an adjective atom; if that atom is missing, it is necessary to restore it before carrying out the logical analysis. In the word *agréable-ment* 'pleasant-ly', or symbolically **agrabl-e**, the adjectival idea **a** is implicitly contained in the root adjective **agrabl**. Actually this molecule is of the type (**â-e**) just like all adverbs derived from adjectives with the suffix *ment.*

8. *Prefixes.* − Prefixes are in general prepositions; they are thus atoms that do not contain in themselves a general idea. However, these prefixes present in particular the fact that they play the role of an adverb in the formation of compound words. Thus *avant-poste* 'outpost' = "(post) − (forward)", *prédire* = "(to say) − (in advance)",

«beau-frère» = «(frère) — (à la manière *beau*)». c'est-à-dire «(frère) — (par alliance)», «bon vouloir» = «(vouloir) — (à la manière *bonne*)», «malheureux» = «(heureux)— (à la manière *contraire*)», etc., etc. On peut donc dire que tous les préfixes contiennent implicitement en eux-mêmes l'idée adverbiale **e** (= à la manière); un mot composé tel que «avant-poste» est donc un molécule bi-atomique du type (ê-ô), etc.

9. *Des atomes à caractère grammatical douteux.* — La plupart des atomes ont un caractère grammatical très net; ainsi les atomes «homme», «table», «science», «âme». contiennent évidemment l'idée substantive. D'autres ont un caractère moins net; ainsi l'atome **bros**, considéré en lui-même, pourrait aussi bien être classé comme verbal que comme substantif; mais il suffit, pour lever le doute, de considérer la famille des molécules dérivées de l'atome «bros» : le mot «brosserie», par exemple, signifie «lieu où l'on tient, où l'on vend des brosses», et ceci montre que le radical **bros** est substantif (tout au moins en français), car si ce radical était verbal, «brosserie» aurait un autre sens et signifierait «lieu où l'on brosse», comme «laverie» signifie «lieu où l'on lave», parce que le radical **lav** est verbal. Et, en effet, le verbe «bross-er» est dérivé du substantif «brosse», comme «couronn-er» est dérivé du substantif «couronne»; ces deux verbes sont des molécules du type (ô-i).

Il y a cependant des cas où l'on a quelque peine à fixer le caractère grammatical d'un atome. Ce cas est dû simplement au fait que toute langue est un organisme vivant qui évolue et se transforme constamment; il arrive donc au bout d'un certain temps que des molécules perdent leur sens primitif, celui qui résulte de leur étymologie, c'est-à-dire de leur composition atomique, et acquièrent un sens nouveau, parce que l'ancienne molécule, en changeant de sens, est devenue un simple atome, qui peu à peu donne naissance à

beau-frère 'brother-in-law' = "(brother) — (in a *beautiful* way)", that is, "(brother) — (by marriage)", *bon vouloir* 'good will' = "(will) — (in a *good* way)", *malheureux* 'unhappy' = "(happy) — (in the *opposite* way)", etc. etc. We can thus say that all prefixes implicitly contain in themselves the adverbial idea **e** (= in the manner); a compound word like *avant-poste* 'outpost' is thus a bi-atomic molecule of the type (ê-ô), etc.

9. *Atoms of doubtful grammatical character.* — Most atoms have a very clear grammatical character; thus the atoms *homme, table, science, âme* 'soul' obviously contain the nominal idea. Others have a less clear character: thus, the atom **bros** considered in itself could just as well be classified as verbal as nominal; but it suffices, to remove doubt, to consider the family of molecules derived from the atom *bros*. The word *brosserie*, for example, means "place where one keeps, or where one sells, brushes", and that shows that the root **bros** is nominal (at least in French), for if this root were verbal, *brosserie* would have a different sense and would mean "place where one brushes", just as *laverie* 'laundry' means "place where one washes", because the root **lav** is verbal. And indeed, the verb *bross-er* is derived from the noun *brosse*, as *couronn-er* is derived from the noun *couronne*; these two verbs are molecules of the type (ô-i).

There are, however, cases in which one has some difficulty in determining the grammatical character of an atom. This is due simply to the fact that every language is a living organism which is constantly evolving and changing. It happens thus that after a time some molecules lose their original sense, that which results from their etymology, and acquire a new sense, because the old molecule, in changing its sense, has become a simple atom, which little by little gives rise to

une nouvelle famille de mots dérivés; mais tant que cette transformation ne s'est pas complètement effectuée, le caractère grammatical du nouvel atome reste plus ou moins caché.

Tel est le cas pour tous les mots français tels que «logique», «physique», «musique», etc., qui sont d'anciens adjectifs dérivés du type moléculaire (ô-a) : «log-ique», «phys-ique», «mus-ique», etc. Mais en prenant un sens précis différent du sens étymologique, ces mots sont devenus ou deviendront de simples atomes substantifs (ô), et ont donné ou donneront de nouveaux adjectifs dérivés; c'est ainsi que le nouvel atome «musique» a engendré le nouvel adjectif «music-al» du type (ô-a), parce que «music» est maintenant un simple atome du type (ô); les nouveaux atomes substantifs «logique», «physique», etc., n'ont pas encore donné naissance à des adjectifs régulièrement dérivés, puisqu'on dit encore «logique», «physique», etc., au sens adjectif : du moins en français, car en anglais on dit régulièrement «logic-al», «physic-al», etc. Il semble donc que ce n'est qu'une question de temps, et que lorsque le caractère substantif des atomes tels que «logique» se sera suffisamment affirmé en français, les adjectifs tels que «logic-al» apparaîtront aussi en français, tout comme l'adjectif «music-al».

Le caractère grammatical douteux de certains atomes en état de transformation n'infirme donc en rien le principe de la spécificité grammaticale des atomes en général.

10. *Du critère par pléonasme.* — Le mot *pléonasme* vient du grec et signifie «être surabondant». Littré définit le pléonasme : «l'emploi simultané de plusieurs mois ayant le même sens. Le pléonasme est une négligence ou un moyen de donner plus de force à la pensée. Il y a lieu de distinguer le pléonasme inconscient et le pléonasme employé comme procédé de style. Le premier est souvent une faute de langage résultant de l'ignorance ou de l'irréflexion (exem-

a new family of derived words; but insofar as this transformation has not been completely carried out, the grammatical character of the new atom may remain more or less hidden.

This is the case for all of the French words like *logique*, *physique*, *musique*, etc., which are old derived adjectives of the molecular type (ô-a): *log-ique*, *phys-ique*, *mus-ique* etc. But in taking on a specific sense different from the etymological sense, these words have become or will become simple nominal atoms (ô) and have given or will give new derived adjectives: thus the new atom *musique* has generated the new adjective *music-al* of type (ô-a), because *music* is now a simple atom of type (ô). The new nominal atoms *logique*, *physique*, etc. have not yet given rise to regularly derived adjectives, since we still say *logique*, *physique*, etc. in the adjectival sense — at least in French, because in English we say regularly "logic-al", "physic-al", etc. It thus seems that it is just a question of time, and that once the nominal character of atoms such as *logique* is sufficiently established in French, adjectives such as "logic-al" will also appear in French, just like the adjective *music-al*.

The doubtful grammatical character of certain atoms undergoing transformation does not at all infringe the principle of the grammatical specificity of atoms in general.

10. *On the criterion of pleonasm.* — The word *pleonasm* comes from Greek, and means "superfluity". The *Littré* defines pleonasm": "the simultaneous use of several words having the same sense. Pleonasm is careless, or a way of giving additional force to the thought. There is cause to distinguish unconscious pleonasm and pleonasm used as a stylistic technique. The first is often a linguistic mistake resulting from ignorance or thoughtlessness (exam-[ple]

[exam]ple: a hemorrhage of blood). But it sometimes happens that usage sanctions involuntary pleonasms, once the etymological value of the terms ceases to be understood (example: aujourd'hui ['today'; orig. literally 'on the day of today'])."

Pleonasms play an important role in the formation of words, and it is necessary to avoid them insofar as possible. This is not, however, absolutely necessary, because even though pleonasm weighs down words and expressions, it does not change their sense; pleonasm is often inevitable, and it is sometimes useful to reinforce the expression or to make it clearer.

We can make use of the notion of pleonasm as a criterion in the analysis of words, because if the pleonasm does not change the sense of a molecule, we can conclude in turn that: *if the addition of an atom to a molecule does not at all change the molecule's sense, that atom forms a pleonasm*: that is, the idea contained in this atom is already contained in the molecule.

Thus from the fact that the expression "hemorrhage of blood" has the seme meaning as the simple word *hemorrhage* we can conclude that the idea "blood" is already contained in the idea *hemorrhage*. From the fact that "big" = "which is big", we conclude that the idea "which is" is already contained in the adjective "big", and since that applies to any adjective at all, we therefore conclude that the expression "which is" is one of the forms of the general adjectival idea a. The equation "big" = "(which is) — (big)" can be written symbolically:

$$\text{big} = (a) - (\text{big}) = (\text{big-a})$$

Similarly the idea "the entity", "an entity" (concrete or abstract) is one of the forms of the general nominal idea o, because for every noun, such as for example *homme*,

on a : «homme» = «le (ou un) être homme»[1]. ou symboliquement :

hom = (o) − (hom) = (hom-o).

De même l'idée «faire l'action» est une des formes de l'idée verbale générale **i**, parce que pour tout verbe, comme par exemple «écri», on a : «écri» = «(faire l'action) − (écri)» = «(écri-re)», puisque la finale «re» exprime aussi l'idée verbale. Donc symboliquement :

skrib = (i) − (skrib) = (skrib-i).

Par contre **skrib** n'est pas égal à **skrib-o**, car de l'équation **skrib = skrib-i**, on tire : **skrib-o** (ou *écri-ture*) = **skrib-i-o** = (i-o) − (skrib) = (*ac-tion*) − (*écri*) ou *action d'écrire*, puisque la molécule (**i-o**) = *ac-tion*.

De même de l'équation **grand = grand-a**, on tire **grand-o** (ou *grand-eur*) = **grand-a-o** = (a-o) − (**grand**) = (*qualité*) − (*grand*).

---

[1] Comme l'idée substantive **o** peut être traduite par «ce qui est», on peut aussi dire que «homme» = «ce qui est homme», mais il faut toujours se garder de confondre «qui est» (l'idée adjective **a**) avec «ce qui est» (idee substantive **o**). Ainsi «grand» = «qui est grand», mais non pas «ce qui est grand», car «ce qui est grand» est «l'être idéel grand», «la grandeur», et «grand» n'est pas «grand-eur» ; en d'autres mots : **grand = grand-a**, mais non **grand-o**. De même «homme» = «ce qui est homme», mais non pas «qui est homme», car «qui est homme» est une forme de l'adjectif «hum-ain», et «homme» n'est pas égal à «hum-ain» ; en d'autres termes symboliques : **hom = hom-o** mais non pas **hom-a**.

FIN DE LA PREMIÈRE PARTIE

we have: "man" = "the (or an) entity man"[1], or symbolically:

man = (o) − (man) = (man-o).

Similarly the idea "to perform the action" is one of the forms of the general verbal idea **i**, since for every verb, like for example *écri*, we have: *écri* = "(perform the action) − (écri)" = "(écri-re)" because the ending *re* also expresses the verbal idea. Thus symbolically:

skrib = (i) − (skrib) = (skrib-i).

In contrast, **skrib** is not equal to **skrib-o**, for from the equation **skrib = skrib-i**, we derive: **skrib-o** (or *écri-ture*) = **skrib-i-o** = (i-o) − (skrib) = (*ac-tion*) − (*écri*) or *action d'écrire*, since the molecule (**i-o**) = *ac-tion*.

Similarly from the equation **grand = grand-a**, we derive **grand-o** (or *grand-eur*) = **grand-a-o** = (a-o) − (**grand**) = (*quality*) − (*grand*).

---

[1] Since the nominal idea **o** can be translated by "that which is", we can also say that "man" = "that which is man", but it is always necessary to avoid confusing "which is" (the adjective idea **a**) with "that which is" (nominal idea **o**). Thus "big" = "which is big", but not "that which is big", because "that which is big" is "the ideal entity big", "bigness, size", and "big" is not "big-ness". In other words, **big = big-a** but not **big-o**. Similarly "man" = "that which is man" but not "which is man", because "which is man" is a form of the adjective *hum-ain* 'hum-an' and *homme* 'man' is not equal to *hum-ain*, or in symbolic terms **hom = hom-o** and not **hom-a**.

END OF THE FIRST PART

Reviews of de Saussure 1911

WE KNOW OF TWO REVIEWS of René de Saussure's 1911 work, both brought to our attention by remarks in its successor, the 1919 work. The first of these appeared in the 20 November, 1911 edition of the *Journal de Genève* on page 3, signed "A.O"[1] and followed a week later in the same newspaper by a brief exchange between that author and René de Saussure. The second was a short note by Antoine Meillet that appeared in volume 18/2 of the *Bulletin* of the Société de linguistique de Paris for 1912-1913 (not as indicated by de Saussure (1919: 5) as appearing in the society's *Mémoires* for 1911). We reproduce those reviews here, with translation.

---

[1] A reviewer suggests that this was probably the same individual as the "A. Oltramare" whose review of de Saussure (1916) is cited by de Saussure (1919: 4; pg. 140 below). The scholar in question appears to have been A[ndré] Oltramare (1884–1947), a Latinist and Socialist politican in Geneva at the time.

René de Saussure

Review in *Journal de Genève*

Principes logiques de la formation des mots, par René DE SAUSSURE, privat-docent à l'Université de Genève. — Première partie. — Genève, librairie Kündig, 1911.

Des travaux récents nous ont fait connaître des «formules» de psychologie, d'économie politique et même d'esthétique ; il fallait prévoir que tôt ou tard les lois de langage seraient de même exprimées sous une forme mathématique. Pour M. René de Saussure le problème de la formation des «dérivés» est un problème de chimie : chaque mot est une molécule ; on découvrira sa nature en le décomposant en ses atomes (radicaux et affixes), auxquels un axiome complaisant octroie une valeur invariable. L'ensemble des significations atomiques donnera le sens de la molécule.

C'est l'analyse traditionelle des laboratoires dans toute son audacieuse simplicité : Soit le mot *labourage* à étudier dans l'éprouvette ; il se décomposera aisément en un radical *labour-* et un suffixe *-age*. Pour fixer chacun de ces deux éléments, on les remplace par des atomes «types» qui n'expriment que les idées grammaticales (celle d'adjectif : symbole *a*, celle de verbe : *i*, ou de substantif : *o*) contenues dans *labour-* et dans *-age*. On arrive ainsi à la formule :

Labour-age = ac-tion (de l'espèce particulière *labour-*) = (*i-o*)

La synthèse n'est guère plus compliquée. Étant donnée une idée complexe comme *action de labourer,* on cherche le mot qui l'exprimera : il appartiendra au type moléculaire : (*i-o*) ; je connais le radical verbal à employer(*i*) ; je choisis un suffixe de substantif (*o*) et je forme : *labourage*. Si l'idée à désigner était nouvelle, le mot serait naturellement nouveau ; tous les inventeurs qui voudront donner à leur découverte un mot logiquement formé devront, conclut M. R. de Saussure, se conformer à ces principes.

Il est difficile de porter un jugement sur un ouvrage dont la première partie est seule publiée ; je crois cependant pouvoir déjà dire que si celui-ci contient dans quelques-unes de ses digressions plusieurs idées intéressantes et même nouvelles (principalement sur la position relative des éléments verbaux), il est faussé dans son ensemble par une erreur très grave de méthode : certes, la linguistique n'est plus une discipline exclusivement historique ; les ouvrages de M. Bally ont démontré qu'elle devient en partie une science d'observation actuelle ; on a le droit désormais d'étudier les faits du langage contemporain en les isolant du passé, d'expliquer par exemple, comment au moyen de suffixes on crée maintenant les mots nouveaux ; ceux-là sont naturellement pour notre conscience de vrais dérivés : nous sentons immédiatement que *labourage* équivaut à *action de labourer,* car du suffixe *-age* notre génération a formé *dérap-age, sabot-age*, etc.

Faire la nomenclature des suffixes de ce genre, qui sont «actuellement vivants», déterminer parmi les moyens de formation quel sont ceux qui peuvent être conçus comme des règles logiques, c'est à cela qu'eût dû se borner l'effort de l'auteur ... Hélas ! son ambition a été plus haute ; il a cru que les observations qu'il faisait étaient valables pour toutes les époques du français et nous a donné surtout en exemples des mots créés dans les siècles antérieurs au moyen de suffixes qui sont morts aujourd'hui ; ces dérivés-là sont «sentis» par nous comme des mots simples : *beauté* n'est plus pour notre conscience un dérivé, car l'élément *-té* est remplacé maintenant comme suffixe créateur de substantifs abstraits par *-ité*.

Principes logiques de la formation des mots, par René DE SAUSSURE, privat-docent à l'Université de Genève. — Première partie. — Genève, librairie Kündig, 1911.

Some recent works have brought to our attention the «formulas» of psychology, political economy and even æsthetics: it had to be expected that sooner or later the laws of language would be similarly expressed in mathematical form. For Mr. René de Saussure, the problem of the formation of "derived words" is a chemical problem: each word is a molecule; we will discover its nature by decomposing it into its atoms (roots and affixes), to which a convenient axiom allocates an invariant value. The collection of atomic meanings will give the sense of the molecule.

This is the traditional laboratory analysis in all its audacious simplicity. Let us suppose that the word we have to analyze in our test tube is *labourage* 'plowing': it will be easily decomposed into a root *labour-* '(to) plow' and a suffix *-age*. To determine each of these two elements, we replace them by "type" atoms which express only grammatical ideas (that of the adjective: symbolized a; that of the verb, i; or the noun: o) contained in *labour-* and in *-age*. We thus arrive at the formula:

Labour-age = *ac-tion* (of the specific type *labour-*) = (i-o)

Synthesis is hardly more complicated. Given a complex idea such as *action of plowing*, we look for the word that expresses it: it will belong to the molecular type (i-o). I know the verbal root to use (i); I choose a nominal suffix (o) and I form *labourage*. If the idea to be represented is novel, the word would naturally be new: all inventors who would wish to give to their discovery a logically formed word will, concludes Mr. René de Saussure, have to comply with these principles.

It is difficult to judge a work of which only the first part has been published; I think, however, that I can say that although this contains in its digressions several ideas that are interesting and even novel (especially concerning the relative position of verbal elements), it is distorted overall by a very serious methodological error. Certainly, linguistics is no longer an exclusively historical discipline: the works of Mr. Bally have shown that it is becoming in part a science of observation of the here and now. We have henceforth the right to study the facts of contemporary language in isolation from the past, to explain, for example, how by means of suffixes we now create new words. These are naturally for our awareness true derivatives: we sense immediately that *labourage* is equivalent to *action of plowing*, because our generation has formed *dérap-age* 'skid-ing', *sabot-age* 'sabotage-ing', etc. with the suffix *-age*.

To make a taxonomy of sufixes of this type, which are "currently living", to determine by the means of formation which are the ones that can be conceived as logical rules, it is to this that the author's efforts ought to have been limited ... Alas! his ambition has been higher. He has believed that the observations he has made were valid for all epochs of French and has given us as examples words created in past centuries by means of suffixes which are dead today. These derivatives are "felt" by us as simple words: *beauté* 'beauty' is no longer a derivative for our intuition, because the element *-té* is now replaced as the suffix creating abstract nouns by *ité*.

René de Saussure

Toutes les lois que M. René de Saussure découvre avec raison dans les formations actuelles tombent à faux quand on veut les appliquer à plusieurs époques. L'axiome même de l'invariabilité des éléments, sur lequel repose tous ses raisonnements, est contredit par le premier exemple venu : le suffixe -*age*, dont j'ai parlé plus haut, a changé de sens et même de catégorie grammaticale dans l'histoire du français. Il était autrefois adjectif (*a*) ; il formait par exemple l'expression de *lait formage* (lait qui prend une forme), d'où est venu notre mot *fromage* ; il a pris ensuite la signification substantive (*o*) de collectif (*herbage, feuillage*) pour devenir enfin aujourd'hui un créateur de nom d'action (*labourage*).

Si son objet avait été plus logiquement délimité, l'opuscule de M. René de Saussure eût été très utile aux linguistes et aux inventeurs. Conçu comme il l'est, il semble avoir comme but de prouver qu'une langue naturelle comme le français forme ses mots de la même manière qu'un langage artificiel comme l'esperanto et ses succédanés.

A. O.

All of the laws which Mr. René de Saussure rightly discovers in current formations break down when we try to apply them to several epochs. Even the axiom of the invariability of elements, on which all of his reasoning rests, is contradicted by the first example that comes up: the suffix -*age*, which I spoke of above, has changed its sense and even its grammatical category in the history of French. It was formerly an adjective (*a*); it formed for example the expression *lait formage* (milk which takes a shape), from which comes our word *fromage* 'cheese'; it subsequently took on the nominal meaning (*o*) of collective (*herbage* 'pasture', *feuillage* 'foliage'), finally becoming today the creator of action nouns (*labourage* 'plowing').

If his objective had been more logically delimited, the work of Mr. René de Saussure would have been very useful for linguists and inventors. Conceived as it is, it seems to have as its end to prove that a natural language like French forms words in the same way as an artificial language like Esperanto and its alternatives.

A. O.

Response by R. de Saussure, *Journal de Genève* 27 November, 1911

Principes logiques de la formation des mots, par René de Saussure. — (Genève, Kündig).

Sous la signature A. O. le *Journal de Genève* a donné de cet ouvrage un compte rendu à propos duquel une courte réponse sera permise à l'auteur. Celui-ci peut estimer, en effet, que cette critique lui attribue des idées qu'il n'a point émises, ou qui sont même directement contraire au sens de sa brochure. J'ai peine à m'expliquer le malentendu, quoique ayant eu tort peut-être de ne pas prendre toutes les précautions pour qu'une méprise sur le point de vue choisi fût impossible.

«Si cet ouvrage, dit M. A. O., contient plusieurs idées interessantes et même nouvelles, il est faussé dans son ensemble par une erreur très grande de méthode... Toutes les lois que M. René de Saussure découvre avec raison dans les formations actuelles (de mots) tombent à faux quand on veut les appliquer à plusieurs époques. L'axiome même de l'invariabilité des éléments, sur lequel reposent tous ses raisonnements, est contredit par le premier exemple venu.»

Le malentendu est flagrant, vu qu'à aucun moment les principes logiques que la brochure cherchait à poser n'ont prétendu s'appliquer à une succession d'époques, diverses dans le temps. Déjà le mot de *logique*, et le fait que l'essai se déroule dans le point de vue logique pur, excluraient une pareille supposition, qui est d'ailleurs écartée explicitement au premier paragraphe, à propos de la valeur étymologique des mots simples déclarée indifférente. L'*invariabilité* des éléments n'est pas relative au temps, mais aux divers mots considérés comme coexistants à un moment donné. C'est d'un mot de la langue à l'autre, non d'une époque à l'autre, qu'elle pose un principe.

Quant au mot de *fromage*, dont le suffixe sert à donner des exemples de ma mauvaise méthode, il n'est pas cité dans ma brochure. Considéré au sein de l'époque présente, ce mot est évidemment un mot simple (atome substantif), et n'offre, par suite, aucune sorte de suffixe.

Je saisis du reste comme un acquiescement précieux ce mot de M. A. O., que toutes les lois énoncés dans l'ouvrage sont valables pour les *formations actuelles*. Il ne m'en faut davantage. Si ces lois sont valables pour les formations actuelles, c'est dire en effet qu'elles ont toute chance de l'être pour une époque donnée quelconque, chose qui reste éminemment distincte d'une pluralité d'époques, avec l'évolution qu'elle comporte. Ainsi, une fois levée l'équivoque initiale qui obscurcissait le début, je crois pouvoir dire que mon honorable critique se trouve plus près qu'il ne pense lui-même de donner raison à ce qui forme le vrai fond de l'ouvrage qu'il condamne.

R.S.

—

L'auteur de l'article, auquel répond M. R. de Saussure, nous écrit :

«M. René de Saussure déclare que ses «Principes logiques» n'ont jamais prétendu s'appliquer à diverses époques. J'avais parfaitement compris son intention : c'est pourquoi je lui ai reproché d'avoir emprunté des exemples à toutes les phases de l'évolution linquistique au lieu de se borner à étudier les procédés actuels de formation verbale.»

Principes logiques de la formation des mots, par RENÉ DE SAUSSURE. — (Genève, Kündig).

Under the name A. O. the *Journal de Genève* has given this work a review with regard to which a short reply will be permitted to the author. The latter may consider, indeed, that this critique attributes to him ideas that he has not at all put forth, or which are even directly contrary to the sense of his booklet. I find it hard to explain the misunderstanding to myself, despite perhaps having been wrong not to take all precautions that a mistake concerning the point of view chosen should have been impossible.

"If this work" says Mr. A. O., "contains several ideas that are interesting and even novel, it is distorted overall by a very serious methodological error ... All of the laws which Mr. René de Saussure rightly discovers in the current formation (of words) are falsified when we wish to apply them to several epochs. Even the axiom of the invariability of elements, on which all of his reasoning rests, is contradicted by the first example that comes up."

The misunderstanding is blatantly obvious, since at no point were the logical principles that the booklet sought to present claimed to apply to a succession of epochs, diverse in time. Already the word *logical*, and the fact that the essay is developed from the point of view of pure logic, would exclude such a supposition, which however is explicitly dismissed in the first paragraph, where the etymological value of simple words is declared irrelevant. The *invariability* of elements is not relevant to time, but to the various words considered to coexist at a given moment. It is from one word of the language to another, not from one time period to another, that the principle applies.

As for the word *fromage*, whose suffix serves to provide examples of my bad method, it is not mentioned in my booklet. Considered within the present period, this word is obviously a simple word (nominal atom), and does not present, in consequence, any sort of suffix.

I take as a valuable acknowledgement, however, Mr. A. O.'s remark that all of the laws set out in the work are valid for *current formations*. No more is necessary for me. If these laws are valid for curent formations, that is to say indeed that there is every chance they will be so for any given period, something that remains entirely distinct from a plurality of periods, with the evolution that this involves. Thus, once the initial misunderstanding is removed which obscured the starting point, I think I can say that my honorable critic finds himself closer than he thinks to agreeing with that which forms the true basis of the work he condemns.

R.S.

—

The author of the article to which Mr. R. de Saussure replies writes to us:

"Mr. René de Saussure declares that his "Logical principles" were never intended to apply to different periods. I have understood his intention perfectly well: that is why I have reproached him for having borrowed examples form all phases of linguistic development rather than limiting himself to the study of current processes of verbal formation."

René de Saussure

Antoine Meillet's Review in the *Bulletin de la Société de linguistique de Paris* (vol. 18/2 [1912-1913], pp. xxii-xxiii)

René DE SAUSSURE. — *Principes logiques de la formation des mots*. Première partie. Genève (chez Kündig), 1911, in-8 ; 122 p.

M. René de Saussure n'est pas linguiste de profession, et c'est l'étude de l'espéranto qui l'a conduit à examiner les principes de la formation des mots. Il se préoccupe, non de ce qui est, mais de ce qui doit être. Presque chacun des principes qu'il pose est en quelque mesure en contradiction ou au moins en désaccord avec les faits positifs des langues naturelles. Un mot n'est pas proprement le symbole d'une idée, mais un signe phonique associé à un ensemble complexe de faits psychiques de toutes sortes. Ce qui fait qu'une notion est représentée par un mot simple ou un mot composé n'est pas le degré de complexité qu'elle présente, c'est le caractère plus ou moins familier de la notion : quand on a nommé pour la première fois le bateau à vapeur, on lui a donné une désignation complexe ; maintenant, on l'appelle volontiers un vapeur. L'analyse de M. René de Saussure porte la plupart du temps sur le français, auquel elle s'applique souvent mal. Par exemple, il distingue, p. 60, dans *agir*, un radical *ag* et un suffixe *ir* ; or, jamais un Français ne saurait analyser ainsi *agir* ; rien ne lui permet d'isoler *ag* , et *-i-* se trouvant dans toutes les formes du verbe en fait partie intégrante ; l'abstrait *action* n'est pas dérivé de *agir* ; c'est un mot qui, en latin, appartenait au groupe de *agere*, mais qui, au point de vue français, en est en somme indépendant. Si *agir* a en français un dérivé abstrait, c'est *agissement*. *Action* n'est pas plus dérivé d'*agir* que *qualité* ne l'est de *quel*. — Si l'on veut bien faire abstraction et des langues telles qu'elles sont et de leur passé, le petit livre de M. René de Saussure fera réfléchir utilement sur les rapports qui existent entre les mots simples et leurs dérivés ou leurs composés.

A. MEILLET.

René DE SAUSSURE. — *Principes logiques de la formation des mots.* Première partie. Genève (chez Kündig), 1911, in-8 ; 122 p.

Mr. René de Saussure is not a linguist by profession, and it is the study of Esperanto that has led him to examine the principles of word formation. He is concerned not with what is, but with what ought to be. Nearly every one of the principles that he asserts is in some way in contradiction or at least in disagreement with the empirical facts of natural languages. A word is not properly the symbol of an idea, but a phonic sign associated with a complex set of psychic facts of all sorts. What causes a notion to be expressed as a simple word or as a compound word is not the degree of complexity that it presents; it is the more or less familiar character of the notion. When a name was given for the first time to the steam boat, it was given a complex designation; now, we happily call it a steam[er]. Mr. René de Saussure's analysis bears most of the time on French, to which it is often poorly applicable. For example, he discerns, p. 60, in *agir* 'to act', a root *ag* and a suffix *ir*; now no Frenchman would analyze *agir* in that way; nothing allows him to isolate *ag*, and since -*i*- is found all of the forms of the verb, it constitutes an integral part of it. The abstract noun *action* is not derived from *agir*; it is a word which in Latin belonged to the family of *agere*, but which, from the point of view of French, is quite independent. If *agir* has a derived abstract noun in French, it is *agissement*. *Action* is no more derived from *agir* than *qualité* is from *quel*. — If one is willing to abstract away both from languages as they are and from their past, the little book of Mr. René de Saussure will provoke useful reflection on the relations that exist between simple words and their derived forms and compounds.

A. MEILLET.

[Paul Jules] Antoine Meillet (1866–1936)

Part II

The 1919 text

La structure logique des mots – The logical structure of words

On the last page of René de Saussure's 1911 book, this is indicated as the "Première partie" of a larger project. The implicitly promised "deuxième partie" of such a project is represented by the first chapter of the work that follows here. We reproduce (and translate) only the initial chapter of this little book; its second chapter concerns the application of René de Saussure's theory of word structure to artificially constructed languages, and this is followed by an appendix providing "all the grammar, the syntax and the formation of words in *Esperantido*" [René de Saussure's revised version of Esperanto], along with a short text in that language. As this material is not directly relevant to our concerns with René de Saussure's theory of word structure in natural languages, we do not include it here.

The conventions for translation adopted are largely the same as for the first book: French words cited as examples have been preserved, with the first instance of a given word provided with an English gloss. Since only a rather small set of French words are invoked, however, and many of these are closely cognate with their English equivalents, we have frequently dispensed with glosses after a word's first appearance. French words cited as concepts or ideas have generally been translated except where this would impair the sense of the text (in which case they have been treated in the same manner as examples). As before, our goal in the translation provided here is to provide access to the French text for the English reader, rather than a new English version of René de Saussure's work. The pagination of the original text has been preserved and indicated at the top of the page, although no attempt has been made to maintain the division of pages into lines. As in the case of the 1911 text, we have retained the original typography as far as possible, with inserted obviously missing material enclosed in square brackets.

We have not included the original cover, whose content and organization are identical with the title page here except for identifying the work as published by "Librairie A. LEFILLEUL, Christoffelgasse — Berne, 1919." As noted in the introduction, we assume the publication date of 1919 should take priority over the printing date of 1918 in referring to the book. Although some references to this work in the literature treat it as having appeared in 1918, it is clear that 1919 is more accurate: this is confirmed by the closing at the end of chapter 2 (not included here), signed on page 58 "Berne, 17 mars 1919. ANTIDO" (this last being René de Saussure's *nom de plume* in his esperantist writings).

René de Saussure

LA STRUCTURE
LOGIQUE
DES MOTS

DANS LES LANGUES NATURELLES,
CONSIDÉRÉE AU POINT DE VUE DE SON
APPLICATION AUX LANGUES ARTIFICIELLES

PAR

RENÉ de SAUSSURE

Ancien élève de l'Ecole Polytechnique de Paris,
Ph. D. and Fellow by courtesy of the Johns Hopkins University,
Lauréat de l'Institut de France

„*Une analyse exacte de la signification des mots ferait mieux connaître que toute autre chose les opérations de l'entendement.*"
LEIBNITZ.

IMPRIMERIE BÜCHLER & CIE, BERNE
1918

THE LOGICAL STRUCTURE OF WORDS

IN NATURAL LANGUAGES,
CONSIDERED FROM THE POINT OF VIEW OF ITS
APPLICATION TO ARTIFICIAL LANGUAGES

BY

RENÉ de SAUSSURE

Former student at the École Polytechnique de Paris,
Ph. D. and Fellow by courtesy of the Johns Hopkins University,
Lauréat of the Institut de France

"An exact analysis of the meaning of words would make known better than any other thing the operations of understanding."
LEIBNITZ.

IMPRIMERIE BÜCHLER & CIE, BERNE
1918

René de Saussure

LA STRUCTURE
LOGIQUE
DES MOTS

dans les langues naturelles,

considérée au point de vue de son

application aux langues artificielles.

Préliminaire.

Les idées développées dans le présent essai ont été en partie déjà exposées dans une publication antérieure, parue sous le titre de *Principes logiques de la formation des mots*.[1]

Au lieu de publier aujourd'hui la deuxième partie de ce travail, il m'a paru préférable de refondre le tout en un seul article, plus condensé et mieux ordonné. Je profite de cette occasion pour faire quelques remarques préliminaires, qui m'ont été suggérées par la lecture des compte-rendus auxquels ma première brochure a donné lieu.

Les linguistes considèrent généralement les faits linguistiques au point de vue historique, évolutif, tandis que mon but est d'étudier la structure des mots dans les langues considérées à une époque donnée de leur existence. Une telle étude appartient plutôt au domaine du logicien qu'à celui du linguiste ; seule la matière qui entre en jeu est la même.

Ainsi, par exemple, lorsque j'admets que les éléments simples (racines ou aflixes), qui entrent dans la composition des mots, sont des éléments *invariables*, cela ne signifie pas que ces éléments sont invariables dans le temps,[2] mais que, dans une langue considérée à une époque donnée, ces éléments restent les mêmes lorsqu'on les transporte d'un mot dans un autre. Ceci revient à dire que, par exemple, le mot *grand* reste toujours le même mot-adjectif, qu'on le considère soit comme mot autonome,

---

[1] Genève, 1911. Librairie Kündig.
[2] Comme me le faisait dire l'auteur du compte-rendu de ma brochure, paru dans le *Journal de Genève* du 20 novembre 1911.

The Logical Structure of Words

in natural languages,
considered from the point of view of its
application to artificial languages.

Preliminaries.

The ideas developed in the present essay have already been presented in part in a previous publication, which appeared with the title *Logical Principles of Word Formation*.[1]

Instead of publishing now the second part of that work, it has seemed preferable to me to recast the whole in a single article, more condensed and better organized. I take advantage of this occasion to make some preliminary remarks, which have been suggested to me in reading the reviews to which my first booklet gave rise.

Linguists have generally considered linguistic facts from the historical, evolutionary point of view, while my aim is to study the structure of words in languages considered at a given time in their existence. Such a study belongs to the domain of the logician rather than that of the linguist; only the material that comes into play is the same.

Thus, for example, when I suppose that the simple elements (roots or affixes) that enter into the composition of words are *invariable* elements, that does not mean that these elements are invariable over time,[2] but that, in a language considered at a given point in time, these elements remain the same when one transports them from one word into another. This amounts to saying, for example, that the word *grand* 'large, tall' still remains the same adjectival word whether we consider it as an autonomous word

---

[1] Geneva, 1911, Librairie Kündig.
[2] As the author of the review which appeared in the *Journal de Genève* for 20 November, 1911, would have me say. [See pp. 130ff. of the present volume]

soit comme faisant partie des mots *grand'eur, grand'ir, s'a'grand'ir, grand'duc*, etc. Cette remarque est importante : elle montre par exemple, que des verbes comme *couronn'er, bross'er, clou'er*, etc., ne sont pas des verbes simples comme *frapp'er, écri're*, etc., mais de vrais mots composés, formés d'un substantif (*couronne, brosse, clou*, etc.) et d'un affixe verbal (*er*); en d'autres termes, dans le verbe *frapper* l'idée verbale pénètre non seulement la désinence *er*, mais aussi le radical *frapp*, tandis que dans le verbe *couronn'er* l'idée verbale est contenue exclusivement dans la désinence *er* (tout comme elle est contenue uniquement dans le dernier élément *essen* du mot allemand *Abend'essen*). Telle est l'interprétation qu'il faut donner au principe de l'invariabilité des éléments, énoncé à la page 10 sous le n° 7. Ce principe, du reste, revient à considérer les langues naturelles (y compris le français) comme des langues où les mots composés et les mots dérivés sont formés par la soudure d'éléments *invariables* et *indépendants* les uns des autres, éléments qui sont de véritables mots, puisque chacun d'eux est le signe d'une idée qui lui est propre.

On voit qu'il n'est pas question ici d'étymologie ; du reste il semble qu'actuellement les linguistes eux-mêmes admettent l'existence de deux sortes de recherches en linguistique. C'est du moins ce qui ressort clairement de l'article écrit par Monsieur A. Oltramare[1] à propos du *Cours de linguistique générale*[2] de mon frère Ferdinand de Saussure :

> .... „les historiens du langage, dit l'auteur de cet article, n'ont fixé que l'évolution de certains faits isolés ; les grammairiens se sont contenté de déterminer dans la langue ce qui est correct et ce qui ne l'est pas ; les phonologues ont seulement observé le mécanisme de l'instrument vocal .... Comment découvrir ainsi les lois universelles du langage ? — En divisant la difficulté, répond F. de Saussure ; en étudiant la langue non seulement dans son histoire, mais surtout dans son état actuel ; en coordonnant les données de faits linguistiques simultanés. Il faut donc distinguer deux sortes de recherches : l'étude de l'évolution et celle d'une période donnée ; il y a deux linguistiques : l'une est *diachronique* (évolution), l'autre est *synchronique* (état). La première détermine comment les vocables se substituent les uns aux autres dans le temps ; elle conditionne la seconde dialectique, qui décrit les rapports de termes contemporains les uns des autres."

Et Monsieur Oltramare ajoute :

> „C'est dans le domaine de la linguistique synchronique que F. de Saussure innove radicalement. L'analyse doit ici être subjective : elle ne s'occupe que des faits perçus par la conscience de la moyenne des sujets parlants. Un mot comme *enfant* doit y être considéré comme un bloc indivisible, alors que l'analyse objective, en usage dans la diachronique, eût décomposé le même terme (*en'fant*) et l'eût rapproché de *in'fans* (non doué de la parole)".

---

[1] Voir la *Semaine littéraire* du 27 mai 1916, p. 258. Genève.
[2] Oeuvre posthume, publiée par les soins de messieurs Ch. Bally, professeur, et A. Sechehaye, privat-docent, à l'Université de Genève. Librairie Payot, Lausanne, 1916.

or as constituting part of the words *grand'eur* 'size', *grand'ir* 'to grow', *grand'duc* 'grand duke', etc. This remark is important: it shows, for example, that verbs like *couronn'er* 'to crown', *bross'er* 'to brush', *clou'er* 'to nail', etc. are not simple verbs like *frapp'er* 'to strike', *écri're* 'to write', etc., but real compound words, formed with a noun (*couronne* 'crown', *brosse* 'brush', *clou* 'nail', etc.) and a verbal affix (*er* 'INFINITIVE'); in other terms, in the verb *frapper* the verbal idea enters into not only the desinence *er*, but also the root *frapp*, while in the verb *couronn'er* the verbal idea is exclusively contained in the desinence *er* (just as it is uniquely contained in the final element *essen* 'eat' of the German word *Abend'essen* 'dinner'). This is the interpretation that must be given to the principle of the invariability of elements, set out on page 10 under number 7. This principle, besides, amounts to considering natural languages (including French) as languages where compound words and derived words are formed by joining *invariable* and *independent* elements with one another, elements which are genuine words, since each of them is the sign of an idea that is proper to it.

We see that it is not a question here of etymology; besides, it seems that currently linguists themselves admit the existence of two kinds of investigation in linguistics. At least that is what clearly emerges from the article written by Mr. A. Oltramare[1] in connection with the *Cours de linguistique générale*[2] of my brother Ferdinand de Saussure:

> ..."historians of language, says the author of this article, have only determined the evolution of certain isolated facts; grammarians have been content to determine what is correct and what is not in the language; phonologists have only observed the mechanism of the vocal instrument ... How are the universal laws of language to be discovered in this way? — In dividing up the problem, F. de Saussure responds; in studying language not only in its history, but especially in its current state; in coordinating the elements of simultaneous linguistic facts. It is thus necessary to distinguish two sorts of investigation: the study of evolution, and that of a given period; there are two sorts of linguistics: one is *diachronic* (evolution), and the other is *synchronic* (state). The first determines how spoken words substitute for one another over time; this depends on the second approach, which describes the relations of contemporaneous terms to one another."

And Mr. Oltramare adds:

> "It is in the domain of synchronic linguistics that F. de Saussure makes radical innovations. The analysis here must be subjective: it is concerned only with facts perceived by the average speaker. A word like *enfant* 'child' must here be considered as an indivisible whole, while the objective analysis, as employed in diachrony, would have decomposed the same term (*en'fant*) and would have compared it with *in'fans* (not endowed with speech)."

---

[1] See the *Semaine littéraire* for 27 May, 1916, p. 258, Geneva.
[2] Posthumous work, published by the good offices of Ch. Bally, professor, and A. Sechehaye, privat-docent [roughly, Lecturer], at the University of Geneva. Librairie Payot, Lausanne, 1916.

J'avais fait moi-même la même remarque à propos du mot *musique*[1] (*mus'ique*, ancien adjectif de *muse*) que l'on doit considérer actuellement comme un mot simple substantif, donnant naissance lui-même à de nouveaux adjectifs, tels que *music'al, music'ien*, etc., où le radical *music* joue le rôle d'un élément simple.

D'une manière générale, on peut dire que tous les mots composés tendent à devenir simples, car tout mot en évoluant tend à perdre sa signification primitive et à en acquérir une nouvelle, qui n'est par conséquent plus conforme à sa structure; mais cette évolution n'empêche pas l'analyse logique des mots en linguistique synchronique, parce qu'elle est très lente; on peut même dire, qu'elle est négligeable pour tous les mots composés qui rentrent dans un type général. Ainsi les mots tels que *beau'té, plén'itude*, en français, *equal'ity*, en anglais, *Schön'heit*, en allemand, etc., forment toute une catégorie de mots dont la structure est encore aujourd'hui exactement la même que celle des mots latins correspondants *ver'itas, pulchr'itudo*, etc.; leur signification, est bien restée conforme à leur structure, puisque les suffixes *ité, itude, heit*, etc., expriment tous l'idée substantive générale de „*chose (en général)*", „*chose abstraite*", et que tous les mots que nous venons de citer sont bien destinés à représenter, sous la forme d'une chose abstraite („*beau-té*"), une idée adjective („*beau*"), qui par elle-même n'est pas une chose.

Dans un court compte-rendu[2] que Monsieur le professeur Meillet a bien voulu faire de mon premier travail, je trouve la remarque suivante: „M. R. de Saussure, dit-il, recherche non ce qui est, mais ce qui doit être."

Si c'est là une critique, je puis répondre que les grammairiens font à peu près la même chose, puisqu'ils déterminent dans la langue ce qui est correct et ce qui ne l'est pas. Mais tandis que le grammairien se place au point de vue de l'usage établi dans une langue particulière, nous nous plaçons au point de vue international des langues en général, et nous recherchons, parmi toutes les formes existantes, celles qui ont un caractère incontestable de généralité. En tout cas, la remarque faite par Monsieur Meillet est intéressante, et elle nous donne l'occasion de préciser l'objet que nous avons en vue: c'est par la constatation de ce qui *est* général dans les langues naturelles que nous trouverons ce qui *doit être* dans une langue artificielle pour que son mécanisme se rapproche le plus possible de celui des langues naturelles.

Evidemment, les lois générales sont aussi difficiles à percevoir dans les faits linguistiques que les lois de la physique dans les phénomènes biologiques ou physiologiques, à cause de la complexité et de la variabilité des organismes vivants; mais cela ne veut pas dire que ces lois n'existent pas; le tout est de les découvrir sous l'apparente complexité des formes.

Dira-t-on, par exemple, qu'il n'existe pas de loi de numération dans les langues naturelles, parce que certains noms de nombres, comme *onze, douze, treize*, etc., n'ont pas leur forme régulière (*dix-un, dix-deux, dix-trois*, etc.)? ou parce que d'autres ont pris des formes excep-

---

[1] Voir *Formation des mots*, p. 120.
[2] Voir les Mémoires de la Société de linguistique, 1911, Paris.

I had myself made the same comment with respect to the word *musique* 'music'[1] (*mus'ique*, former adjective from *muse*), which must now be considered a simple noun, itself giving rise to new adjectives such as *music'al* 'musical', *music'ien* 'musician', etc., where the root *music* plays the role of a simple element.

In general, we can say that all compound words tend to become simple, because every word tends in its evolution to lose its original meaning and to acquire a new one, which as a result no longer conforms to its structure; but this evolution does not prevent the logical analysis of words in synchronic linguistics, because it is very slow; we can even say that it is negligible for all compound words that fit into a general type. Thus, words like *beau'té* 'beauty', *plén'itude* 'fullness' in French, *equal'ity* in English, *Schön'heit* 'beauty' in German, etc. all make up a category of words whose structure is still today exactly the same as that of corresponding Latin words *ver'itas, pulchr'itudo*, etc.; their meaning has remained conformant to their structure, since the suffies *ité, itude, heit,* etc. all express the genral nominal idea of "*thing (in general)*", "abstract thing", and all the words that we have just cited are well designed to represent, in the form of an abstract thing ("*beau-té*") an adjectival idea ("*beau*" 'beautiful') which by itself is not a thing.

In a short review[2] that Professor Meillet has been so kind as to provide of my first work, I find the following remark: "Mr. R. de Saussure, he says, studies not what is, but what must be."

If that is a criticism, I can reply that grammarians do almost the same thing, since they determine in language what is correct and what is not. But while the grammarian takes the point of view of the usage established in a particular language, we take the international point of view of languages in general, and we study, among all existing forms, those that have an incontestable character of generality. In any case, the remark made by Mr. Meillet is interesting, and it gives us the opportunity to clarify the object we have in mind: it is by the investigation of what *is* general in natural languages that we find what *must be* in an artificial language for its mechanism to come as close as possible to that of natural languages.

Obviously, general laws are as difficult to perceive in linguistic facts as are physical laws in biological or physical phenomena, because of the complexity and variability of living organisms; but that does not mean that these laws do not exist. The main thing is to uncover them under the apparent complexity of forms.

Will we say, for example, that there does not exist a law of numeration in natural languages, because the names of certain numbers like *onze* 'eleven ', *douze* 'twelve', *treize* 'thirteen, etc. do not have their regular form (*dix-un* 'ten-one', *dix-deux* 'ten-two', *dix-trois* 'ten-three', etc.)? Or because others take excep[tional] forms,

---

[1] See *Formation des mots*, p.120
[2] See the Mémoires de la Société de linguistique, 1911[sic], Paris. [Reproduced on pp. 136f. of the present volume]

tionnelles, comme *soixante-dix*, *quatre-vingt*, etc.? Evidemment non. Il est clair que si quelques nombres font exception à la règle, cela vient uniquement de la fréquence de leur emploi, qui les a détériorés en vertu de la loi du moindre effort.[1] Mais la loi de numération n'en existe pas moins et la preuve, c'est qu'on la trouve encore intacte dans certaines langues, comme l'albanais, où elle a conservé une forme absolument régulière:

1 (*nje*), 2 (*dú*), 3 (*tri*), 4 (*kater*), 5 (*pés*), 6 (*kjast*), 7 (*stát*), 8 (*tét*), 9 (*nánt*), 10 (*diét*); 11 (*diét e nje*), 12 (*diét e dú*), 13 (*diét e tri*), 14 (*diét e kater*), etc.; 20 (*dú-diet*), 21 (*dúdiét e nje*), 22 (*dúdiét e dú*), etc.; 30 (*tri-diét*), etc.; 40 (*kater-diét*), etc., etc.

Ainsi c'est bien ce qui „est" généralement dans les langues naturelles, et en particulier en albanais, qui conditionne ce que „doit être" le système de numération dans une langue artificielle.

De même, pour juger de la structure des mots dans une langue artificielle, il est nécessaire d'étudier d'abord cette structure dans les langues naturelles. Mais cela ne signifie pas que dans ces dernières tous les mots composés suivent la loi générale, ou qu'ils aient tous une signification conforme à leur structure. Dans le *Cours de linguistique générale* cité plus haut, l'auteur (parlant des langues naturelles) fait remarquer avec raison (p. 187) que les mots sont des signes linguistiques plus ou moins *motivés*; entre le signe tout à fait arbitraire et le signe tout à fait motivé il y a des degrés. Qu'est-ce à dire, si ce n'est que les signes *arbitraires*, ou *immotivés*, sont les mots simples qui servent de point de départ à la formation des mots composés (comme en algèbre des lettres arbitraires a, b, x, y, etc. servent de point de départ aux formules); que les mots *complètement motivés* sont les mots composés qui ont une signification conforme à leur contenu, et que les mots *partiellement motivés* sont ceux dont la signification n'est que partiellement expliquée par leur contenu.[2]

Les différentes langues naturelles sont plus ou moins riches en mots complètement motivés. Pour dégager les lois générales de la formation des mots, on devra donc s'appuyer de préférence sur les langues qui, comme l'allemand, sont riches en mots de cette espèce. C'est ce que nous ferons dans le présent essai, parce que nous avons l'intention d'appliquer ensuite ces lois aux langues artificielles, et il est bien évident qu'une langue artificielle sera d'autant plus à la portée de tout le monde, qu'elle sera plus riche en mots motivés, car alors le

---

[1] Ces exceptions n'infirment pas la loi générale; elles sont dues uniquement à l'intervention d'autres causes entrant en conflit avec cette loi. On peut comparer la loi générale à un système de tranchées défensives dans l'art militaire: un tel système est établi suivant un plan logique et ce plan logique subsiste alors même que d'autres causes, par exemple une attaque ennemie, en aurait détruit une partie.

[2] L'expression *complètement motivé* ne doit pas être prise dans un sens absolu, car un mot composé n'est jamais la description complète d'une idée; il exprime seulement, par une sorte de logique différenciative, ce en quoi cette idée diffère des autres de même espèce. On peut dire qu'un mot est *complètement motivé* lorsqu'il satisfait aux deux principes de nécessité et de suffisance, exposés à la page 13.

[excep]tional [forms], such as *soixante-dix* 'sixty-ten: seventy', *quatre-vingt* 'four-twenty: eighty', etc.? Obviously not. It is clear that if some numbers constitute exceptions to the rule, that comes solely from the frequency of their use, which has caused them to deteriorate as a result of the law of least effort.[1] But the law of numeration exists nonetheless, and the proof is that we find it still intact in certain languages, such as Albanian, where it has been preserved in absolutely regular form:

1 (*nje*), 2 (*dú*), 3 (*tri*), 4 (*kater*), 5 (*pés*), 6 (*kjast*), 7 (*stát*), 8 (*tét*), 9 (*nánt*), 10 (*diét*); 11 (*diét e nje*), 12 (*diét e dú*), 13 (*diét e tri*), 14 (*diét e kater*), etc.; 20 (*dú-diet*), 21 (*dúdiét e nje*), 22 (*dúdiét e dú*), etc.; 30 (*tri-diét*), etc.; 40 (*kater-diét*), etc., etc.

Thus it is just what "is" in general in natural languages, and in particular in Albanian, that conditions what "must be" the system of numeration in an artificial language.

Similarly, to evaluate the structure of words in an artificial language, it is necessary first to study this structure in natural languages. But that does not mean that in the latter all compound words will follow the general law, or that they all should have a meaning in conformance with their structure. In the *Cours de linguistique générale* cited above, the author (speaking of natural languages) observes correctly (p. 187) that words are more or less *motivated* linguistic signs: between the completely arbitrary sign and the completely motivated sign there are degrees. Which is to say that if it is not *arbitrary* or *unmotivated* signs, it is simple words that serve as the point of departure for the formation of compound words (as in algebra the arbitrary letters *a, b, x, y*, etc. serve as the point of departure for formulas); that *completely motivated* words are compound words that have a meaning in accord with their content, and that *partially motivated* words are those for which the meaning is only partially explained by their content.[2]

Different natural languages are more or less rich in completely motivated words. To bring out the general laws of the formation of words, we will thus have to depend preferably on languages, like German, that are rich in words of that type. That is what we will do in the present essay, because we intend to apply these laws subsequently to artificial languages, and it is quite obvious that an artificial language will be more accessible to everyone the richer it is in motivated words, because then the

---

[1] These exceptions do not weaken the general law; they are only the result of the intervention of other causes that are in conflict with that law. We can compare the general law to a system of defensive trenches in the art of war: such a system is established according to a logical plan, and this logical plan remains even when as a result of other causes, such as an enemy attack, a part of it is destroyed.

[2] The expression *completely motivated* must not be taken in an absolute sense, because a compound word is never the complete description of an idea; it only expresses, by a sort of differentiative logic, that in which this idea differs from others of the same sort. We could say that a word is *completely motivated* when it satisfies the two principles of necessity and sufficiency, presented on page 13 below.

nombre des signes arbitraires de la langue, c'est-à-dire le vocabulaire des mots simples que l'on est obligé d'apprendre par cœur, sera réduit à un minimum. L'exemple, choisi plus haut, du système de numération dans les langues naturelles est tout à fait frappant : en albanais, tous les noms de nombres sont entièrement motivés, à l'exception des nombres 0, 1, 2, 3, 4, 5, 6, 7, 8, 9, 10, 100, 1000, etc., qui sont immotivés ; en français, outre les nombres précédents, le nombre 20 est immotivé ; les nombres 13, 14, 15, 16, 30, 40, 50, etc. ne sont que partiellement motivés ; en allemand, la numération est encore moins bonne : certains nombres, comme *dreizehn*, sont bien complètement motivés, mais il le sont à rebours de la loi générale, et il en résulte que des noms de nombre à structure semblable, comme *dreizehn* et *dreihundert* n'ont pas du tout des significations semblables. Cette remarque est importante, car elle montre qu'en étudiant la structure des mots dans les langues naturelles, on pourra rencontrer dans telle ou telle langue particulière des exceptions à la loi générale ; mais ces exceptions n'infirment pas la règle, si l'on se place au point de vue des langues en général, ou, si l'on veut, au point de vue international.

En résumé, si nous adoptons le terme de *lexicologique* pour désigner les langues riches en mots immotivés et celui de *grammatical* pour désigner celles qui sont riches en mots motivés,[1] nous arrivons à cette conclusion qu'une langue artificielle doit être construite sur le type „grammatical" et qu'elle est capable de réaliser ce type infiniment mieux qu'aucune langue naturelle, puisque dans une langue artificielle rien n'empêche de réduire au minimum le nombre des mots immotivés, et de remplacer tous les mots qui ne sont que partiellement motivés par des mots qui le sont entièrement, comme nous le verrons au second chapitre.

R. de S.

---

[1] Voir le *Cours de ling. gén.* déjà cité, pag. 189.

number of arbitrary signs in the language, that is, the vocabulary of simple words that one is obliged to learn by heart, will be reduced to a minimum. The example chosen above of the system of numeration in natural languages is quite striking: in Albanian, all of the names of numbers are entirely motivated, with the exception of the numbers 0, 1, 2, 3, 4, 5, 6, 7, 8, 9, 10, 100, 1000, which are unmotivated; in French, besides the preceding numbers, the number 20 is unmotivated; the numbers 13, 14, 15, 16, 30, 40, 50 etc. are only partially motivated; in German, the numeration is still less good: certain numbers, like *dreizehn* 'thirteen' are completely motivated, but they are so contrary to the general law, and the result is that number names with similar structure, like *dreizehn* 'thirteen' and *dreihundert* 'three hundred' do not at all have similar meanings. This remark is important, because it shows that in studying the structure of words in natural languages, we may encounter in one or another language exceptions to the general law; but these exceptions do not weaken the law, if we take the point of view of languages in general, or, if you like, the international point of view.

In summary, if we adopt the term *lexicological* to designate languages rich in unmotivated words, and the term *grammatical* to designate those that are rich in motivated words,[1] we will arrive at the conclusion that an artificial language must be constructed to be of the "grammatical" type and that it is capable of realizing this type infinitely better than any natural language, since in an artificial language, nothing prevents us from reducing to a minimum the number of unmotivated words, and replacing all the words that are only partially motivated with words that are entirely so, as we will see in the second chapter.

R. de S.

---

[1] See the *Cours de linguistique générale*, cited above, page 189.

René de Saussure

[Blank page in original]

The 1919 Text

CHAPITRE PREMIER.

La structure logique des mots dans les langues naturelles.

§ 1. Principes généraux.

A. Définitions.

1. *Un mot est le signe usuel au moyen duquel on exprime une idée.* — Faire l'*analyse* d'un mot, c'est rechercher l'idée exprimée par ce mot. Au contraire, faire la *synthèse* d'un mot, c'est construire le mot qui doit évoquer une idée donnée. L'analyse est donc faite par le lecteur ou l'auditeur, tandis que la synthèse est faite par l'écrivain ou l'orateur.

2. *Un mot simple est un mot qui ne contient qu'un seul élément* (ex. : maison). — Il existe trois espèces de mots simples ou éléments : les mots *racines* ou mots autonomes (ex. : **homme**); les mots *préfixes* qui se placent avant une racine (ex. : **re** dans **re'tirer**); enfin les mots *suffixes* et les mots[1] *désinences*, qui se placent après une racine (ex. : **iste** dans **violon'iste**; **er** dans **couronn'er**).

En général, les affixes (préfixes, suffixes ou désinences) ne sont pas des mots autonomes; cependant les préfixes-prépositions, comme **sous** dans **sou'tirer**, et certains suffixes, comme **full** dans le mot anglais **beauti'ful**, sont des mots autonomes.

3. *Un mot composé est un mot formé par la soudure de plusieurs mots simples ou éléments* (ex. : **hum'an'ité**, **steam'ship**, etc.). — Il n'y a pas de différence essentielle entre un mot „composé" de plusieurs mots autonomes, comme **Schreib'tisch**, et un mot „dérivé" d'un mot autonome par l'adjonction d'affixes, comme **grand'eur**, **couronn'er**, **hum'an'ité**, etc. On peut donc considérer tous les mots dits „dérivés", comme des mots „composés" par soudure. Ainsi, dans l'analyse des mots, il ne faut pas dire que **couronn** est le

---

[1] Nous prenons le mot „*mot*" dans le sens d'*unite significative*. Voir la définition ci-dessus (N° 1).

CHAPTER ONE.

The logical structure of words in natural languages.

§ 1. General principles.

A. Definitions.

1. *A word is the usual sign by means of which we express an idea.* — To *analyze* a word is to look for the idea expressed by that word. Conversely, to *synthesize* a word is to construct the word that evokes a given idea. The analysis is thus performed by the reader or the hearer, while the synthesis is performed by the writer or the speaker.

2. *A simple word is a word that contains only a single element* (e.g. maison 'house'). — There are three types of simple words or elements: *root* words or autonomous words (e.g. **homme** 'man'); *prefix* words, which are placed before a root (e.g. **re** in **re'tirer** 'remove'); and finally *suffix* words and *desinence* words[1] which are placed after a root (e.g. **iste** in **violon'iste** 'violinist'; **er** in **couronn'er** 'to crown').

In general, affixes (prefixes, suffixes and desinences) are not autonomous words; however preposition-prefixes, like **sous** 'under' in **sou'tirer** 'extract', and certain suffixes, like **full** in the English word **beauti'ful**, are autonomous words.

3. *A compound word is a word formed by joining together several simple words or elements* (e.g. **hum'an'ité** 'humanity', **steam'ship**, etc.). — There is no essential difference between a word "compounded" of several autonomous words, like *Schreib'tisch* 'writing table: desk' and a word "derived" from an autonomous word by the addition of affixes, like **grand'eur** 'size', **couronn'er** 'to crown', **hum'an'ité** 'humanity' etc. We can thus consider all words called "derived" as words "compounded" by joining. Thus, in the analysis of words, it is not necessary to say that **couronn** 'crown' is the

---
[1] We take the word "word" in the sense of *meaningful unit*. See the definition above (# 1).

radical du verbe **couronner**, mais que **couronn** est un substantif, qui avec l'affixe verbal **er** forme le verbe **couronner**.[1]

4. *On nomme pléonasme la répétition de la même idée au moyen de mots superflus.* — En général, les pléonasmes n'ont pas d'utilité et ne font qu'alourdir l'expression (ex. : le mot allemand **Prinz'ess'in** contient un pléonasme, puisque les suffixes **ess** et **in** expriment tous deux la même idée féminine). Toutefois, comme les pléonasmes ne modifient pas la signification du mot ou de la phrase qui les contient, on les emploie souvent pour renforcer l'idée à exprimer (ex. : **non, non!** est une expression plus forte que simplement **non!**).

Réciproquement, si à un mot (ou à une phrase) on ajoute un ou plusieurs mots, et que cette addition ne change pas le sens du mot (ou de la phrase) donné, on peut en déduire que les mots ajoutés forment un simple pléonasme, c'est-à-dire que l'idée qu'ils expriment était déjà contenue dans les données primitives.[2]

5. *On dit que deux mots sont synonymes lorsqu'ils évoquent la même idée, ou des idées presque identiques.* — La synonymie peut donc être traduite par le signe =, à condition de ne pas attribuer à ce signe une valeur aussi absolue qu'en mathématique (ex. : **bonheur** = **félicité**, signifiera simplement que ces mots sont des synonymes).

6. *La signification d'un mot est l'idée évoquée par ce mot, tandis que son sens n'est que l'un des aspects opposés sous lesquels ce mot peut être considéré.* — Ainsi par exemple, tout mot peut être pris au sens propre ou au sens *figuré*; tout nom peut être pris au sens *concret* ou au sens *abstrait*, etc.

B. Analyse des mots.

7. Principe de l'invariabilité les éléments. *Tout élément simple (racine ou affixe) forme un tout invariable, qui a sa signification propre.* — Par exemple, dans les mots **grand, grandeur, agrandir**, etc., l'élément **grand** est toujours le même individu ; le mot **grandeur** n'est donc pas un substantif simple comme **maison** ; c'est un mot composé d'un élément adjectif, **grand**, et d'un élément substantif, **eur**.

8. *Un mot-racine exprime plutôt une idée particulière* (ex. : **éléphant**), *tandis qu'un mot-affixe exprime toujours une idée générale* (ex. : le suffixe **ine**, dans **héro'ïne**, exprime l'idée

---

[1] Cette remarque revient à dire que les langues dites *à flexion* sont en réalité des langues *à soudure*, lorsqu'on fait une analyse rationnelle de leurs mots.

[2] Cette remarque est importante et nous aurons plusieurs fois l'occasion de l'appliquer à l'analyse des mots.

root of the verb **couronner** 'to crown', but that **couronn** 'crown' is a noun, which with the affix **er** forms the verb **couronner**.[1]

4. *We use the term pleonasm to designate the repetition of the same idea by means of superfluous words.* — In general, pleonasms are not useful and only serve to weigh down the expression (e.g.: the German word **Prinz'ess'in** 'princess' contains a pleonasm, since the suffixes **ess** and **in** both express the same idea of feminine). Nonetheless, as pleonasms do not modify the meaning of the word or phrase that contains them, they are often used to reinforce the idea to be expressed (e.g. **non, non!** 'no, no!' is a stronger expression than just **non!** 'no!').

Conversely, if we add one or several words to a word (or to a phrase), and this addition does not change the sense of the given word (or phrase), we can deduce from this that the idea they express is already contained in the basic material.[2]

5. *We say that two words are synonyms when they evoke the same idea, or nearly identical ideas.* — Synonymy can thus be translated by the sign =, provided we do not attribute to that sign a value as absolute as in mathematics (e.g. **bonheur** 'happiness' = **félicité** 'bliss' means simply that these words are synonyms).

6. *The meaning of a word is the idea evoked by that word, while its sense is only one of the opposed aspects from which the word can be considered.* — Thus for example every word can be taken in the *proper* sense or in the *figurative* sense; every noun can be taken in the *concrete* sense or in the *abstract* sense, etc.

B. Analysis of words.

7. PRINCIPLE OF THE INVARIABILITY OF ELEMENTS. *Every simple element (root or affix) forms an invariable whole, which has its own meaning.* — For example, in the words **grand** 'large', **grandeur** 'size', **agrandir** 'enlarge', etc., the element **grand** is always the same individual; the word **grandeur** is thus not a simple noun like **maison** 'house'; it is a word composed of an adjectival element **grand** and a nominal element **eur**.

8. *A root word generally expresses a particular idea* (e.g. **éléfant** 'elephant') *while an affix word always expresses a general idea* (e.g.: the suffix **ine** in **héroïne** expresses the [general] idea

---

[1] This remark amounts to saying that languages called *flexional* are in reality *joining* languages, when we make a rational analysis of their words.

[2] This remark is important and we will have several occasions to apply it to the analysis of words.

générale du féminin). — Les affixes qui expriment les idées les plus générales sont ceux qui correspondent aux idées grammaticales de *substantif*, d'*adjectif* et de *verbe* (ex. : l'affixe-désinence **er** dans **couronn'er** exprime l'idée *verbale* générale ; le suffixe **ain** dans **hum'ain** exprime l'idée *adjective* générale ; le suffixe **eur** dans **grand'eur** exprime l'idée *substantive* générale) ; ces suffixes généraux peuvent donc aussi être considérés comme des désinences *grammaticales*.

Beaucoup de mots simples sont synonymes (ex. : **peur** = **crainte**). — Il y a aussi des suffixes synonymes (ex. : les suffixes **ité** dans **égalité**, **esse** dans **rich'esse**, **eur** dans **grand'eur**, etc., sont évidemment des synonymes ; théoriquement ces suffixes sont interchangeables entre eux).

Enfin *les mots simples ne sont pas tous des éléments indépendants les uns des autres*. — Les idées qu'ils expriment forment des hiérarchies, qui procèdent du particulier au général. Ainsi, les mots **pomme** et **fruit** sont dépendants l'un de l'autre, en ce sens que l'idée particulière „pomme" implique en elle-même l'idée plus générale de „fruit" ; à son tour, l'idée évoquée par le mot **fruit** implique l'idée encore plus générale d'„objet", de „chose", c'est-à-dire finalement l'idée générale de „*substantif*", de „*substance*" ; en résumé, dans tout mot simple évoquant une idée particulière, comme **pomme**, se trouvent à l'état latent des idées plus générales, exprimables par d'autres mots, tels que **fruit**, **chose**, **substantif**. On n'ajoute donc rien à l'idée „pomme" en lui accolant l'idée de „fruit" ou l'idée de „chose" ; en anglais, par exemple, on pourrait écrire **apple** = **apple'fruit**, ce qui montre que l'addition du mot **fruit** ne produit qu'un pléonasme (voir règle 4), c'est-à-dire que l'idée „fruit" se trouvait déjà implicitement contenue dans le mot **apple**.

9. *Avant de faire l'analyse d'un mot on doit le débarrasser des pléonasmes inutiles qu'il peut contenir.* — Ainsi, par exemple, avant d'analyser le mot allemand **Prinz'ess'in**, on supprimera l'un des deux suffixes synonymes **ess** ou **in**.

10. LOI DU RENVERSEMENT. *Pour faire l'analyse d'un mot composé de deux éléments, on sépare ces éléments et l'on renverse leur ordre* (ex. : **survol** = „vol sur" ; la forme **survol** est la forme synthétique, tandis que la forme „vol sur" est la forme analytique). — On peut aussi énoncer la loi du renversement en disant que : *l'ordre analytique de deux éléments est inverse de leur ordre synthétique* ; ou encore, que pour dessouder deux éléments réunis en un mot, il suffit de renverser leur ordre.

Cas logique d'exception. Il peut arriver toutefois (quand le premier élément du mot à analyser est une préposition, un nombre ou un verbe), que le second élément soit le *complément direct* du premier ; dans ce cas, l'analyse consiste en une simple séparation des deux

general [idea] of the feminine. The affixes that express the most general ideas are those that correspond to the grammatical ideas of *noun, adjective* and *verb* (e.g.: the desinence affix **er** in **couronn'er** 'to crown' expresses the general *verbal* idea; the suffix **ain** in **hum'ain** 'human' expresses the general *adjectival* idea; the suffix **eur** in **grand'eur** 'size' expresses the general *nominal* idea); these general suffixes can also be considered *grammatical* desinences.

Many simple words are synonyms (e.g.: **peur** 'fear' = **crainte** 'fear'). — there are also synonymous suffixes (e.g.: the suffixes **ité** in **égal'ité** 'equality', **esse** in **rich'esse** 'wealth', **eur** in **grand'eur** 'size', etc., are of course synonyms; theoretically these suffixes are interchangeable with one another).

Finally *simple words are not all elements that are independent of one another.* — The ideas that they express form hierarchies which proceed from the specific to the general. Thus, the words **pomme** 'apple' and **fruit** 'fruit' are dependent on one another, in the sense that the specific idea "*apple*" implies in itself the more general idea of "*fruit*"; in turn, the idea evoked by the word **fruit** implies the more general idea of "*object*", of "*thing*" and finally the general idea of "*noun*", of "*substance*"; in sum, in every simple word evoking a particular idea, like **pomme**, is to be found underlyingly more general ideas, expressible in other words such as **fruit, thing, noun**. We thus add nothing to the idea "*apple*" by adjoining to it the idea of "*fruit*" or the idea of "*thing*"; in English, for example, we could write **apple** = **apple'fruit**, which shows that the addition of the word **fruit** only produces a pleonasm (see rule 4). that is, the idea "*fruit*" is already contained implicitly in the word **apple**.

9. *Before analyzing a word it is necessary to clear away the useless pleonasms that it may contain.* — Thus, for example, before analyzing the German word **Prinz'ess'in** 'princess', we eliminate one of the two synonymous suffixes **ess** or **in**.

10. LAW OF REVERSAL. *To analyze a word composed of two elements, we separate the elements and reverse their order* (e.g.: **survol** 'overflight' = "*flight over*"; the form **survol** is the synthetic form, while the form "*flight over*" is the analytic form). — We can thus formulate the law of reversal in saying that: *the analytic order of two elements is the inverse of their synthetic order*; or else that to disconnect two elements brought together in one word, it suffices to reverse their order.

Logically exceptional case. It can sometimes happen (when the first element of the word to be analyzed is a preposition, a number or a verb) that the second element is the *direct complement* of the first; in that case, the analysis consists of a simple separation of the two

éléments, *sans renversement* de leur ordre (ex. : **inter'règne** — „*entre règnes*" parce qu'ici le mot **règne** est le complément de la préposition **entre** ; ce cas d'exception est logique parce que les deux éléments **entre** et **règne** formaient déjà un seul tout avant même d'être réunis ; au contraire, dans l'exemple **survol** = „vol sur", il y a renversement parce qu'ici le mot **vol** n'est pas le complément de la préposition **sur** ; les deux idées „*vol*" et „*sur*" représentent dans ce mot des idées autonomes et indépendantes l'une de l'autre.[1]

11. Le procédé d'analyse qui consiste à séparer les deux éléments d'un mot composé (avec ou sans renversement) n'est pas toujours suffisant. *Pour pousser plus loin l'analyse, il faut mettre en évidence l'idée sous-entendue qui se cache dans la soudure entre les deux éléments du mot composé* (ex. : **Schreib'tisch** — „*table [pour] écrire*", **steam'ship** = „*bateau [mû par la] vapeur*" etc. — La nature de l'idée sous-entendue varie beaucoup d'un mot à un autre ; toutefois, cette idée peut presque toujours être traduite par l'expression : „*de l'espèce caractérisée par*" (ex. : **Schreib'tisch** = „*table [de l'espèce caractérisée par] écrire*").

Dans le cas particulier des mots composés sans renversement, comme **inter'règne**, il n'y a pas d'idée sous-entendue dans la soudure entre les deux éléments, puisque dans ce cas le second élément est complément direct du premier.[2]

12. *Pour faire une analyse encore plus complète, il faut mettre en évidence les idées générales qui existent à l'état latent dans toute idée particulière*.[3] — Ainsi pour analyser le mot **cheval**, on peut mettre en évidence une idée plus générale, telle que „*quadrupède*", „*vertébré*", „*animal*", etc., qui est contenue implicitement dans l'idée „*cheval*" ; on a alors les diverses possibilités d'analyse :

cheval = „*quadrupède* [*espèce*] *cheval*",
cheval = „*vertébré* [*espèce*] *cheval*",
cheval = „*animal* [*espèce*] *cheval*", etc.

On a en effet, par la loi de renversement : „*animal cheval*" = **horse'animal** ; or, **horse'animal** n'est qu'une forme pléonasmatique de **horse**, comme **apple'fruit** de **apple**. On a donc bien le droit d'écrire : „*animal cheval*" — **cheval**, ou réciproquement.

Remarque. Il faut bien faire la distinction entre les mots composés du type **Pferd'tier**, qui contiennent un pléonasme et les

---

[1] Pour les autres cas d'exceptions, voir p. 16.
[2] Par contre, dans la langue française, il y a toujours dans ce cas une idée sous-entendue *avant* le mot composé. Ainsi : **inter'règne** = [*temps*] *entre règnes*, **coupe-papier** = „[*objet qui*] *coupe papier*", **sous-pied** = „[*objet qui est*] *sous pied*", **tri'angle** = „[*chose qui est*] *trois angles*", **tri'corne** = „[*objet qui est*] *trois cornes*", etc.
[3] Voir le n° 8.

elements, *without reversing* their order (e.g.: **inter'règne** 'interregnum' — "*between reigns*" because here the word **règne** 'reign' is the complement of the preposition **entre** 'between'; this exceptional case is logical because the elements **entre** and **règne** would already form a unit before even being joined; on the contrary, in the example **survol** 'overflight' = "flight over", there is reversal because here the word **vol** 'flight' is not the complement of the preposition **sur** 'over'; the two ideas "*flight*" and "*over*" represent in this word autonomous ideas independent of one another.[1]

11. *The process of analysis which consists of separating the two element of a compound word (with or without reversal) is not always sufficient. To carry the analysis further, it is necessary to highlight the underlying idea which is concealed under the juncture between the two elements of the compound word* (e.g.: **Schreib'tisch** = "*table[for] writing*", **steamship** = "*ship [driven by] steam*", etc.[)] — the nature of the idea that is understood varies considerably from one word to another; however, this idea can nearly always be translated by the expression "*of the type characterized by*" (e.g.: **Schreib'tisch** = "*table [of the type characterized by] writing*").

In the special case of words composed without reversal, like **inter'règne**, there is no idea understood in the juncture between the two elements, since in this case the second element is the direct complement of the first.[2]

12. *To make an analysis still more complete, it is necessary to highlight the general ideas that exist in a latent state within each specific idea.*[3] — Thus, to analyze the word **cheval** 'horse', we can bring out a more general idea, such as "*quadruped*", "*vertebrate*", "*animal*", etc. which is implicitly contained in the idea "*horse*": we thus have various possibilities of analysis:

    cheval = "*quadruped*   [*of the type*] *horse*",
    cheval = "*vertebrate*   [*of the type*] *horse*",
    cheval = "*animal*   [*of the type*] *horse*", etc.

Indeed, by the law of reversal, we have: "*animal horse*" = **horse'animal**; now **horse'animal** is only a pleonastic form of **horse**, as **apple'fruit** is of **apple**. We thus are justified in writing: "*animal horse*" = **cheval**, or vice versa.

Remark: It is necessary to make the distinction between compound words of the type **Pferd'tier**, which contain a pleonasm, and

---

[1] For other exceptional cases, see p. 16.
[2] On the other hand, in French, there is always an understood idea in this case *before* the compound word. Thus **inter'règne** = "[*period*] *between reigns*", **coupe-papier** 'paper cutter' = "[*object which*] *cuts paper*", **sous-pied** 'foot strap' = "[*object which is*] *under foot*", **tri'angle** 'triangle' = "[*thing which is*] *three angles*", **tri'corne** 'three-cornered hat' = "[*object which is*] *three horns*", etc.
[3] See number 8.

mots du type **Fell'tier**, qui n'en contiennent pas. Dans le premier cas, on a simplement : **Pferd'tier** = „*animal [de l'espèce] cheval*" ; dans le second cas, on a : **Fell'tier** = „*animal [de l'espèce caractérisée par] une fourrure*".

13. Enfin, *dans les cas peu fréquents où les règles précédentes d'analyse sont encore insuffisantes, on mettra en évidence les idées cachées dans le contexte du mot à analyser.* — En particulier, on rétablira dans le contexte les mots sous-entendus (ex. : **un riche** signifie „*un homme riche*", **un mille-pied** signifie „*un animal qui a mille pieds*").

C'est aussi le contexte qui décide si un mot doit être pris au sens *propre* ou au sens *figuré*,[1] au sens *concret* ou au sens *abstrait*. Ainsi la signification d'un mot dépend aussi de son contexte, ou plus généralement des circonstances dans lesquelles ce mot est employé.

14. *Lorsqu'un mot composé contient plus de deux éléments, son analyse peut toujours être ramenée à celle de plusieurs mots ne contenant chacun que deux éléments.*

Ainsi le mot **Schrauben'dampfer'aktien'gesellschaft** se décompose d'abord en deux parties (**Schraubendampfer** et **Aktiengesellschalt**) auxquelles on appliquera la loi de renversement en considérant chacune des deux parties comme un mot simple ; on analysera ensuite chaque partie séparément par le même procédé, et l'on répétera l'opération jusqu'à ce qu'il ne reste plus que des mots simples comme résidu.

C. Synthèse des mots.

15. La synthèse, ou construction, des mots est basée sur les deux principes suivants, qui ne sont du reste que l'expression de la *loi du moindre effort* :

PRINCIPE DE NÉCESSITÉ. *Dans la construction d'un mot composé il faut introduire* (au moyen de la loi de renversement) *tous les éléments simples* (racines et affixes) *qui sont nécessaires pour évoquer clairement l'idée que ce mot doit exprimer* (dans des circonstances données).

PRINCIPE DE SUFFISANCE : *On doit aussi, dans cette construction, éviter l'introduction de pléonasmes inutiles, ainsi que celle d'idées étrangères à l'idée que l'on veut exprimer.*

En d'autres termes, si un mot est construit suivant les deux principes de nécessité et de suffisance, *la signification de ce mot sera conforme à son contenu*, c'est-à-dire que le mot construit sera un mot *entièrement motivé* (dans les circonstances données).

16. *Pour faire la synthèse d'un mot, on se servira de procédés exactement inverses, de ceux qui ont servi à en faire l'analyse.*

---

[1] Ainsi dans le mot **mille-pied**, le mot **mille** est pris au sens figuré.

words of the type **Fell'tier** which do not. In the first case, we have simply: **Pferd'tier** = "*animal [of the type] horse*"; in the second, we have: **Fell'tier** = "*animal [of the type characterized by] a fur*".

13. Finally, *in the infrequent cases where the preceding rules of analysis are still insufficient, we will bring out the ideas concealed in the context of the word to be analyzed.* — In particular, we will restore the words understood in the context (e.g.: **un riche** 'a rich' means "*a rich man*", **un mille-pied** 'a millipede' = "*an animal that has a thousand legs*").

It is also the context that decides whether a word should be taken in its *proper* sense or in a *figurative* sense,[1] in the *concrete* sense or the *abstract* sense. Thus, the meaning of a word also depends on its context, or more generally, on the circumstances in which the word is used.

14. *When a compound word contains more than two elements, its analysis can always be reduced to that of several words each containing no more than two elements.*

Thus, the word **Schrauben'dampfer'aktien'gesellschaft** 'screw-steamer joint stock company' breaks down first into two parts (**Schrauben'dampfer** and **Aktiengesellschaft**) to which we apply the law of reversal, considering each of the two parts as a simple word; we then analyze each part separately through the same procedure, and we repeat the operation until only simple words remain as the result.

C. Synthesis of words

15. The synthesis, or construction, of words is based on the two following principles, which are only the expression of the *law of least effort*:

PRINCIPLE OF NECESSITY. *In the construction of a compound word it is necessary to introduce* (by means of the law of reversal) *all of the simple elements* (roots and affixes) *necessary to evoke clearly the idea that the word is to express* (in the given circumstances).

PRINCIPLE OF SUFFICIENCY: *We must also, in this construction, avoid the introduction of useless pleonasms, as well as ideas foreign to the idea that we wish to express.*

In other terms, if a word is constructed according to the two principles of necessity and sufficiency, *the meaning of the word will conform to its content*, that is, the constructed word will be an *entirely motivated* word (in the given circumstances).

16. *To perform the synthesis of a word, we make use of procedures that are the exact inverses of those we make use of to perform its analysis.*

---

[1] Thus in the word **mille-pied**, the word **mille** 'thousand' is taken in the figurative sense.

Prenons comme exemple le mot **couronner** et faisons en d'abord l'analyse. Ce mot se compose de deux éléments : le substantif **couronn** et l'affixe verbal **er**. On a donc d'abord : **couronner** = **couronn'er**. Appliquant ensuite la loi de renversement (règle n° 10), on obtient :

couronn'er = „*er couronn*"[1]

La désinence **er** exprime l'idée verbale générale ; cette désinence est donc synonyme du mot **faire**, dans le sens général de „faire une action" ; on exprimera cette synonymie en posant

er = „*faire l'action*".

D'autre part, en faisant sortir du mot **couronne** l'idée plus générale d'„objet", qui y est contenue (règle n° 12) et „appliquant encore une fois la loi de renversement (règle n° 10), on a :

couronne = **couronne(objet)** = „*objet couronne*"

Reportant ces résultats dans la première égalité, il vient :

couronn'er = „*er couronne*" = „(*faire l'action*) (*objet couronne*)".

Enfin, appliquant la règle n° 11, d'après laquelle la soudure d'un mot composé renferme à l'état latent l'idée générale „*de l'espèce caractérisée par*", on a comme résultat final de l'analyse :

couronn'er — „*faire l'action* [de l'espèce caractérisée par]
l'*objet couronne*".

Réciproquement, si l'on veut faire la synthèse de l'idée „*faire l'action caractérisée par l'objet couronne*", c'est-à-dire construire le mot qui exprime cette idée, on effectuera en ordre inverse des opérations inverses :

On remarquera d'abord que l'idée donnée contient deux idées indépendantes : „*faire l'action*" et „*objet couronne*", réunies par l'expression „*caractérisée par*", dont il n'y a pas lieu de tenir compte, puisqu'elle est destinée à disparaître dans la soudure du mot composé, d'après la règle 11. L'idée dont il faut faire la synthèse peut donc être réduite à la forme :

„(*faire l'action*) (*objet couronne*)".

Or, d'une part, on a par la règle de renversement (n° 10) et par suppression de pléonasme (n° 12) :

„*objet couronne*" = **couronn(objet)** = **couronne** ;

d'autre part, l'idée „*faire une action*" est l'idée verbale générale, et cette idée peut être exprimée soit par les mots racines **faire**, **agir**, soit par des suffixes, tels que **ir** (dans **blanch'ir**), **er** (dans **clou'er**), etc. On doit évidemment mettre l'idée verbale sous la forme d'un suffixe, toutes les fois que l'élément qui la représente doit occuper en fin de synthèse la place d'un suffixe ; c'est bien ce qui a lieu dans l'exemple choisi, car, en remplaçant l'idée verbale „*faire l'action*" par l'affixe **er**, il ne reste plus qu'à faire la synthèse de l'expression analytique :

„(*er*) (*couronne*)",

---

[1] La forme analytique „*er couronn*" n'existe pas en français, mais elle existe en anglais : „*to crown*", car dans cette expression c'est le mot *to* qui exprime l'idée verbale.

Let us take as an example the word **couronner** 'to crown', and first perform the analysis. This word consists of two elements: the noun **couronn** and the verbal affix **er**. Thus we have initially: **couronner** = **couronn'er**. Applying next the law of reversal (rule number 10), we obtain:

$$\textbf{couronn'er} = \text{``}er\ couronn\text{''}^1$$

The desinence **er** expresses the general verbal idea; this desinence is thus synonymous with the word **faire** 'to do', in the general sense of "*perform an action*"; we express this synonymy by asserting

$$\textbf{er} = \text{``}perform\ the\ action\text{''}.$$

On the other hand, in extracting from the word **couronne** the more general idea of "*object*" which is contained in it (rule number 12) and applying once more the law of reversal (rule number 10), we have:

$$\textbf{couronne} = \textbf{couronne(objet)} = \text{``}object\ crown\text{''}$$

Returning these results to the first equation, it becomes:

$$\textbf{couronn'er} = \text{``}er\ crown\text{''} = \text{``}(perform\ the\ action)\ (object\ crown)\text{''}.$$

Finally, applying rule number 11, according to which the juncture of a compound word contains latently the general idea "*of the type characterized by*", we have as the final result of the analysis

$$\textbf{couronn'er} - \text{``}perform\ the\ action\ [of\ the\ type\ characterized\ by]$$
$$\text{the}\ object\ crown\text{''}.$$

Conversely, if we wish to perform the synthesis of the idea "*perform the action characterized by the object crown*", that is, construct the word that expresses that idea, we carry out the inverse operations in the inverse order:

We observe first that the given idea contains two independent ideas: "*perform the action*" and "*object crown*", linked by the expression "*characterized by*", which need not be taken into account because it is destined to disappear in the junction of the compound word, according to rule number 11. The idea whose synthesis must be performed can thus be reduced to the form:

$$\text{``}(perform\ the\ action)\ (object\ crown)\text{''}$$

Now on the one hand, we have by the rule of reversal (number 10) and by suppression of pleonasm (number 12):

$$\text{``}object\ crown\text{''} - \textbf{couronn(objet)} = \textbf{couronn};$$

on the other hand, the idea "*perform an action*" is the general verbal idea, and this idea can be expressed either by the roots **faire** 'to do', **agir** 'to act', or by suffixes such as **ir** (in **blanch'ir** 'to whiten'), **er** (in **clou'er** 'to nail'), etc. We must obviously introduce the verbal idea in the form of a suffix every time the element that represents it occupies, at the end of the synthesis, the position of a suffix; this is what takes place in the example chosen, because, in replacing the idea "*perform the action*" by the suffix **er**, it only remains to perform the synthesis of the analytic expression:

$$\text{``}(er)\ (crown)\text{''},$$

---

[1] The analytiic form "*er couronn*" does not exist in French, but it does exist in English: „*to crown*", because in this expression it is the word *to* that expresses the verbal idea.

qui, conformément à la loi de renversement (n° 10), se condense en un seul mot : **couronn'er**. (On laissé tomber l'*e* muet de **couronne**, comme on laisse tomber une bavure, après que la soudure est effectuée.) La synthèse est ainsi terminée : le mot **couronner** représente bien, par sa structure et son contenu, l'idée donnée.

En résumé, *analyser un mot, c'est tirer de l'intérieur même de ce mot* (au moyen des règles posées plus haut) *toute une phrase explicative de la signification de ce mot* ; réciproquement, *faire la synthèse d'un mot, c'est recondenser cette phrase explicative en un seul mot par des opérations inverses.*

Remarques sur l'interprétation des principes généraux. Dans l'application des principes généraux que nous venons de résumer, on devra procéder avec circonspection dans chaque cas particulier, car les mots (racines ou affixes), qui forment la matière régie par ces principes, ne sont pas des éléments aussi rigides et précis que des signes mathématiques : ceux-ci ont par leur nature même une valeur parfaitement définie, tandis que celle des signes linguistiques est toujours plus ou moins élastique. Ainsi, toutes les fois que l'on emploie le signe = on doit se rappeler que ce signe signifie simplement „synonyme de", d'après la définition donnée au n° 5. Il est rare que deux mots synonymes aient exactement la même valeur ; ce cas ne se présente guère que pour certain suffixes : par exemple, les suffixes **ité** (dans **égal'ité**), **eur** (dans **grand'eur**), **esse** (dans **rich'esse**), etc., sont exactement équivalents, car ces suffixes ont partout le même rôle et la même signification. On comprend du reste facilement pourquoi deux mots synonymes n'ont presque jamais une signification identique : la langue profite précisément de la différence de forme de deux mots synonymes pour établir entre ces mots une différence de sens, quoique leur signification générale soit la même. Par exemple, au point de vue logique, le mot allemand : **süss'lich** = **süss**, parce qu'en ajoutant l'idée adjective **lich** à une racine adjective, comme **süss**, on produit un simple pléonasme ; mais cela ne veut pas dire, qu'il n'y ait, dans la pratique, aucune différence de valeur entre ces deux formes. De même, si l'on écrit **mouton** = **sheep**, cela signifie que le mot anglais **sheep** est la traduction du mot français **mouton**, mais il n'en résulte pas que ces deux mots aient une valeur identique ; il y a des cas par exemple où **mouton** est traduit, non par **sheep**, mais par **mutton**.

Il peut arriver, au contraire, que des mots ayant la même forme extérieure (*homonymes*) aient des significations absolument différentes (Ex. : **son**, pronom possessif ; **son**, phénomène physique ; **son**, de grain[1], etc. ; de même, le suffixe **eur** dans **grandeur** n'a aucun rapport avec le suffixe **eur** dans **acheteur**, etc.). Il est à peine besoin d'insister sur ces distinctions, tant elles sont évidentes.

Ce qui importe donc pour le logicien, c'est beaucoup moins la forme extérieure d'un mot que sa signification. Il peut arriver, par exemple, que la forme d'un élément se modifie pour rendre plus facile la prononciation du mot, dont cet élément fait partie. Ainsi dans la série **homme**, **hum'ain**, **hum'an'ité**, le mot **homme** prend la forme **hum**, et le suffixe **ain** la forme **an** ; il n'y a pas de doute, cependant que nous avons à faire là aux mêmes éléments, puisqu'en allemand, par exemple, on retrouve la même série de mots encore intacte : **Mensch, mensch'lich, Mensch'lich'keit**. Il peut même arriver qu'un mot français ait conservé sa forme latine dans les mots dérivés (Ex. : **père, pater'nel**) ; peu

---

[1] On voit que pour distinguer des homonymes, on recourt à la règle d'analyse n° 12, car en spécifiant un des sens du mot son au moyen de l'épithète „*de grain*", on ne fait que mettre en évidence une idée plus générale, qui était déjà implicitement contenue dans le mot son.

which, in conformity with the law of reversal (number 10), condenses to a single word: **couronn'er** 'to crown'. (We drop the mute *e* of **couronne** 'crown' as we drop a smudge, after the juncture is effected.) The synthesis is thus finished: the word *couronner* represents well, by its structure and its content, the given idea.

In sum, *to analyze a word is to take from the very interior of that word* (by means of the rules presented above) *an entire phrase explanatory of the the meaning of that word; conversely, to synthesize a word is to condense that explanatory phrase back into a single word by the reverse operations.*

Remarks on the interpretation of the general principles. In the application of the general principles that we have just summarized, we must proceed with circumspection in each particular case, because the words (roots or affixes that form the material governed by these principles are not elements as rigid and precise as mathematical signs: the latter have, by their very nature, a perfectly defined value, while that of linguistic signs is always more or less elastic. Thus, every time we use the sign = we have to remember that that sign means simply "*synonym of*", according to the definition given in number 5. It is rare that two synonymous words have exactly the same value; this case hardly presents itself except for certain suffixes: for example the suffixes **ité** (in *égal'ité* 'equality'), **eur** (in **grand'eur** 'size'), **esse** (in **rich'esse** 'wealth'), etc. are exactly equivalent, because the suffixes all have the same role and the same meaning. Otherwise, we understand easily why two synonymous words almost never have an identical meaning: language profits precisely from the difference in form of two synonymous words to establish a difference of sense between them, even though their general meaning may be the same. For example, from a logical point of view, the German word **süsslich** 'sweetish' = **süss** 'sweet', because by adding the adjectival idea **lich** to an adjectival root like **süss**, we produce a simple pleonasm, but that does not mean that there is, in practice, no difference in value between these two forms. Similarly, if we write **mouton** = **sheep**, that means that the English word **sheep** is the translation of the French word **mouton**, but it does not follow that the two words have an identical value: there are circumstances, for example, where **mouton** is translated not by **sheep** but by **mutton**.

On the other hand, it can happen that words with the same external form (*homonyms*) have absolutely different meanings (e.g.: **son**, possessive pronoun; **son** 'sound' physical phenomenon; **son** 'bran' of grain[1], etc.; similarly, the suffix **eur** in **grandeur** is unrelated to the suffix **eur** in **acheteur** 'buyer', etc.). It is hardly necessary to insist on these distinctions, since they are so obvious.

What matters therefore for the logician is much less the external form of a word than its meaning. It can happen for instance, that the form of an element can change to make the pronunciation of the word of which it is a part easier. Thus, in the series **homme, hum'ain, hum'an'ité** 'man, human, humanity', the word **homme** takes the form **hum** and the suffix **ain** the form **an**; there is, however, no doubt that we have to do there with the same elements, since in German for example we find the same series of words still intact: **Mensch, mensch'lich, Mensch'lich'keit**. It can even happen that a French word may have preserved its Latin form in derived words (e.g.: **père** 'father', **pater'nel** 'paternal'); that does not

---

[1] We see that to distinguish homonyms, we go back to rule of analysis number 12, because in specifying one of the senses of the word **son** by means of the qualifier "*of grain*", we are only bringing out a more general idea which was already implicitly contained in the word **son**.

importe, car le principe de l'invariabilité des éléments (n° 7) se rapporte plutôt au signifié qu'au signifiant.

Nous avons vu qu'il existe deux sortes de mots composés : ceux du type **survol**, dont les éléments sont des mots qui expriment des idées indépendantes l'une de l'autre (cas général), et ceux du type **inter'règne**, où l'un des éléments est le complément direct de l'autre (cas particulier). Il n'en faut pas conclure toutefois qu'il n'existe pas d'autres types dans les langues naturelles ; ainsi, dans les langues latines, les mots composés contenant deux mots-racines (**timbre-poste**, **assurance-vieillesse**, etc.), sont formés à rebours de la loi générale. Ces formes ne sont pas vraiment synthétiques ; ce sont de simples abréviations de la forme analytique : „*timbre (de) poste*", „*assurance (pour la) vieillesse*", etc. Si notre étude portait uniquement sur la langue française, il nous faudrait admettre deux lois de formation des mots : une loi de renversement pour les mots composés contenant une racine et un affixe (par ex. : **sou'tenir** = „*tenir sous*", **util'ité** = „*ité* [espèce] *util*", etc.), et une loi de formation directe pour les mots composés contenant deux racines (**timbre-poste**, etc.) ; mais comme nous nous plaçons au point de vue international des langues en général, nous sommes fondés à considérer la loi de renversement comme la seule loi générale de formation des mots composés, par le fait que cette loi est générale pour les langues germaniques, slaves, etc., et qu'elle existe même dans les langues latines pour composer une racine avec des affixes[1]. Au point de vue international, des mots composés à la manière de **timbre-poste** sont anormaux ; ils proviennent du manque d'habitude qu'ont les Latins de faire des mots composés, et en effet lorsqu'on veut former le pluriel de ces mots, le signe du pluriel tombe au milieu du mot (des **timbres-poste**), ce qui est une anomalie au point de vue logique et pratique. Du reste, les mots du type **timbre-poste**, **va-nu-pied**, etc. ne sont pas de vrais mots composés, en ce sens que leurs éléments ne sont pas *soudés* (comme dans les mots **survol**, **Apfelbaum**, etc.), mais seulement réunis par un trait d'union. Or, d'après la définition (n° 3, p. 9) un mot composé est formé par *soudure* de ses éléments.

Remarque. L'espèce grammaticale d'un mot est déterminée par son *dernier* élément ; ainsi **Schreib'tisch** est un substantif, parce que **Tisch** est un substantif. Cette règle suppose évidemment que le mot considéré est construit conformément à la loi de renversement ; si le mot composé a une structure anormale, la règle est naturellement inapplicable ; ainsi dans le mot **timbre-poste** c'est le premier élément **timbre** qui détermine l'espèce grammaticale du mot. Du reste, il suffit pour lever le doute, de redonner au mot composé sa forme analytique ; l'élément qui détermine l'espèce grammaticale occupe alors toujours la première place. Ex. : „*table* à écrire", „*timbre* de poste", etc.

Enfin, nous avons vu que tout mot composé de plus de deux éléments est divisible en deux parties, analysables séparément. Mais cette division ne peut pas être effectuée d'une manière arbitraire. Ainsi, par exemple, le mot **passenger'steam'ship** ne peut pas être divisé en (**passenger'steam**) et **ship**, mais seulement en **passenger** et (**steam'ship**). De même le mot **hum'an'it'ar'isme** ne peut être analysé que par la série suivante de mots à deux parties :

humanitarisme = humanitar'isme,
humanitaire = humanit'aire,
humanité = human'ité,
humain = hum'ain.

---

[1]Ainsi, par exemple, le mot **pomm'ier** est aussi conforme à la loi de renversement que le mot allemand **Apfel'baum**, ou le mot anglais **apple'tree**, car le suffixe **ier** signifie „*un arbre*", „*un objet qui porte*". Ex. : **chandel'ier** = „*ier chandel*" = „*objet qui porte* (des) *chandelles*".

matter, because the principle of the invariability of elements (number 7) relates to the signified rather than to the signifier.

We have seen that there are two sorts of compound words: those of the type **survol** 'overflight', where the elements are words that express ideas independent of one another (the general case), and those of the type **inter'règne** 'interregnum', where one of the elements is the direct complement of the other (the special case). It should not be concluded from this that other types do not exist in natural languages; thus, in the Romance languages, compound words containing two root words (**timbre-poste** 'stamp-post: postage stamp', **assurance-vieillesse** 'insurance-old age', etc.), are formed in the wrong way from the general law. These forms are not really synthetic: they are simply abbreviations of the analytic form: "*stamp (of) post(age)*", "*insurance (for) old age*", etc. If our study bore uniquely on French, we would have to admit two laws of word formation: a law of reversal for compound words containing a root and an affix (for example: **sou'tenir** 'to support' = "*to hold under*", **util'ité** 'usefulness' = "*ity* [of type] *useful*"), and a law of direct formation for compound words containing two roots (**timbre-poste**, etc.); but since we are taking the international perspective on languages in general, we are justified in taking the law of reversal as the only general law for the formation of compound words, by the fact that this law is general for the Germanic, Slavic, etc. languages, and that it exists also in the Romance languages for combining a root with affixes.[1] From the international point of view, words composed in the manner of **timbre-poste** are abnormal: they come from the lack of a habit in Latin speakers to form compound words, and indeed when we want to form the plural of these words, the sign of the plural falls in the middle of the word (**timbres-poste** 'postage stamps'), which is anomalous from the logical and practical point of view. Besides, words of the type **timbre-poste, va-nu-pied** 'go-bare-foot: tramp', etc. are not true compound words, in the sense that their elements are not *joined* (as in the words **survol, Apfelbaum**, etc.), but just combined by a hyphen. Now according to the definition (number 3, p. 9) a compound word is formed by the *juncture* of its elements.

Remark. The grammatical category of a word is determined by its *final* element: thus, **Schreib'tisch** 'writing table' is a noun because **Tisch** 'table' is a noun. This rule obviously presumes that the word under consideration is built in accord with the law of reversal: if the compound word has an abnormal structure, the rule is naturally inapplicable; thus, in the word **timbre-poste** it is the first element **timbre** that determines the grammatical category of the word. Besides, to remove doubt it suffices to give the compound word back its analytic form; the element that determines the grammatical category always occupies the first position. E.g.: "*table* for writing", "*stamp* of postage", etc.

Finally, we have seen that every compound word composed of more than two elements is divisible into two parts, analyzed separately. But this division must not be made arbitrarily. Thus, for example, the word **passenger'steam'ship** cannot be divided into **(passenger'steam)** and **ship**, but only into **passenger** and **(steam'ship)**. Similarly the word **hum'an'it'ar'isme** 'humanitarianism' can only be analyzed by the following series of two part words:

humanitarisme = humanitar'isme,
humanitaire = humanit'aire,
humanité = human'ité,
humain = hum'ain.

---

[1] Thus, for example, the word **pomm'ier** 'apple tree' is as much in conformace with the law of reversal as the German word **Apfel'baum**, or the English word **apple'tree**, because the suffix **ier** means "*a tree*", "*an object that bears*". E.g.: **chandelier** = "*ier candle*" = "*object that bears candles*".

§ 2. — Les mots fondamentaux.

Les mots, ou plutôt les idées qu'ils expriment, ne sont pas tous indépendants les uns des autres ; ils forment, nous l'avons vu (N° 8) des hiérarchies. Plus une idée est générale, plus le mot qui la représente a une place élevée dans cette hiérarchie. Considérons par exemple les mots : **chat, chien, cheval, lion, corbeau, fourmi,** etc. ; tous ces mots contiennent en eux-mêmes l'idée plus générale d'„*animal*". L'idée „*animal*" est donc en quelque sorte le chef de file auquel sont subordonnées les idées particulières : „*chat*", „*chien*", „*cheval*", etc. : c'est pourquoi le mot **animal** peut être considéré comme ayant dans la hiérarchie des mots un grade plus élevé que les mots **chat, chien,** etc.

Il est important de remarquer à ce propos, que c'est l'idée particulière „*chat*" qui contient en elle-même l'idée plus générale „*animal*" (en effet, tous les chats sont des animaux, et en adjoignant à l'idée „*chat*" celle d'„*animal*", on produit un simple pléonasme : **cat** = **cat'animal**) ; au contraire, on ne peut pas dire que l'idée générale „*animal*" contienne en elle-même l'idée particulière „*chat*", car les animaux ne sont pas tous des chats ; l'idée „*chat*" est une spécialisation de l'idée „*animal*" (chat = „*animal*, espèce chat").

Au sommet de la hiérarchie se trouvent donc les idées les plus générales, les plus abstraites. Ces idées sont l'idée substantive (*chose, substance*), l'idée adjective (*qualité*) et l'idée verbale (*action*), avec, si l'on veut, l'idée adverbiale (*manière*). Les mots qui expriment ces idées sont donc les mots *fondamentaux* de la langue. Ils en constituent les éléments les plus simples ; en effet, tandis que tous les autres mots simples (par exemple : **chat**) contiennent en eux-mêmes une série d'idées plus générales („*mammifère*", „*vertébré*", „*animal*", etc.), les mots fondamentaux, comme **chose**, ne contiennent qu'une seule idée, puisque l'idée qu'ils expriment est déjà elle-même la plus générale possible.

Les mots fondamentaux sont donc les éléments ultimes formant la base de l'analyse des mots, comme les atomes des corps simples forment la base de l'analyse chimique. Cherchons quels sont les mots fondamentaux de la langue française.

I. Idée substantive. L'idée substantive peut être exprimée par le mot **chose**, pris dans son sens le plus général de „*chose concrète*" (vivante ou non-vivante) ou de „*chose abstraite*".

L'idée substantive est souvent exprimée aussi par l'*article*, placé devant un adjectif ou un verbe ; s'il s'agit d'une chose concrète, on emploie l'article indéfini **un** (Ex. : „**un** *blanc*", „**un** *noir*") ; s'il s'agit d'une chose abstraite, on emploie l'article défini **le**, en allemand **das** (Ex. : „**le** *boire* et **le** *manger*", „l'*utile* et l'*agréable*").

§ 2. — Basic words.

Words, or rather the ideas that they express, are not all independent of one another. They form hierarchies, as we have seen (number 8). The more general an idea is, the more the word that represents it has a high place in this hierarchy. Let us consider for example the words **chat** 'cat', **chien** 'dog', **cheval** 'horse', **lion** 'lion', **corbeau** 'crow', **fourmi** 'ant', etc. All of these words contain in themselves the more general idea of "*animal*". The idea "*animal*" is thus in a way the leading form to which the specific ideas "*cat*", "*dog*", "*horse*", etc. are subordinated: this is why the word **animal** can be considered to have a higher rank in the hierarchy of words than the words **chat, chien**, etc.

It is important to note in this connection that it is the specific idea "*cat*" that contains in itself the more general idea "*animal*" (actually, all cats are animals, and in adding to the idea "*cat*" that of "*animal*", we produce a simple pleonasm: **cat** = **cat'animal**. On the other hand, we cannot say that the general idea "*animal*" contains in itself the specific idea "*cat*", because not all animals are cats: the idea "*cat*" is a specialization of the idea "*animal*" (**cat** = "*animal*, type *cat*").

At the top of the hierarchy are found all of the most general ideas, the most abstract. These ideas are the nominal idea (*thing, substance*), the adjectival idea (*quality*), and the verbal idea (*action*), together with, if you like, the adverbial idea (*manner*). The words that express these idea are thus the *basic* words of the language. They constitute the simplest elements of it; indeed, while all other simple words (for example, **chat**) contain in themselves a series of more general ideas ("*mammal*", "*vertebrate*", "*animal*", etc.), the basic words like **chose** 'thing' only contain a single idea, since the idea they express is itself already the most general possible.

The basic words are thus the ultimate elements making up the analysis of words, just as atoms are the simple substances that form the basis of chemical analysis. Let us seek the basic words of the French language.

I. Nominal idea. The nominal idea can be expressed by the word **chose**, taken in its most general sense of "*concerete thing*" (alive or not alive), or of "*abstract thing*".

The nominal idea is often expressed by the *article*, placed before an adjective or a verb; if it is a question of a concrete thing, we use the indefinite article **un** (e.g. "**un** *blanc*" 'a white (one)', "**un** *noir*" 'a black (one)'); if it is a question of an abstract thing, we use the definite article **le**, in German **das** (e.g. "**le** *boire* et **le** *manger*" 'drink and food', "*l'utile* et *l'agréable*" 'the useful and the pleasant').

L'idée substantive peut aussi être exprimée par le pronom **ce** (ceci, cela), dans le sens de „ce qui est", „ce qui existe".

Enfin l'idée substantive générale („*chose abstraite*") est encore exprimable au moyen de suffixes, tels que **ité** ou **té** (dans **beau'té**), **eur** (dans **grand'eur**), **tion** ou **ation** (dans **pré-par'ation**), **ture** (dans **écri'ture**), etc. En effet, **beauté** signifie „la chose abstraite *beau*", „le beau"; or, par la loi de renversement : **beau'té** = „**té beau**", c'est-à-dire que le suffixe **té** (ou **ité**) exprime bien l'idée substantive générale de „*la chose abstraite*". Nous reviendrons du reste sur l'analyse des mots tels que **beau'té** et **écri'ture**.

II. Idée adjective. On dit souvent que l'adjectif exprime la *qualité*, la *propriété* (*Eigenschaft*). Mais il y a lieu de remarquer que les mots **qualité**, **propriété**, sont des substantifs ; ils représentent donc, non l'idée adjective elle-même (qui n'est pas une chose), mais l'idée adjective substantifiée. Ainsi, ce ne sont pas les adjectifs **égal**, **grand**, **riche**, etc., qui expriment des „*qualités*", des „*propriétés*", mais ce sont les substantifs **égal'ité**, **grand'eur**, **rich'esse**, etc. Or, ceci signifie que hiérarchiquement les mots généraux **qual'ité** et **propri'été**, sont chefs de file des mots particuliers **égal'ité**, **grand'eur**, **rich'esse**, etc.; ou encore que les mots **qual** et **propre**, sont chefs de file des adjectifs **égal**, **grand**, **riche**, etc.; autrement dit, tout adjectif contient en lui-même l'idée „*qual*" (ou l'idée „*propre*") à l'état latent ; le radical **qual**[1] (qui n'est autre que l'adjectif latin **qualis**) et le mot **propre** sont donc des éléments fondamentaux, qui expriment l'idée adjective générale, car ils expriment l'idée commune à tous les adjectifs.

On peut arriver au même résultat d'une autre manière, en comparant les deux séries suivantes :

FRANÇ'AIS,   QUAL'ITÉ (PROPRI'ÉTÉ),
Lyonn'ais,   *util'ité*,
Marseill'ais,   *égal'ité*,
Toulon'ais,   *médiocr'ité*,
Orléan'ais,   *van'ité*,
       etc.   etc.

La première colonne montre que le mot **Franç'ais** est le chef de file des mots **Lyonn'ais**, **Marseill'ais**, etc., et la seconde colonne, que le mot **qual'ité** est le chef de file des mots **égal'ité**, **util'ité**, etc. Or, si le mot **Lyonn'ais** contient l'idée de „*Franç'ais*", c'est évidemment parce que le mot **Lyon** contient l'idée de „*France*" ; de même, si le mot **util'ité** contient l'idée de „*qual'ité*" ou de „*propri'été*" c'est parce que le mot **util** contient l'idée „*qual*", ou l'idée „*propre* [à]".

---

[1] Le mot-racine **qual** n'existe pas en français comme adjectif autonome (car le mot français **quel** n'a pas tout à fait la même signification), mais nous verrons plus loin (p. 22) que **qual** est synonyme de **qualitatif**.

The nominal idea can also be expressed by the pronoun **ce** (ceci 'this', cela 'that'), in the sense of "that which is, that which exists".

Finally, the general nominal idea ("*abstract thing*") is also expressible by means of suffixes, such as **ité** or **té** (in **beau'té**), **eur** (in **grand'eur**), **tion** or **ation** (in **prépar'ation**), **ture** (in **écri'ture**), etc. Actually, **beauté** means "the abstract thing *beautiful*", "the beautiful"; or thus by the law of reversal **beauté** = "**té beau**", that is the suffix **té** (or **ité**) expresses the general nominal idea of "*the abstract thing*". We will come back additionally to the analysis of words such as **beau'té** and **écri'ture**.

II. ADJECTIVAL IDEA. We often say that the adjective expresses a *quality*, a *property* (*Eigenschaft*). But it should be noted that the words **qualité, propriété** are nouns: they thus represent not the adjectival idea itself (which is not a thing) but the nominalized adjectival idea. Thus it is not the adjectives **égal, grand, riche** etc. that express "qualities" or "properties", but rather the nouns **égal'ité, grand'eur, rich'esse** etc. Now that means that hierarchically the general words **qualité** and **propriété** are the leading forms for the specific words **égal'ité, grand'eur, rich'esse** etc.; or again that the words **qual** and **propre** are the leading forms for the adjectives **égal, grand, riche** etc. To put it another way, every adjective contains in itself the idea "qual" (or the idea "propre") in a latent state: the root **qual**[1] (which is nothing more than the Latin word **qualis**) and the word **propre** are thus basic elements which express the general adjectival idea, since they express the idea common to all adjectives.

We can arrive at the same result in another way, by comparing the two series below:

FRANÇ'AIS,	QUAL'ITÉ (PROPRI'ÉTÉ),
Lyonn'ais,	*util'ité,*
Marseill'ais,	*égal'ité,*
Toulon'ais,	*médiocr'ité,*
Orléan'ais,	*van'ité,*
etc.	etc.

The first column shows that the word **Franç'ais** 'French'man' is the leading form for the words **Lyonn'ais, Marseill'ais**, etc., and the second column that the word **qual'ité** is the leading form for the words **égal'ité, util'ité,** etc. Now if the word **Lyonn'ais** contains the idea of "French'man" it is obviously because the word **Lyon** contains the idea of "France": similarly, if the word **util'ité** contains the idea of "qual'ité" or of "propri'été", it is because the word **util** 'useful' contains the idea "qual" or the idea "proper [to]".

---

[1] The root word **qual** does not exist in French as an autonomous adjective (for the French word **quel** does not have at all the same meaning), but we will see below (p. 22) that **qual** is a synonym of **qualitatif**.

On voit maintenant pourquoi **utilité** signifie „qualité *util*". En appliquant la loi de renversement, on a : „*qualité util*" = **util'qual'ité**; or, l'idée „*qual*" existant déjà dans l'adjectif **util** produit un pléonasme superflu, qu'on peut supprimer : le mot **util'qual'ité** se réduit donc à **util'ité**[1]. On démontrerait de même que :

Lyonn'ais = „*Franç'ais de Lyon*", car, d'après la loi de renversement : „*Franç'ais Lyon*" = **Lyon'Franç'ais**; mais l'idée „*France*" existant déjà dans le mot **Lyon** produit un pléonasme inutile, qu'on peut supprimer : le mot **Lyon'Franç'ais** se réduit donc à **Lyonn'ais**.

En résumé, l'idée adjective générale doit être représentée, non par les substantifs **qualité**, **propriété**, mais par les adjectifs **qual**, **propre (à)**.

L'idée adjective est en outre exprimable par de nombreux suffixes, tels que **ain** (dans **hum'ain**), **ique** (dans **symbol'ique**), **eux** (dans **chanc'eux**), **al** (dans **nation'al**), etc. Tous ces suffixes sont donc synonymes de l'idée adjective exprimée par les mots racines **qual**, **propre** (à), c'est-à-dire qu'ils sont théoriquement interchangeables avec ces racines. Ainsi, par exemple, on a par la loi de renversement :

hum'ain — „*ain hom*" — „*propre [à] [l']homme*"; ou encore, en remplaçant le suffixe **ain** par la racine **qual**, dans le mot **humanité** :

hum'an'ité = **hom'qual'ité** = „*qualité [d']homme*".

L'idée adjective générale est aussi exprimable par la préposition **de**. En effet :

„pied hum'*ain*" = „pied *d'*homme";
„amour pater'*nel*" = „amour *de* père";

ces égalités montrent, en tenant compte de la loi de renversement, que la préposition **de** est bien synonyme des suffixes **ain**, **el**, **ique**, etc.

Enfin l'idée adjective peut encore être exprimée par le mot **qui** dans le sens de „*qui est*". Pour s'en rendre compte, il suffit de remarquer qu'on n'ajoute rien à un adjectif en lui adjoignant l'expression „*qui est*". Par exemple, „un homme grand" = „un homme *qui est* grand". L'expression „*qui est grand*" contient donc un pléonasme, puis qu'elle est réductible à **grand** (voir n° 4, p. 10); or, ceci revient à dire que l'idée „*qui est*" est implicitement contenue dans tout adjectif[2].

III. Idée verbale. Le verbe, dit-on généralement, exprime l'„*action*" ou l'„*état*". Mais les mots **action** et **état** sont des sub-

---

[1] Ainsi donc ce n'est pas le suffixe **ité** qui apporte dans un mot l'idée de „*qualité*". Ce suffixe n'apporte que l'idée substantive, et l'idée „*qual*" est apportée implicitement par l'adjectif qui est accolé au suffixe **ité**.

[2] Ne pas confondre l'idée „*qui est*" (idée adjective) avec l'idée „*ce qui est*" (idée substantive, voir plus haut).

We see now why **utilité** means "quality *util*". Applying the law of reversal, we have: "*quality util*" = **util'qual'ity**; now since the idea "*qual*" already present in the adjective **util** produces an unnecessary pleonasm, we can remove it, and the word **util'qual'ity** reduces to **util'ity**[1] We can similarly demonstrate that:

Lyonn'ais = "*Franç'ais* 'French'man' *from Lyon*", since according to the law of reversal, "*Franç'ais Lyon*" = **Lyon'Franç'ais**, but since the idea "*France*" exists already in the word **Lyon**, this produces an unnecessary pleonasm which we can eliminate: the word **Lyon'Franç'ais** thus reduces to **Lyonn'ais**.

To summarize, the general adjective idea must be represented not by the nouns **quality, property**, but by the adjectives **qual, proper (to)**.

The adjectival idea can also be represented by a number of suffixes, such as **ain** (in **hum'ain**), **ique** (in **symbol'ique**), **eux** (in **chanc'eux**), **al** (in **nation'al**), etc. All of these suffixes are thus synonyms of the adjectial idea expressed by the root words **qual, proper (to)**; that is, they are theoretically interchangeable with these roots. Thus, for example, we have by the law of reversal:

hum'ain = "*ain hom*" = "*proper [to] man*"; or again, replacing the suffix **ain** by the root **qual**, in the word **humanité**:

hum'an'ité = **hom'qual'ité** = "*quality [of] man*".

The general adjectival idea is also expressible by the preposition **de** 'of'. Thus:

"pied hum'*ain*" = "pied *d'*homme ('foot *of* man')";
"amour pater'*nel*" = "amour *de* père ('love *of* father')";

These equations show, taking the law of reversal into account, that the preposition **de** is indeed synonymous with the suffixes **ain, el, ique**, etc.

Finally, the adjectival idea can also be expressed by the word **qui** in the sense of "*qui est*" 'who/which is'. To recognize this, it is sufficient to note that we add nothing to an adjective when we adjoin the expression "*who/which is*". For example, "un homme grand" 'a tall man' = "a man *who is* tall". The expression "*who is tall*" thus contains a pleonasm, since it can be reduced to **tall** (see number 4, p. 10); now this comes down to saying that the idea "*who/which is*" is implicitly contained in every adjective[2].

III. VERBAL IDEA. The verb, we usually say, expresses "*action*" or "*state*". But the words **action** and **state** are no[uns]

---

[1] Thus it is not the suffix **ité** that carries the idea of "*quality*" in a word. This suffix only carries the nominal idea, and the idea "*qual*" is implicitly borne by the adjective which is attached to the suffix **ité**.
[2] Do not confuse the ides "*who/which is*" (adjectival idea) with the idea "*that which is*" (nominal idea, see above).

stantifs; ils représentent donc, non l'idée verbale elle-même (qui n'est pas une „chose"), mais l'idée verbale substantifiée. L'idée verbale ne peut être définie que par les verbes correspondant aux substantifs **action** et **état**, c'est-à-dire par les verbes **agir**, **faire** (*une action*) ou **être** (*dans un état*). Mais les mots **ag'ir**, **fai're**, **êt're**, se composent encore de deux éléments : un mot-racine **ag**, **fai** ou **êt**, et une désinence **ir** ou **re**. Cette désinence, qui sert à exprimer le temps du verbe, est évidemment superflue pour l'objet que nous avons en vue. Donc, en dernière analyse, les éléments fondamentaux qui expriment l'idée verbale générale sont les racines **ag**, **fai**, ou **êt**.

On peut arriver à ce résultat d'une autre manière : de même que le mot **qualité**, ou le mot **propriété**, représente l'idée commune à tous les adjectifs substantifiés (**égalité**, **utilité**, etc.), de même le mot **action**, ou le mot **état**, représente l'idée commune à tous les verbes substantifiés. Formons le tableau de ces substantifs :

AC'TION,	ÉT'AT
abdic'ation,	*abond'ance,*
fabric'ation,	*exist'ence*
pénétr'ation,	*suffis'ance,*
etc.	etc.

Puisque le mot **pénétr'ation**, par exemple, contient en lui-même l'idée d'„*ac'tion*", le radical **pénétr** doit contenir l'idée „*ac*" (ou „*ag*", racine du verbe **ag'ir**). Ainsi, toutes les racines verbales contiennent implicitement en elles-mêmes l'une des deux idées générales „*ag*" ou „*êt*". On retrouve bien ainsi le même résultat, et l'on comprend maintenant pourquoi on peut écrire : **pénétr'ation** = „*ac'tion pénétr*"; en effet, en vertu de la loi de renversement, le second membre de cette égalité peut s'écrire : **pénétr'ac'tion**, mot composé qui se réduit à : **pénétr'tion** puisque l'idée „*ac*" (ou „*ag*") est déjà contenue dans la racine verbale pénétr. Ainsi les deux égalités :

pénétr'ation = „*ac'tion* [espèce] *pénétr*"
util'ité   = „*qual'ité* [espèce] *util*"

sont en tous points semblables à l'égalité :

Lyonn'ais = „*Franç'ais* [espèce] *Lyon*".

Considérons maintenant les verbes tels que **couronn'er**, **clou'er pâl'ir**, etc., dérivés d'un substantif ou d'un adjectif. Comme les substantifs **couronne**, **clou**, etc., ne contiennent pas d'idée verbale, celle-ci ne peut être contenue que dans les suffixes verbaux **er**, **ir**, etc., des verbes **couronn'er**, **pâl'ir**, etc. On en conclut donc que l'idée verbale générale peut être exprimée aussi par les suffixes

[no]uns; they thus represent not the verbal idea itself (which is not a "thing") but the nominalized verbal idea. The verbal idea can only be defined by the verbs corresponding to the nouns **action** and **state**, that is by the verbs **agir** 'to act', **faire** 'to do, perform (*an action*)' or **être** 'to be (*in a state*)'. But the words **ag'ir, fai're, êt're** are again made up of two elements: a root word **ag, fai,** or **êt** and a desinence **ir** or **re**. This desinence, which serves to express the tense of the verb, is obviously superfluous for our object here. Thus, in the last analysis, the basic elements that express the general verbal idea re the roots **ag, fai,** or **êt**.

We can reach this result in another way: just as the word **quality** or the word **property** represents the idea common to all nominalized adjectives, so the word **action** or the word **state** represents the idea common to all th nominalized verbs. Let us make up the table of these nouns:

AC'TION,   ST'ATE
abdic'ation,   *abond'ance,*
fabric'ation,   *exist'ence*
pénétr'ation,   *suffis'ance,*
etc.   etc.

Since the word **pénétr'ation**, for example, contains in itself the idea of "*ac'tion*", the root **pénétr** must contain the idea "*ac*" (or "*ag*", root of the verb **ag'ir**). Thus all verbal roots implicitly contain in themselves one of the two genreal ideas "*ag*" or "*êt*". We thus find again the same result, and we now understand why we can write: **pénétr'ation** = "*ac'tion pénétr*"; actually, by virtue of the law of reversibility the second member of this equation can be written: **pénétr'ac'tion**, a compound word that reduces to: **pénétr'tion** since the idea "*ac*" (or "*ag*") is already contained in the root **pénétr**. Thus the two equations:

pénétr'ation = "*ac'tion* [type] *pénétr*"
util'ité   = "*qual'ité* [type] *util*"

are in every respect similar to the equation:

Lyonn'ais = „*Franç'ais* [type] *Lyon*".

Let us now consider verbs such as **couronn'er, clou'er pâl'ir** 'to turn pale', etc., derived from a noun or an adjective. As the nouns **couronne, clou,** etc. do not contain a verbal idea, this must only be contained in the verbal suffixes **er, ir,** etc. of the verbs **couronn'er, pâl'ir,** etc. We conclude from this that the general verbal idea can also be expressed by the suffixes

er, **ir**, **re**, etc., exactement comme l'idée adjective l'est par les suffixes **ain**, **ique**, **eux**, etc.[1]

Résumé. Les mots ou éléments fondamentaux, derniers résidus de l'analyse des mots dans la langue française, sont les suivants : 1. le mot **chose**, l'article **un** ou **le**, le pronom **ce**, les suffixes **ité**, **eur**, etc., **tion**, **ture**, etc., qui expriment l'idée générale *substantive*; 2. le mot **propre** (à), la racine **qual**, le pronom-adjectif **qui** (est), la préposition **de**, les suffixes **ain**, **ique**, **al**, **eux**, etc., qui expriment l'idée générale *adjective*; 3. les racines **ag**, **fai**, **êt**, les suffixes verbaux **er**, **ir**, **re**, etc., qui expriment l'idée générale *verbale*; à ces mots fondamentaux on peut encore ajouter, comme n° 4, le suffixe **ment** (dans **agréable'ment**) qui exprime l'idée générale *adverbiale*, et qui est synonyme de l'idée „*à la manière*".

Comme on le voit ci-dessus, et comme il est naturel, tous les mots fondamentaux sont des mots ou éléments simples. En effet, les mots fondamentaux, en tant que derniers résidus d'analyse, doivent être non seulement des mots simples, mais parmi les mots simples ils doivent être ceux dont la constitution est la plus simple ; ainsi, tout mot fondamental, comme **chose** par exemple, ne contient en lui-même aucune autre idée plus générale, tandis qu'un mot simple, non fondamental, comme **chat**, contient implicitement en lui une série d'autres idées plus générales, tels que „mammi-fère", vertébré, „animal", etc. Le mot **chose** est comparable en quelque sorte à une boule pleine et homogène, tandis que tout mot simple et non fondamental (comme **chat**) peut être comparé à ces boules creuses, qui contiennent à leur intérieur une série de boules plus petites, emboîtées les unes dans les autres et correspondant aux idées plus générales (*mammifère, vertébré, animal,* etc.) implicitement contenues dans ce mot.

Or, le but de l'analyse des mots est d'expliquer la signification des mots à structure complexe, par celle des mots à structure simple; on explique donc les mots composés par les mots simples, et les mots simples par les mots fondamentaux. Il en résulte que ces derniers ne peuvent être définis autrement que par eux-mêmes ; les mots fondamentaux sont les signes représentatifs de l'idée substantive, de l'idée adjective ou de l'idée verbale, et toute autre définition serait illusoire, car elle impliquerait l'emploi de mots plus complexes que les mots fondamentaux qu'il s'agit de définir; on tomberait dans un cercle vicieux, comme le chimiste qui après avoir expliqué les molécules des corps par les atomes, voudrait définir ces atomes à leur tour par des molécules[2].

---

[1] Dans tout cet essai nous ne considérons les verbes qu'à l'infinitif, car ce qui nous intéresse dans les désinences verbales, ce ne sont pas les différents temps du verbe, mais uniquement le fait que ces désinences expriment aussi l'idée verbale générale.

[2] Voir à ce propos la note de la page 25.

er, **ir**, **re**, etc., exactly as the adjectival idea is by the suffixes **ain**, **ique**, **eux**, etc.[1]

Summary. The basic words or elements, the final residue of the analysis of words in the French language, are the following: the word **chose** 'thing', the article **un** or **le**, the pronoun **ce**, the suffixes **ité**, **eur**, etc., **tion**, **ture**, etc., which express the general *nominal* idea; 2. the word **propre** 'proper (to)', the root **qual**, the pronoun-adjective **qui** 'who/which (is)', the preposition **de**, the suffixes **ain**, **ique**, **al**, **eux**, etc., which express the general *adjectival* idea; 3. the roots **ag**, **fai**, **êt**, the verbal suffixes **er**, **ir**, **re**, etc., which express the general *verbal* idea; to these basic words we can also add, as number 4, the suffix **ment** (in **agréable'ment**) which expresses the general *adverbial* idea, and which is synonymous with "*in the manner*".

As we see above, and as is natural, all of the basic words are simple words or elements. Indeed, the basic words, as the final residue of the analysis, must be not only simple words, but among the simple words, they must be ones whose constitution is the simplest. Thus, every basic word, like **chose** 'thing' for example, does not contain in itself any more general idea, while a simple but non-basic word like **chat** 'cat' implicitly contains in itself a series of other more general ideas, such as "*mammal*", "*vertebrate*", "*animal*", etc. The word **chose** is in a way comparable to a solid, homogenous ball, while a simple but non-basic word (like **chat**) can be compared to those hollow balls, which contain within them a series of smaller balls, enclosed within one another and corresponding to the more general ideas (*mammal, vertebrate, animal,* etc.) implicitly contained in this word.

Now the goal of the analysis of words is to explain the meaning of structurally complex words by that of structurally simple words. We thus explain compound words by simple words, and simple words by the basic words. The result is that these last cannot be defined otherwise than by themselves: the basic words are the signs representative of the nominal idea, the adjectival idea or the verbal idea, and any other definition would be illusory, for it would imply the use of words more complex than the basic words which are to be defined; we would fall into a vicious circle, like the chemist who after explaining the molecules of a body by atoms, would wish to define these atoms in turn by molecules[2].

---

[1] Throughout this essay we only consider verbs in the infinitive, because what interests us in the verbal desinences is not the different tenses of the verb, but only the fact that these desinences also express the general verbal idea.

[2] In this connection, see the note on page 25.

Remarque sur les mots fondamentaux. Mais ici une remarque s'impose : les mots fondamentaux, qui définissent les idées générales de substantif, d'adjectif ou de verbe, sont des éléments simples, dont quelques-uns (par exemple les éléments **qual, ag, êt,** etc.) ne sont pas des mots autonomes, et ne peuvent pas par conséquent être employés tels quels dans le langage courant. C'est pourquoi, dans la pratique, les grammairiens définissent quelquefois les idées substantive, adjective et verbale par des mots en apparence non fondamentaux, voire même par des mots composés, ou des expressions encore plus complexes. Ainsi, on peut définir, par exemple, l'idée adjective comme étant l'idée exprimée par le mot **qualitatif** ou par les expressions „*de qualité*", „*qui est de qualité*" (**hum'ain** = „**ain homme**["**]** = „*de qualité* homme", „*qui est de qualité* homme"). Mais il est facile de voir que toutes ces expressions ne sont complexes qu'en apparence ; elle sont toutes logiquement réductibles à l'adjectif fondamental **qual** : en effet, si d'un adjectif comme **beau** on dérive le substantif **beau'té**, en anglais **beauty**, et qu'ensuite du substantif **beauty** on dérive l'adjectif **beauti'ful**, on aura **beau'ti'ful** = **beau**, parce que les deux opérations s'annulent réciproquement, l'une étant l'inverse de l'autre ; de même, si de l'adjectif latin **qual** on forme le substantif **qual'itas**, en français **qualité**, et qu'ensuite du subtantif **qualité** on dérive l'adjectif **qualita'tif**, on aura **qual'ita'tif** = **qual**, pour la même raison que **beau'ti'ful** = **beau**. Ainsi, le mot **qualitatif** est bien un mot fondamental, qui représente l'idée adjective, et la complexité de sa structure n'est qu'apparente.

Il en est de même des expressions d'apparence encore plus complexes : „*de qualité*" ou „*qui est de qualité*". En effet, nous savons que l'expression „*qui est*" équivaut à l'idée adjective (voir p. 19) ; en outre, on a par la loi de renversement : ,

$$\text{„}de\ qualité\text{"} = \text{„}qualita\text{'}tif\text{"}$$

puisque la préposition **de** et le suffixe **tif** expriment tous deux l'idée adjective ; enfin, nous venons de voir que **qualitatif** se réduit à **qual**, donc en résumé l'expression „*qui est de qualité*" se réduit à „*qui est qual*", expression qui se réduit elle-même à „*qual*". On arriverait directement au même résultat, en remarquant que l'on n'ajoute rien à un adjectif en lui adjoignant l'expression „*qui est*" ou, „*de qualité*" ; ainsi :

„un homme *grand*" = „un homme *qui est grand*"
= „un homme *qui est de qualité grand*".

On peut faire des remarques semblables à propos de l'idée verbale et des éléments fondamentaux **ag, fai** ou **êt**, qui la représentent. Les grammairiens définissent généralement l'idée verbale au moyen des expressions en apparence complexes : „*faire une action*" ou „*être dans un état*" ; mais „*faire une action*" se réduit à **faire**, le mot „action" servant seulement à indiquer que le verbe **faire** doit ici être pris dans le sens d'*agir* ; de même l'expression „*être dans un état*" se réduit à **être**, le mot „état" servant seulement à indiquer que le verbe **être** ne doit pas être pris ici dans le sens d'„*exister*". Finalement les verbes **fai're, ag'ir, êt're**, qui expriment l'idée verbale renferment encore un pléonasme, car les suffixes verbaux comme **re, ir**, etc., n'expriment eux-même que l'idée verbale ; les expressions „*faire une action*" et „*être dans un état*" sont donc bien réductibles aux éléments fondamentaux **fai, ag** ou **êt**.

§ 3. — Exemples d'analyses et de synthèses.

1. Faire l'analyse du mot : **grandeur**.

D'après la loi de renversement, **grand'eur** = „*eur grand*", c'est-à-dire „*la chose grand*", puisque le suffixe **eur** exprime l'idée substantive générale de „chose". Cette analyse est insuffisante.

Remark on the basic words. But here a remark is necessary: the basic words, which define the general ideas of noun, adjective, or verb are simple elements, of which some (for example **qual**, **ag**, **êt**, etc.) are not autonomous words, and cannot as a consequence be used as such in everyday language. This is why, in practice, grammarians sometimes define the basic nominal, adjectival, and verbal ideas with words that do not appear basic, even with compound words or expressions even more complex. Thus we can define, for example, the adjectival idea as as being expressed by the word **qualitatif** or by the expressions "*of quality*", "*which is of quality*" (**hum'ain** = "**ain homme**" = "*of quality* man", "*which is of quality* man"). But it is easy to see that all of these expressions only appear complex; they are all logically reducible to the basic adjective **qual**. Actually, if from an adjective like **beau** we derive the noun **beau'té**, in English **beauty**, and if then from the noun **beauty** we derive the adjective **beautiful**, we will have **beau'ti'ful** = **beau**, because the two operations cancel each other, the one being the inverse of the other. Similarly, if from the Latin adjective **qual** we form the noun **qual'itas**, in French **qualité**, and then from the noun **qualité** we derive the adjective **qualita'tif**, we will have **qual'ita'tif** = **qual**, for the same reason that **beau'ti'ful** = **beau**. Thus the word **qualitatif** is indeed a basic word which represents the adjectival idea, and its structural complexity is only apparent.

The same is true for the apparently even more complex expressions "*of quality*" or "*which is of quality*". Actually, we know that the expression "*who/which is*" is equivalent to the adjectival idea (see p. 19). Besides, by the law of reversal we have:

$$\text{"}de\ qualité\text{"} = \text{"}qualita'tif\text{"}$$

since the preposition **de** and the suffix **tif** both express the adjectival idea. Finally, we have just seen that **qualitatif** reduces to **qual**, and so in sum the expression "*qui est de qualité*" reduces to "*qui est qual*", an expression which itself reduces to "*qual*". We would arrive at the same result in noting that we add nothing to an adjective when we add to it the expression "*qui est*" or "*de qualité*", thus:

"un homme *grand*" = "un homme *qui est grand*"
 = "un homme *qui est de qualité grand*".

We can make similar remarks concerning the verbal idea and the basic elements **ag**, **fai** or **êt** which represent it. Grammarians generally define the verbal idea by means of apparently complex expressions: "*to perform an action*" or "*to be in a state*", but "*faire une action*" 'to perform an action' reduces to **faire** 'to do', the word "action" serving only to indicate that the verb **faire** must here be taken in the sense of **agir** 'to act'. Similarly the expression "*être dans un état*" 'to be in a state' reduces to **être**, the word "état" 'state' serving only to indicate that the verb **être** must not here be taken in the sense "to exist". Finally, the verbs **fai're**, **ag'ir**, **êt're** which express the verbal idea again contain a pleonasm, since the suffixes like **re**, **ir**, etc. themselves only express the verbal idea; the expressions "*faire une action*" and "*être dans un état*" are thus reducible to the basic elements **fai**, **ag**, or **êt**.

§ 3. — Examples of analyses and syntheses.

1. Analyze the word: **grandeur**

According to the law of reversal, **grand'eur** = "*eur grand*", that is "*la chose grand*" 'the thing large', since the suffix **eur** expresses the general nominal idea of "thing". This analysis is insufficient.

183

Pour pousser l'analyse plus à fond, il faut, d'après la règle 12, mettre en évidence les idées générales qui existent à l'état latent dans les divers éléments du mot à analyser. Ainsi, nous savons que tout adjectif contient en lui-même l'idée générale „*qual*"; on peut donc écrire : **grand** = **grand(qual)**, comme nous avons écrit : **cat** = **cat(animal)**, ou **apple** = **apple(fruit)**. Par suite :

grand'eur = **grand(qual)'ité**,

puisque les suffixes **eur** et **ité** sont équivalents; enfin, en appliquant la loi de renversement :

grandeur = „*qualité grand*"

= „*qualité* [de l'espèce] *grand*"

2. Faire la synthèse de l'idée : „*qualité grand*".

Par la loi de renversement on a :

„*qualité grand*" = **grand'qual'ité**.

Or, le mot **grandqualité** contient un pléonasme inutile puisque l'idée „*qual*" existe déjà dans l'adjectif **grand**; ce mot se réduit donc à **grand'ité**, c'est-à-dire à **grand'eur**, en remplaçant le suffixe **ité** par son synonyme **eur**.

3. Faire l'analyse du mot : **écriture**.

Le mot **écriture** se compose du verbe **écri** et du substantif **ture**. D'après la loi de renversement, **écri'ture** = „*ture écri*", c'est-à-dire : „*la chose écri*", puisque le suffixe **ture** exprime l'idée substantive générale de „*chose*". Or, **écri** = **écri're**, puisque l'idée verbale „*re*" est déjà contenue dans le verbe **écri**. On peut donc dire que **écriture** signifie „*la chose écrire*".

Si l'on veut pousser plus loin l'analyse, il faut mettre en évidence l'idée verbale générale „*ag*" (ou „*ac*"), qui existe dans tout verbe, c'est-à-dire que : **écri** = **écri(ag)**, tout comme **grand** = **grand(qual)**, ou **apple** = **apple(fruit)**. D'autre part, le suffixe **ture** est synonyme du suffixe **tion**, on a donc :

écri'ture = **écri(ag)'tion** = **écri(ac)'tion**,

et enfin, en appliquant la loi de renversement :

écriture = „*action écri*" ou „*action écrire*" = „*action* [de l'espèce] *écrire*".

4. Faire la synthèse de l'idée : „*action écrire*" : Le mot **écrire** contient un pléonasme, car si l'on compare le verbe **écri're** au verbe **pâl'ir**, par exemple, on voit que dans ce dernier verbe l'élément **pâl** est un adjectif, tandis que dans le premier, l'élément **écri** est lui-même un verbe; l'idée verbale exprimée par le suffixe **re** existe donc déjà dans l'élément **écri**, c'est-à-dire que **écrire** est réductible logiquement à **écri**, lorsqu'on ne se préoccupe pas du temps de la conjugaison. La loi de renversement donne ensuite la synthèse :

„*action écri*" = **écri'action** = **écri'ac'tion**.

Or, l'idée „*ac*" (ou „*ag*") est encore l'idée verbale, laquelle est déjà contenue dans le verbe **écri**, c'est-à-dire que **écri'ac** est une forme pléonasmatique réductible à **écri**, de sorte que **écri'ac'tion** est réductible à **écri'tion**, ou encore **écri'ture**, puisque les suffixes **tion** et **ture** sont synonymes.

5. Faire l'analyse du mot : **humanité**.

Pour faire cette analyse, il est bon de considérer la série **homme, hum'ain, hum'an'ité**. On voit alors que dans le mot **humanité** l'élément **hum** n'est qu'une altération du substantif **homme**, et l'élément **an** une altération du suffixe adjectif **ain** (ou vice-versa).

Or, le suffixe **ain**, exprimant l'idée adjective générale, est synonyme du mot-racine **qual**; on a donc, **hum'an'ité** = **hom'qual'ité**, c'est-à-dire, par la loi de renversement : „*qualité homme*".

6. Faire l'analyse du mot **maniement**.

Si l'on considère la série : **main, mani'er, mani'e'ment**, on voit que dans le mot **mani'e'ment**, l'élément **mani** n'est qu'une altération du substantif **main**, et l'élément **e** est une altération du suffixe verbal **er**.

To push the analysis deeper, it is necessary, according to rule 12, to bring out the general ideas that exist in a latent state in the different elements of the word to be analyzed. Thus, we know that every adjective contains in itself the general idea "*qual*"; we can therefore write: **grand** = **grand(qual)** just as we have written **cat** = **cat(animal)**, or **apple** = **apple(fruit)**. Consequently:

$$\textbf{grand'eur} = \textbf{grand(qual)'ité},$$

since the suffixes **eur** and **ité** are equivalent. Finally, applying the law of reversal:

$$\textbf{grandeur} = \text{``}qualité\ grand\text{''}$$
$$= \text{``}qualité\ [\text{of the type}]\ grand\text{''}$$

2. Synthesize the idea "*qualité grand*".

By the law of reversal, we have:

$$\text{``}qualité\ grand\text{''} = \textbf{grand'qual'ité}.$$

Now the word **grandqualité** contains an unnecessary pleonasm since the idea "*qual*" already exists in the adjective **grand**; this word thus reduces to **grand'ité**, that is **grand'eur** on replacing the suffix **ité** with its synonym **eur**.

3. Analyze the word: **écriture**.

The word **écriture** is composed of the verb **écri** and the noun **ture**. According to the law of reversal, **écri'ture** = "*ture écri*", that is "*the thing write*", since the suffix **ture** expresses the general nominal idea "thing". And **écri** = **écri're** 'to write' since the verbal idea "*re*" is already contained in the verb **écri**. We can thus say that **écriture** means "*the thing [—] to write*".

If we want to push the analysis further, it is necessary to bring out the general verbal idea "*ag*" (or "*ac*") that exists in every verb — that is, **écri** = **écri(ag)**, just as **grand** = **grand(qual)**, or **apple** = **apple(fruit)**. Additionally, the suffix **ture** is a synonym of **tion**, and we thus have:

$$\textbf{écri'ture} = \textbf{écri(ag)'tion} = \textbf{écri(ac)'tion},$$

and finally, applying the law of reversal:

$$\textbf{écriture} = \text{``}action\ écri\text{''}\ \text{or}\ \text{``}action\ écrire\text{''} = \text{``}action\ [\text{of the type}]\ écrire\text{''}.$$

4. Synthesize the idea: "*action écrire*". The word **écrire** contians a pleonasm, for if we compare the verb **écri're** with the verb **pâl'ir** 'to turn pale' for example, we see that in this last verb the element **pâl** 'pale' is an adjective, while in the first, the element **écri** is itself a verb. The verbal idea expressed by the suffix **re** thus already exists in the element **écri**, that is **écrire** is logically reducible to **écri**, since we are not concerned with the tense of the conjugation. The law of reversal thus gives the synthesis:

$$\text{``}action\ écri\text{''} = \textbf{écri'action} = \textbf{écri'ac'tion}.$$

Now the idea "*ac*" (or "*ag*") is again the verbal idea which is already contained in the verb **écri**, that is **écri'ac** is a pleonastic form reducible to **écri**, so that **écri'ac'tion** is reducible to **écri'tion**, or rather **écri'ture**, since the suffixes **tion** and **ture** are synonyms.

5. Analyze the word: **humanité**.

To carry out this analysis, it is good to consider the series **homme**, **hum'ain**, **hum'an'ité**. We see then that in the word **humanité** the element **hum** is merely a modification of the noun **homme**, and the element **an** is a modification of the adjective suffix **ain** (or vice versa).

Now the suffix **ain**, expressing the general adjectival idea, is synonymous with the root word **qual**. We thus have **hum'an'ité** = **hom'qual'ité**, that is, by the law of reversal "*quality man*".

6. Analyze the word: **maniement** 'handling'

If we consider the series **main** 'hand', **mani'er** 'handle', **mani'e'ment**, we see that in the word **mani'e'ment** the element **mani** is just a modification of the noun **main**, and the element **e** is a modification of verbal suffix **er**.

Or, le suffixe **er**, exprimant l'idée verbale générale, est synonyme du mot-radical **ag** (agir) ; on a donc : **mani'e(r)'ment**= **main'ag'ment**, ou mieux : **main'ag'tion**, à cause de la synonymie des suffixes **ment** et **tion**. Enfin, par la loi de renversement : **main'ag'tion** = „*agtion main*", d'où : **mani'e'ment** = „*action* [de l'espèce caractérisée par] *la main*".

7. Analyser les mots : **moderniser, béatifier, agrandir, épurer**.

Les suffixes **is** et **ifi** sont des suffixes verbaux synonymes du mot-racine **rend**, c'est-à-dire qu'on peut écrire **is'er** = **ifi'er** = **rend're**. On a donc, par la loi de renversement :

modern'iser = „*iser modern*" — „*rendre moderne*",

béat'ifier = „*ifier béat*" = „*rendre béat*".

D'autre part, les préfixes **a** (dans **a'grand'ir**) et **é** (dans **é'pur'er**) sont aussi synonymes des suffixes **is** et **ifi** ; **agrandir** signifie donc : „*rendre grand*", et **épurer** = [„]*rendre pur*" ; on a donc **épurer** = **purifier**.

Remarque. Le mot **qual'ifier** signifie „*rendre qual*", et comme le mot **qual** sert de chef de file à tous les adjectifs, le mot **qualifier** servira de chef de file à tous les verbes tels que **béatifier, purifier, moderniser**, etc.

8. Analyser les mots : **se moderniser, s'agrandir**.

D'après ce qui précède, **se moderniser** signifie „*se rendre moderne*", c'est-à-dire „*devenir moderne*" ; de même : **s'agrandir** = „*se rendre grand*" = „*devenir grand*".

Remarque. Les mots tels que **pâlir** (devenir pâle), **blanchir** (rendre, ou devenir blanc), etc., ne satisfont pas au principe de nécessité, autrement dit ces mots ne sont que partiellement motivés. Pour les rendre complètement motivés, il faudrait dire : **blanchifier** pour „*rendre blanc*", et **se blanchifier** pour „*devenir blanc*".

9. Analyser le mot : **international**.

Tout mot composé est divisible en deux parties, mais non arbitrairement. Ainsi le mot **internation'al** (et non pas **inter'national**). Le suffixe **al** exprime l'idée adjective, idée que l'on peut traduire ici par l'expression „*qui est*". On a donc par la loi de renversement :

internation'al = „*al internation*" = „*qui est internation*".

Reste à analyser le mot **internation** ; ce mot se compose de la préposition **inter**, ou **entre**, et du substantif **nation**, mais il faut remarquer que ce substantif est le *complément* de la préposition **entre**, c'est-à-dire que l'on se trouve dans le cas particulier où la loi de renversement n'est pas logiquement applicable (cas **inter'règne**, n° 10, p. 11) ; on a donc par simple séparation des éléments : **internation** = „*entre nations*". Donc en résumé : **international** = „*qui est entre nations*".

10. Analyser les mots : **qualité, propriété**.

Le suffixe **ité** est synonyme de l'idée substantive générale : „*ce (qui est)*". On a donc :

qualité = „*ité qual*" — „*ce qui est qual*"

propriété = „*ité propre*" = „*ce qui est propre [à]*".

On ne peut pas pousser l'analyse plus loin, car les éléments **ité, qual, propre**, sont tous des éléments fondamentaux, c'est-à-dire des éléments simples qui ne contiennent pas en eux-mêmes d'idées plus générales. On peut seulement remarquer que l'idée „*qual*", ou „*propre*", est l'idée générale qu'exprime tout adjectif ; on peut donc définir les mots **qualité** et **propriété** comme indiquant „*ce qu'exprime l'adjectif*", ou encore (puisque le suffixe **ité** représente l'idée substantive), on peut dire que les mots **qual'ité** et **propri'été** sont les „*adjectivo-substantifs*" types, servant de chefs de file à tous les adjectivo-substantifs particuliers : **util'ité, vér'ité, grand'eur**, etc.

Now the suffix **er**, expressing the general verbal idea, is a synonym of the root word **ag** (agir); we thus have: **mani'e(r)'ment**= **main'ag'ment**, or better: **main'ag'tion**, because of the synonymy of the suffixes **ment** and **tion**. Finally, by the law of reversal: **main'ag'tion** = "*agtion main*", from which: **mani'e'ment** = "*action* [of the type characterized by] *the hand*".

7. Analyze the words: **moderniser, béatifier, agrandir, épurer**.

The suffixes **is** and **ifi** are verbal suffixes synonymous with the root word **rend** 'make'; that is, we can write **is'er** = **ifi'er** = **rend're** 'to make'. We thus have, by the law of reversal:

>**modern'iser** = "*iser modern*" — "*to make modern*",
>**béat'ifier** = "*ifier béat*" = "*to make blessed*".

Furthermore, the prefixes **a** (in **a'grand'ir** 'to enlarge') and **é** (in **é'pur'er** 'to purify') are also synonymous with the suffixes **is** and **ifi**; **agrandir** thus means "*to make large*" and **épurer** = "*to make pure*"; we thus have **épurer** = **purifier**.

Remark. The word **qual'ifier** means "*to make qual*", and since the word **qual** serves as the leading form for all adjectives, the word **qualifier** serves as the leading form for all of the verbs like **béatifier, purifier, moderniser**, etc.

8. Analyze the words: **se moderniser, s'agrandir**.

From the preceding, **se moderniser** means "*to make self modern*", that is "*to become modern*"; similarly **s'agrandir** = "*to make self large*" = "*to become large*".

Remark. Words like **pâlir** (to become pale), **blanchir** (to make or to become white), etc. do not satisfy the principle of necessity; in other words, these words are only partially motivated. To render them completely motivated, it would be necessary to say **blanchifier** for "*to make white*" and **se blanchifier** for "*to become white*".

9. Analyze the word: **international**.

Every compound word is divisible into two parts, but not arbitrarily. Thus the word **international** = **internation'al** (and not **inter'national**). The suffix **al** expresses the adjectival idea, an idea which we can translate here by the expression "*which is*". We thus have by the law of reversal:

>**internation'al** = "*al internation*" = "*which is internation*".

It remains to analyze the word **internation**. This word is composed of the preposition **inter**, or **entre** 'between', and the noun **nation**, but it is necessary to note that the noun is the *complement* of the preposition **entre**: that is, we find ourselves in the specific case where the law of reversal is not logically applicable (case **inter'règne**, number 10, p. 11). We thus have by simple separation of the elements: **inter'nation** = "*between nations*". Thus in summary: **international** = "*that which is between nations*".

10. Analyze the words: **qualité, propriété**.

The suffix **ité** is a synonym of the general nominal idea "*that (which is)*". We thus have:

>**qualité** = "*ité qual*" — "*that which is qual*"
>**propriété** = "*ité propre*" = "*that which is proper [to]*".

We cannot push this analysis further, since the elements **ité, qual, propre** are all basic elements, that is, simple elements that do not contain more gneral ideas in themselves. We can simply note that the idea "*qual*" or "*propre*" is the general idea that every adjective expresses; or again (since the suffix **ité** represents the nominal idea), we can say that the words **qual'ité** and **propri'été** are the *adjectivo-noun* type, serving as leading forms for all of the specific adjectivo-nouns: **util'ité, vér'ité, grand'eur**, etc.

11. Analyser les mots : **action**, **état**.

Les suffixes **tion**, **at**, sont synonymes de l'idée substantive générale : „*(ce qui est)*.["] On a donc **ac'tion** = „*tion ac*" = „*ce qui est ac*", ou „*ag*", c'est-à-dire : „*ce qui est agir*". De même, **ét'at** = „*at ét*" = „*ce qui est ét*", „*ce qui est être*" (en ayant soin de donner ici au verbe *être* le sens „*être dans un état*", et non le sens d'„*exister*").

On ne peut pousser l'analyse plus loin, puisque les éléments **tion**, **at**, **ac** (ou **ag**), **ét**, sont déjà tous des éléments fondamentaux. On peut seulement remarquer que l'idée „*ag*", ou „*ét*", est l'idée générale exprimée par un verbe, on peut donc définir les mots **action** et **état** comme indiquant „*ce qu'exprime le verbe*"[1], ou encore (puisque les suffixes **tion**, **at**, représentent l'idée substantive), on peut dire que les mots **ac'tion** et **ét'at** sont les „*verbo-substantifs*" types, servant de chefs de file à tous les verbo-substantifs particuliers : **abdic'ation**, **écri'ture**, **abond'ance**, etc.

On voit que les quatre mots *qual'ité*, *propri'été*, *ac'tion*, *ét'at* sont très généraux, puisque chacun de ces mots est composé de deux mots fondamentaux.

§ 4. — Symétrie du verbe et de l'adjectif par rapport au substantif.

Les exercices précédents mettent en évidence une symétrie remarquable de l'adjectif et du verbe vis-à-vis du substantif. Non seulement les mots tels que **qual'ité** et **ac'tion**, **grand'eur** et **écri'ture**, etc., ont des structures symétriques, mais aussi les mots tels que **hum'an'ité** et **mani'e'ment**, qui représentent des substantifs *abstraits* tirés de substantifs *concrets*, soit par adjectivation, soit par verbification ; les séries :

homme, hum'ain hum'an'ité,
main, mani'er, mani'e'ment,

sont tout-à-fait symétriques. On peut citer même les séries doubles :

homme, hum'ain, hum'an'ité, hum'an'it'aire, hum'an'It'ar'isme ;
règle, règl'er, règl'e'ment, règl'e'ment'er, règl'e'ment'a'tion.

Chacune de ces séries doubles est équivalente à deux séries simples : en effet, de l'idée concrète „*homme*" on tire d'abord par adjectivation (*hum'ain*) l'idée abstraite d'„*humanité*", dans le sens de „*qualité d'homme*" ou „*homme en général*" ; mais si l'on prend ce même mot **humanité** dans le sens concret de „*ensemble des hommes*", „*collectivité humaine*" (groupe concret d'individus), alors de cette idée concrète, on peut tirer de nouveau une idée abstraite, „*humanitarisme*", par l'intermédiaire d'une seconde adjectivation („*humanit'aire*").

De même de l'idée concrète „*une règle*" on tire par verbification (*règl'er*) l'idée abstraite „*règlement*", dans le sens „*action de régler*", ou „*la règle en général*" ; prenant ensuite le mot **règlement** dans le sens concret de „*ensemble de règles*", „*groupe concret de règles*", on peut de cette idée concrète tirer de nouveau une idée abstraite „*réglementation*", par l'intermediaire d'une seconde verbification („*réglement'er*").

En résumé, on peut dire que le Substantif forme la substance, le corps du langage, tandis que le Verbe et l'Adjectif sont les deux membres symétriques qui permettent le fonctionnement de ce corps en y introduisant l'action et la qualité.

---

[1]C'est précisément la définition du mot **action**, donnée par Larousse. Seulement Larousse fait d'autre part un cercle vicieux en définissant à son tour le mot **verbe** par les mots composés **action** et **état**. On ne doit pas dire : „le verbe exprime l'action", mais : „le verbe exprime l'idée „*ag*", ou si l'on veut : l'idée „*agir*", puisque **agir** est réductible à **ag**.

11. Analyze the words: **action, état**.

The suffixes **tion, at** are synonyms of the general nominal idea: "*(that which is)*". We thus have **ac'tion** = "*tion ac*" = "*that which is ac*" or "*ag*", that is "*that which is to act*". Similarly, **ét'at** = "*at ét*" = "*that which is ét*", "*that which is to be*" (being careful to give the verb 'to be' here the sense "*to be in a state*" and not the sense of "*to exist*".

We cannot push the analysis further, since the elements **tion, at, ac** (or **ag**), **ét** are all already basic elements. We can only note that the idea "*ag*" or "*ét*" is the general idea expressed by a verb. We can thus define the words **action** and **état** as indicating "*that which the verb expresses*"[1], or again (since the suffixes **tion, at** represent the nominal idea) we can say that the words **ac'tion** and **ét'at** are of the "*verbo-noun*" type, serving as leading forms for all of the specific verbo-nouns: **abdic'ation, écri'ture, abond'ance**, etc.

We see that the four words *qual'ité, propri'été, ac'tion, ét'at* are very general, since each of these words is composed of two basic words.

§ 4. — Symmetry of the verb and the adjective in relation to the noun

The preceding exercises demonstrate a remarkable symmetry of the adjective and the verb with regard to the noun. Not only have words like **qual'ité** and **ac'tion**, **grand'eur** and **écri'ture** symmetrical structures, but also words like **hum'an'ité** and **mani'e'ment**, which represent *abstract* nouns derived from *concrete* nouns either by adjectivalization or verbalization. The series:

homme,	**hum'ain**	**hum'an'ité,**
main,	**mani'er,**	**mani'e'ment,**

are completely symmetrical. We can even cite the double series:

homme,	**hum'ain,**	**hum'an'ité,**	**hum'an'it'aire,**	**hum'an'It'ar'isme;**
règle,	**règl'er,**	**règl'e'ment,**	**règl'e'ment'er,**	**règl'e'ment'a'tion.**

Each of these double series is equivalent to two simple series: indeed, from the concrete idea "*homme*" we first derive by adjectivalization (*hum'ain*) the abstract idea of "*humanité*", in the sense "*quality of man*" or "*man in general*"; but if we take the same word **humanité** in the concrete sense of "*the set of men*" or "*the human collectivity*" (concrete group of individuals), then from that concrete idea, we can derive a new abstract idea, "*humanitarisme*" by means of a second adjectivalization ("*humanitaire*").

Similarly, from the concrete idea "*une règle*" 'a rule' we derive by verbalization (*règl'er* 'to rule') the abstract idea "*règlement*" 'ruling, regulation' in the sense "*action of ruling*" or "*rules in general*"; taking next the word **règlement** in the concrete sense of "*set of rules*" or "*concrete group of rules*", we can now derive from that concrete idea an abstract idea "*règlementation*" 'regulations' by means of a second verbalization (*règlement'er* 'to regulate').

In summary, we can say that the Noun forms the substance, the body of language, while the Verb and the Adjective are the two symmetric limbs that allow this body to function by introducing action and quality.

---

[1] This is precisely the definition of the word **action** given by the *Larousse*. But *Larousse* on the other hand gets into a vicious circle by defining in turn the word **verb** by the compound words **action** and **state**. We must not say "the verb expresses the action" but rather "the verb expresses the idea *ag*" or if you like, the idea "*agir*" since **agir** is reducible to **ag**.

Digression. — Les remarques précédentes nous conduisent naturellement à l'examen des rapports qui existent entre la pensée et le langage. Mr. Couturat, dans un article sur la „Structure logique du langage", dont je ferai la critique au chapitre II, a abordé la même question, et il dit avec raison[1] :

> „De toutes les manifestations de la pensée, le langage est la plus universelle et, malgré tout, la plus adéquate. Si imparfait qu'il soit comme mode d'expression, il est encore le plus commode et le plus complet. Il est impossible que l'esprit humain, qui le façonne et le transforme sans cesse pour son usage, n'y imprime pas la trace de ses tendances et de ses fonctions, et que les formes du langage ne reflètent pas, dans une certaine mesure, les formes de la pensée."

J'exprimerai la même idée autrement, en disant que les catégories „grammaticales" correspondent aux catégories „logiques", et comme les premières sont les mêmes pour toutes les langues, le langage serait ainsi l'expression d'une certaine conception philosophique du monde, conception populaire si l'on veut, mais qui doit avoir des racines très profondes, parce qu'elle émane pour ainsi dire du dedans de l'évolution naturelle.

Il est donc très important de fixer le nombre des catégories ou classes fondamentales de mots.

Mr. Couturat n'en reconnaît que deux fondamentales : les *verbes* et les *noms*[2] ; le professeur Ostwald va plus loin : il ramène tous les concepts au concept de „*chose*" qu'il considère comme le plus général[3], ce qui revient à subordonner l'idée verbale et l'idée adjective à l'idée substantive, puisque l'idée de „chose" est précisément l'idée substantive. Or, cette subordination est impossible, car „agir" par exemple n'est pas une chose.

Il existe en réalité *trois* classes fondamentales de mots (les substantifs, les adjectifs et les verbes) correspondant aux trois concepts les plus généraux de „*chose*", de „*qualité*" et d'„*action*", exprimés plus exactement par les mots fondamentaux **chose**, **qual** et **ag**. Ces trois concepts sont indépendants les uns des autres, comme le sont par exemple en physique les trois concepts de temps, de force et d'espace ; leur nombre est par conséquent irréductible.

Cette division des concepts en trois catégories correspond évidemment à la manière dont nous concevons la réalité. Nous distingons en effet dans tout phénomène : 1° la *chose en soi* qui nous semble être le support du phénomène ; 2° le phénomène *objectif* ; 3° le phénomène *subjectif*.

Considérons par exemple un phénomène lumineux : nous expliquons un tel phénomène par des vibrations très rapides d'atomes ; vibrations qui, se propageant à travers l'éther, viennent frapper notre œil et y produire des sensations de lumière, de couleur, etc. L'„atome" qui vibre, c'est la chose en soi, c'est le concept évoqué par le *substantif* „atome" ; cet atome „vibre", voilà le phénomène objectif, c'est-à-dire le phénomène mécanique (quantitatif), le seul que considère la science, et cette partie du phénomène, qui est un „agir" est exprimée par le *verbe* „vibrer" ; enfin la vibration de cet atome produit sur notre œil l'impression subjective de couleur, par exemple de couleur „jaune", et cette partie subjective (qualitative) du phénomène est traduite par *l'adjectif* „jaune". Telle semble être en gros la correspondance qui existe entre les classes de mots et les catégories de notre pensée.

On peut dire qu'à certains égards la psychologie est la science de l'*adjectif*, car tout ce qui est subjectif est qualitatif, et le „qualitatif" est exprimé par

---

[1] *Revue de métaphysique et de morale*, n° 1, 1912, Paris.
[2] Voir la critique de ce système au chapitre II.
[3] Voir *Esquisses d'une philosophie des sciences*, par W. Ostwald, p. 62 de la traduction française. Félix Alcan, Paris, 1911.

Digression. — The preceding remarks lead us naturally to examine the relations that exist between thought and language. Mr. Coutourat, in an article on the "Logical structure of language", which I will criticize in chapter II, has addressed the same question, and he says correctly[1]:

> "Of all manifestations of thought, language is the most universal, and despite all, the most adequate. As imperfect as it may be as a mode of expression, it is still the easiest and most complete. It is impossible that the human spirit, which shapes and transforms it ceaselessly through usage, should not imprint on it the trail of its tendencies and functions, and that the forms of language should not reflect, to a certain extent, the forms of thought."

I will express the same idea otherwise, in saying that "grammatical" categories correspond to "logical" categories, and since the former are the same for all languages, language must therefore be the expression of a certain philosophical conception of the world, the popular conception if you will, but one that must have very deep roots, because it emanates so to speak from within natural evolution.

It is thus very important to establish the number of basic categories or classes of words.

Mr. Coutourat recognizes only two basic ones: *verbs* and *nouns*[2]. Professor Ostwald goes further: he brings all concepts down to the concept of "*thing*" which he considers the most general[3], which comes down to subordinating the verbal idea and the adjectival idea to the nominal idea, since the idea of "*thing*" is precisely the nominal idea. Now this subordination is impossible, since "to act" for example is not a thing.

In reality, there exist *three* basic classes of words (nouns, adjectives and verbs) corresponding to the three most general concepts of "*thing*", "*quality*" and "*action*", expressed more exactly by the basic words **thing**, **qual** and **ag**. These three concepts are independent of one another, as are for example in physics the three concepts of time, force and space: their number is thus irreducible.

This division of concepts into three categories evidently corresponds to the way in which we conceive reality. We distinguish, indeed, in every phenomenon 1. the *thing in itself* that seems to us to be the support of the phenomenon; 2. the *objective* phenomenon; 3. the *subjective* phenomenon.

Let us consider for example a phenomenon of light: we explain such a phenomenon by the very rapid vibration of atoms, vibrations that propagate across the ether, coming to strike our eye and produce there the sensations of light, of color, etc. The "atom" which vibrates is the thing in itself, it is the concept evoked by the *noun* "atom"; this atom "vibrates", and there is the objective phenomenon, that is the mechanical (quantitative) phenomenon, the only thing that science considers, and this part of the phenomenon, which is an "acting", is expressed by the *verb* "to vibrate"; finally the vibration of this atom produces on our eye the subjective impression of color, for example the color "yellow", and this subjective (qualitative) part of the phenomenon is translated by the *adjective* "yellow". Such seems to be roughly the correspondence that exists between the classes of words and the categories of our thought.

We can say that in certain respects psychology is the science of the *adjective*, since everything that is subjective is qualitative, and the "qualitative" is expressed by

---

[1] *Revue de métaphysique et de morale*, n° 1, 1912, Paris.
[2] See the criticism of this system in chapter II. [not included in the present edition]
[3] See *Esquisses d'une philosophie des sciences*, by W. Ostwald, p. 62 in the French translation. Félix Alcan, Paris, 1911.

l'adjectif. Au contraire, les sciences physiques seraient la science du *verbe* et du *substantif*, car ces sciences ne considèrent que le phénomène objectif, lequel est essentiellement quantitatif et se réduit en dernière analyse à des masses en mouvement, c'est-à-dire à des grammes, des centimètres et des secondes; or, la masse est une „chose", un substantif, et son mouvement est un „agir", un verbe.

Conclusion. Lorsqu'on se place au point de vue international, on peut dire que le type le plus général de structure des mots dans les langues naturelles est le type *par soudure*, c'est-à-dire que les mots composés sont formés par soudure de plusieurs mots simples (racines ou affixes), que l'on peut considérer comme invariables (de forme et de signification) et autonomes. La signification de tout mot composé résulte alors directement de l'analyse de son contenu, et non de la manière dont on suppose ce mot dérivé d'un autre; chaque mot est en soi un édifice propre.

Il est vrai qu'on considère les langues latines plutôt comme des langues à flexion, que comme des langues à soudure, mais cela vient uniquement de ce que l'on regarde en général les affixes comme des éléments qui modifient le sens de la racine, au lieu de regarder la racine et les affixes comme autant de mots, invariables et autonomes, c'est-à-dire comme autant de signes exprimant chacun une idée qui lui est propre. Ainsi l'adjectif **humain**, ou le verbe **couronner**, ne seront plus considérés comme des mots simples dérivés respectivement de **homme** et de **couronne**, mais comme des mots composés du substantif **homme** et du suffixe adjectif **ain**, du substantif **couronne** et de la désinence verbale **er**. La différence est essentielle; dans le premier cas l'idée adjective pénètre le mot **humain** tout entier, et l'idée verbale pénètre de même tout le mot **couronner**, de sorte que ces deux mots sont des mots simples comparables, par exemple, à l'adjectif **utile** ou au verbe **frapper**; dans le second cas, l'idée adjective reste cantonnée dans le suffixe **ain** sans pénétrer la racine **hum**, et l'idée verbale reste cantonnée dans la désinence **er** sans pénétrer la racine **couronn**, de sorte que les mots **hum'ain**, **couronn'er** sont des mots composés très différents des mots simples **utile** et **frapper**. Le mot **couronn'er** est en réalité un substantivo-verbe, de structure semblable à celle du substantivo-verbe **hand'schreiben** en allemand.

En assimilant ainsi les mots dérivés à des mots composés, on réduit la structure générale des différents mots à un seul type, le même pour toutes les langues; ce type est aussi celui qui convient le mieux aux langues artificielles, puisqu'il permet de trouver la signification de chaque mot par la simple analyse de son contenu et sans se soucier de savoir si ce mot est, ou non, dérivé d'un autre.

the adjective. In contrast, the physical sciences would be the science of the *verb* and the *noun*, for these sciences consider only the objective phenomenon, which is essentially quantitative and reduces in the last analysis to masses in movement, that is, to grams, centimeters and seconds; and mass is a "thing", a noun, and its movement is "to act", a verb.

Conclusion. When we take the international point of view, we can say that the most general type of structure of words in natural languages is the type *by juncture*, that is, that compound words are formed by joining several simple words (roots or affixes) which we can consider as invariable (in form and meaning) and autonomous. The meaning of every compound word thus results directly from the analysis of its content, and not from the manner in which we suppose this word to be derived from another; each word is in itself its own structure.

It is true that we consider the Romance languages rather more as flexional languages than as languages by juncture, but that comes exclusively from the fact that we generally think of affixes as elements that modify the sense of the root, instead of regarding the root and the affixes as so many words, invariable and autonomous, that is as so many signs each expressing an idea which is proper to it. Thus the adjective **humain** or the verb **couronner** are no longer to be considered as simple words derived from **homme** and **couronne**, respectively, but as words composed of the noun **homme** and the adjectival suffix **ain**, of the noun **couronne** and the verbal desinence **er**. The difference is essential: in the first case the adjectival idea fills the entire word **humain**, and the verbal idea fills all of the word **couronner** in the same way, such that these two words are simple words comparable, for example, to the adjective **utile** or the verb **frapper**. In the second case, the adjectival idea remains confined to the suffix **ain** without seeping into the root **hum**, and the verbal idea remains confined to the desinence **er** without penetrating the root **couronn**, so that the words **hum'ain**, **couronn'er** are compound words quite different from the simple words **utile** and **frapper**. The word **couronn'er** is really a noun-verb, with structure comparable to that of the noun-verb **hand'schreiben** in German.

In thus assimilating derived words to compound words, we reduce the general structure of different words to a single type, the same for all languages. This type is also the one that is most suitable for artificial languages, since it allows us to find the meaning of each word by the simple analysis of its content and without caring to know if this word is or is not derived from another.

Ce point de vue, du reste, n'est pas nouveau. Dans l'ouvrage déjà cité[1], l'auteur admet qu'il y a deux manières de concevoir les mots dérivés, lorsqu'il dit :

„Il y a conflit entre ces deux conceptions : pour former *indécoràble*, nul besoin d'en extraire les éléments (*in'décor'able*) ; il suffit de prendre l'ensemble et de le placer dans l'équation :

$$\text{pardonner : impardonnable = décorer : x}$$
$$\text{x = indécorable.}$$

Laquelle de ces théories correspond à la réalité ? ... Nos grammaires européennes opèrent avec la quatrième proportionnelle ; elles expliquent par exemple la formation d'un prétérit allemand en partant de mots complets ; on dit à l'élève : sur le modèle de *setzen : setzte*, formez le prétérit de *lachen*, etc. Au contraire la grammaire hindoue étudierait dans un chapitre déterminé les racines (*setz-*, *lach-*, etc.), dans un autre les terminaisons du prétérit (*-te*, etc.) ; elle donnerait les éléments résultant de l'analyse, et on aurait à recomposer les mots complets .... Selon la tendance dominante de chaque groupe linguistique, les théoriciens de la grammaire inclineront vers l'une ou l'autre de ces méthodes.... Le latin avait à un haut degré le sentiment des pièces du mot (radicaux, suffixes, etc.), et de leur agencement. Il est probable que nos langues modernes ne l'ont pas de façon aussi aiguë, mais que l'allemand l'a plus que le français."

Si nous ne craignions pas d'empiéter sur le domaine du linguiste, nous émettrions l'opinion que la méthode de la grammaire hindoue est la seule satisfaisante[2], mais afin de ne pas nous lancer dans un domaine qui nous est étranger, nous nous bornerons à constater que cette méthode est la seule qui convient pour les langues artificielles. En effet, „dans une langue artificielle les mots sont presque tous analysables ; un espérantiste a pleine liberté de construire sur une racine donnée des mots nouveaux". Dans ce jugement exprimé par l'auteur déjà cité,[3] nous n'avons qu'un mot à supprimer : le mot „presque".

---

[1] *Cours de ling. gén.*, p. 235 et 236.

[2] A l'appui de cette opinion je crois pouvoir invoquer les lignes suivantes du *Cours de linguistique générale* (p. 196) : „*les entités abstraites reposent toujours en dernière analyse, sur des entités concrètes* ; aucune abstraction grammaticale n'est possible sans une série d'éléments matériels qui lui sert de substrat, et c'est toujours à ces éléments qu'il faut revenir en fin de compte." Et plus loin (p. 197 et 198) : „Une unité matérielle n'existe que par le sens, la fonction dont elle est revêtue ; .... inversement un sens, une fonction n'existent que par le support de quelque forme matérielle."

[3] *Cours de ling. gén.*, p. 234.

This point of view, moreover, is not new. In the work already cited[1], the author supposes that there are two ways of conceiving derived words when he says:

"There is a conflict between two conceptions: to form *indécorable*, there is no need to extract its elements from it (*in'décor'able*); it suffices to take the whole and place it in the equation:

$$pardonner: impardonnable = décorer: x$$
$$x = indécorable.$$

Which of these theories corresponds to reality? Our European grammars operate with the fourth proportional; they explain, for example, the formation of a German preterite starting from complete words. We tell the student: on the model of *setzen* : *setzte*, form the preterite of *lachen*, etc. On the other hand, Hindu grammar would study in a particular chapter the roots (*setz-*, *lach-*, etc.), in another the preterite endings (*-te*, etc.). It would give the elements resulting from the analysis, and we would have to put the complete words together. ... According to the dominant tendency in each linguistic group, the theoreticians of grammar incline toward the one or the other of these methods. ... Latin had to a high degree a feeling for the pieces of a word (roots, suffixes, etc.) and for their arrangement. It is likely that our modern languages do not have this in as sharp a fashion, but German has it more than French."

If we did not fear to impinge on the domain of the linguist, we would offer the opinion that the method of Hindu grammar is the only satisfying one[2], but in order not to plunge into a domain which is foreign to us, we will limit ourselves to noting that this method is the only one that is suitable for artificial languages. Indeed, "in an artificial language the words are almost all analyzable; an Esperantist is fully at liberty to construct new words from a given root". In this judgment expressed by the author already cited[3], we have only one word to eliminate: "almost".

---

[1] *Cours de ling. gén.*, p. 235 and 236.

[2] In support of this opinion I believe I can invoke the following lines from the *Cours de linguistique générale* (p. 196): "*abstract entities are always based, in the final analysis, on concrete entities*; no grammatical abstraction is possible without a series of material elements which serve as its substrate, and it is always to these elements that it is necessary to return in the end." And later (p. 197 and 198): "A material unit only exists by virtue of the sense, the function with which it is imbued; ... inversely, a sense, a function exists only with the support of some material form."

[3] *Cours de ling. gén.*, p. 234.

Part III

Commentary

R ENÉ DE SAUSSURE'S LITTLE BOOKS ON MORPHOLOGY present a great many points of interest, only some of which can be addressed here. In the sections below, we discuss first the background of René's ideas in his work on Esperanto, and then some ways in which the books anticipate themes that have been developed in subsequent work by other scholars in the study of word structure, and finally some noteworthy features of the theory of meaning presumed (and presented) in the books.

Chapter 1

The Esperantist background of René de Saussure's work

Marc van Oostendorp

Radboud University and The Meertens Institute

René de Saussure was arguably more an Esperantist than a linguist – somebody who was primarily inspired by his enthusiasm for the language of L. L. Zamenhof, and the hope he thought it presented for the world. His interest in general linguistics seems to have stemmed from his wish to show that the structure of Esperanto was better than that of its competitors, and that it reflected the ways languages work in general.

Saussure became involved in the Esperanto movement around 1906, apparently because his brother Ferdinand had asked him to participate in an international Esperanto conference in Geneva; Ferdinand himself did not want to go because he did not want to become "compromised" (Künzli 2001). René became heavily involved in the movement, as an editor of the *Internacia Scienca Revuo* (International Science Review) and the national journal *Svisa Espero* (Swiss Hope), as well as a member of the *Akademio de Esperanto*, the Academy of Esperanto that was and is responsible for the protection of the norms of the language. Among historians of the Esperanto movement, he is also still known as the inventor of the *spesmilo*, which was supposed to become an international currency among Esperantists (Garvía 2015).

At the time, the interest in issues of artificial language solutions to perceived problems in international communication was more widespread in scholarly circles than it is today. In the western world, German was often used as a language of e.g. scholarship and French as a language of diplomacy and it was unclear that German or French politicians would ever allow the "other" language to grow into an international language for all domains. English was becoming a little more used as well, but one could not yet have expected it to attain the position it has

Marc van Oostendorp. 2018. The Esperantist background of René de Saussure's work. In Stephen R. Anderson & Louis de Saussure (eds.), *René de Saussure and the theory of word formation*, 201–208. Berlin: Language Science Press. DOI:10.5281/zenodo.1306494

now. Furthermore, there was still a strong belief in "technological" solutions to social problems, and therefore the idea of a specific artificial language to overcome language barriers did not seem too far-fetched to many (Gordin 2015). In the period until the Second World War, many linguists also became involved in issues of artificial language creation, such as Otto Jespersen, Nikolaj Trubetzkoy and André Martinet (van Oostendorp 2004).

Saussure's work on morphology was very closely related to his interest in Esperanto. This is clear already from a superficial inspection of the terminology he introduces in the 1911 text. The vowels **o, a, i** which he uses to denote nouns, adjectives and verbs, respectively, correspond exactly to the desinences for those lexical categories in Esperanto (see below). A form such as *kron-ag-o*, which Saussure presents as an "abstraction", is actually a well-formed Esperanto word. The idea was that Esperanto very closely mirrored the structure underlying all languages.

One can therefore understand the 1911 text in particular as an extension of Saussure's work on Esperanto (which he had presented earlier in his 1910 book *La construction logique des mots en espéranto* (de Saussure 1910). As Meillet noted in his review of the 1911 book (cf. p. 136 above), Saussure's interest in morphology was triggered by his interest in Esperanto word formation. The 1911 booklet can basically be seen as a way to show that Saussure's analysis of Esperanto morphology was right, by turning it into a universal theory. The 1919 text is clearly a similar introduction to a text in which Saussure presented a (mostly orthographic) reform of Esperanto.

Saussure's 1910 analysis of Esperanto itself was actually intended as an argument against Ido, a proposed reform of Esperanto from 1907 introduced by a team led by the French mathematician, Leibniz scholar and philosopher Louis Couturat (Couturat 1907; 1908). Ido was seen by its proponents as an "improved" form of Esperanto, and several of the improvements concerned morphology. Saussure's aim was to show that the Idists were wrong on this (he published his work under the pseudonym *Antido*, showing his attitude towards the language). Since many of the prominent Idists were French intellectuals, aiming to devise a language that would be more "natural", i.e. more like French, it is interesting that Saussure showed how the "Esperanto" kind of morphology actually underlies French.

Saussure's 1910 text is still seen as foundational to the study of Esperanto word formation, as is a later text from 1915, *Fundamentaj reguloj de la vort-teorio en Esperanto. Raporto al la akademio esperantista* (Foundational rules of the word theory in Esperanto. Report to the Esperanto Academy, de Saussure 1915). His own

1 The Esperantist background of René de Saussure's work

Figure 1: L[udwik] L[ejzer] Zamenhof (1859–1917)

relation with the Esperanto movement was rather unstable, mainly because he presented a large number of different (again, mostly orthographic) reform proposals of the language himself, under names such as Esperantido, Nov-Esperanto and Esperanto II.

In order to understand this more clearly, I will first lay out some of the basics of Esperanto word structure before turning to the criticisms raised against it by Louis de Couturat, the mathematician who proposed Ido instead and Saussure's response to Couturat, as well as the relevance of that response to the texts which are presented in the present volume.

1 The word structure of Esperanto

Esperanto is a language project, published by L. L. Zamenhof in 1887 (Zamenhof 1887). It is fair to say that morphology was the module that got the most attention in Zamenhof's language creation work. The intention was to make an "international language" that could serve as a second language for everybody in the (Western) world who might need it. The language therefore needed to be simple, and this simplicity was mostly a matter of morphology. First, there should be no exceptions, and secondly, the word stock should be as small as possible, by exploiting the combinatory possibilities of the language.

In a "16 rule grammar" that Zamenhof published of his language project (Zamenhof 1905), five rules seem particularly relevant:

- 2. Nouns have the ending -*o*. To form the plural, add the ending -*j*. There are only two cases: nominative and accusative; the latter can be obtained from the nominative by adding the ending -*n*. (...)
- 3. Adjectives end in -*a*. Cases and numbers are as for nouns. (...)
- 6. The verb does not change for person or number. Forms of the verb: present time takes the ending -*as*; past time, -*is*; future time, -*os*; conditional mood, -*us*; imperative mood, -*u*; infinitive mood, -*i*. (...)
- 7. Adverbs can be formed from adjectives by changing the -*a* ending to an -*e* ending (...)
- 11. Compound words are formed by simple juxtaposition of words (the main word stands at the end); the grammatical endings are also viewed as independent words.

Notice that several parts of Saussure's "universal" theory of word formation already find their expression here. I have already noted the correspondence of the nominal, adjectival and verbal (infinitival) endings to the names of categories in Saussure's system. Similarly, adverbs have an ending -*e*, just as in Saussure's system. They are considered not to be on a par with the three main categories: the rule for adverbs explicitly says they are derived from adjectives (the language actually also has adverbs that are not derived from adjectives, and those end in -*aŭ*: e.g. *hieraŭ*, 'yesterday'). This is also mirrored in Saussure's 1911 text, which similarly sees adverbs as derived from adjectives.

The idea that grammatical endings -*o*, -*a*, -*i* can be viewed as independent words is also introduced explicitly in Zamenhof's 1905 rules. Although it is not explicitly stated that the same would be true for other affixes, it seems logically implied that they are. It would be strange to assume that in a form like *lern-ej-o* 'school' (literally: learn-location-noun), only *lern* and *o* count as independent words.

As a matter of fact, affixes in Esperanto can be and are often used as independent words. In the example just given, *ejo* (etymologically derived from the German/Yiddish locational suffix -*ei*) can mean 'place' and be used as such in this way (*La parko estas bela ejo*, 'The park is a nice place'). The language has approximately 45 affixes, all of them productive, because Zamenhof believed that

it would be easier to learn a language when one did not have to learn too many separate morphemes.

This decision was sometimes criticized, because it means that Esperanto words are not directly recognizable to people unfamiliar with the language, even though most morphemes are taken from Indo-European (mostly Romance) languages. For instance a common word for 'hospital' is *mal-san-ul-ej-o* (opposite-healthy-person-place-noun). Apart from *-ej*, the other affixes in this form can also be combined with a desinence to form an independent word (*mal-e* 'to the contrary', *ul-o* 'guy'; for some reason these words often have an informal flavour to them.) Even suffixes that have been borrowed after Zamenhof's time are used like this: the pejorative *-aĉ* suffix (from Italian *-accio*) can be used as an adjective in *aĉa* 'ugly, morally corrupt'.

On the other hand, the desinences themselves cannot really be used as independent words in Esperanto. For instance, the phrase *la o* is not used for 'the thing' as Saussure's theory would perhaps predict; instead people say *la aĵo*, where *-aĵ* is indeed a deadjectival nominalizing suffix (French *-age*).

Replacing one desinence by another, is however, freely admissable: the Esperanto system allows for conversion between all categories, so that, e.g., from the noun *krono* 'crown' one can also form the verb *kroni* 'to crown'.

2 Couturat's criticism and Saussure's answer

The years after 1907 are sometimes referred to as the *Ido crisis* in the literature on the history of the Esperanto movement. In this year, Louis Couturat proposed his reform plan for Esperanto, which attracted a considerable following in particular among the intellectual leadership of the young Esperanto movement at the time. Although the language was still understandable for somebody who knew Esperanto (and as a matter of fact originally thought of as an "improved dialect"), there were changes in the lexicon, the orthography, the syntax (e.g. there was no longer an obligatory accusative for direct objects) and the morphology. The claim was that these changes would make the language more "natural" and hence more palatable for the world which had not accepted Zamenhof's language in the 20 years after he had presented it.

A bitter fight between Esperantists and Idists ensued. Saussure took sides with the former group, although he must have agreed with some of the reform proposals, in particular with respect to orthography (Esperanto has letters like *ĉ*, *ŝ*, *ĝ* which have not always been easy to typeset). He did not, however, at all share Couturat's criticism of the morphological system.

Marc van Oostendorp

Figure 2: Louis Couturat (1868–1914)

In particular, the Idists reject as unnatural the idea that affixes can be used as independent words. This is somewhat ironic, as *ido* is itself an independently used suffix for 'offspring' (*bovo* is 'cow', *bovido* 'calf'); the name of the language thus denotes that it is 'offspring' of Esperanto. However, the active Idist (and Esperantist) Gonçalo Neves (p.c.) informs me that the only suffix that Idists accept as an independent word is the causative -*ig*: *igar* means 'to make (somebody do something)' (the infinitival ending in Ido is -*ar* rather than -*i*).

Even more importantly for Saussure, Couturat (1907) also rejected conversion, in particular forming a verb from a noun directly. Couturat believed that this violated a "principle of reversability" (different from Saussure's "rule of reversal") stating that the relation between words from the same stem should always work in two directions. If one derives a noun from a verb, the meaning of that should always be a nominalitzation. However, *krono* in Esperanto is obviously not the nominalitzation of *kroni*; it does not mean 'coronation' but rather 'a crown'. (The word for 'coronation' is *kronado*, with an explict deverbal nominalizing suffix -*ad*; the form *kronago* which Saussure gives would also be possible, but is not common.)

This problem was solved by essentially banning direct conversion of nouns to verbs in Ido. 'To crown' in that language is *kron-iz-ar* with a suffix -*iz* denoting 'to cover with', and 'coronation' is therefore *kronizo*. This system was considered more "logical" as one always knows how to form a noun from a given verb, viz. by replacing -*ar* by -*o*, whereas this is not possible in Esperanto.

Saussure's answer to this is interesting in its own right. He argues that, since stems without desinences are actually "independent words" (according to Za-

menhof's rule in the case of Esperanto, or according to the universal principles in the 1911 and 1919 texts), they also have their own categorial specification. We can illustrate this the example of *kombi* 'to comb' and *brosi* 'to brush'. The corresponding nouns, *kombo* and *broso* mean 'combing' and 'a brush' respectively. The reason for this, according to Saussure, is that *komb'* is inherently a verb, and *bros'* inherently a noun. If one wants to say 'a comb' one therefore needs to use an instrumental (i-o) suffix *il* to say *kombilo*; similarly, in order to say 'brushing' one needs to say *brosado*. The suffix *ad* is *i-o* and therefore turns the nominal *bros'* into a verb which then gets nominalized (in his 1911 notation we have *bros-o-i-o*).[1]

Instead of Couturat's principle of reversability, Saussure proposed the principles of NECESSITY and SUFFICIENCY in his Esperanto work, which also play a role in the 1911 and 1919 texts as universal principles. In the cases at hand, the principle of necessity says that *broso* does not mean 'brushing', as an explicit suffix denoting the verbal meaning inside that word is missing; the principle of *sufficiency* on the other hand has it that *brosilo* is not the word for 'brush', as *il* is not necessary to express the instrumental meaning that is already contained in *bros*. The two principles actually seem to function as Gricean maxims in the sense that e.g. *brosilo* is a possible word; it just does not mean 'brush' but 'something that can be used to brush, but is probably not a brush' (*Branĉo estas brosilo* 'A branch is an object to brush').

It seems important that in the two texts presented in the present volume, Saussure shows how the analysis can be applied to French, as France was the primary battleground of the Ido crisis, and the main criticism of the Idists was that the Esperanto system was an "unnatural" one. By showing that the Esperanto system was actually also underlying in French, Saussure tried to rebut this argument. It is similarly significant that the 1919 text has a motto by Leibniz; Couturat was an eminent Leibniz scholar and both Couturat and Saussure subscribed to the Enlightenment idea that all languages have the same underlying structure, which is given by the way in which thought functions in all humans, and that all differences are mere layers put on top of that universal structure by history. Leibniz, Couturat and Saussure all believed that the ideal "universal language" should reflect the common grammar as much as possible. The difference in opinion between Couturat and Saussure was whether this universal grammar contained the principle of reversability or those of necessity and sufficiency.

---

[1] For further discussion of these matters, see van Oostendorp (1998).

3 Conclusion

Initially, Saussure's ideas met with universal acclaim among Esperantists. Zamenhof (who would die in 1917), for instance, seems to have approved Saussure's analysis of the morphology. However, Saussure was soon to become estranged from the Esperantists, mainly because of his almost endless attempts to reform the language. In 1921, he was forced to leave the *Akademio* and in 1925 he declared himself to be no longer an Esperantist (although he would always maintain that he was a *disĉiplo de Zamenhof*. Still, the principles of necessity and sufficiency were declared to be official rules of Esperanto grammar by the *Akademio* in 1957 (Garvía 2015; Künzli 2001).

References

Couturat, Louis. 1907. *Étude sur la dérivation en espéranto, dédiée à MM. les membres du comité de la délégation pour l'adoption d'une langue auxiliarie internationale*. Coulommiers: P. Brodard.

Couturat, Louis. 1908. Esperanto ed esperantismo. *Progreso*. 264–267.

de Saussure, René. 1910. *La construction logique des mots en espéranto. Réponse a des critiques suivie de propositions a à'Académie espérantiste*. Genève: Universala Esperantia Librejo.

de Saussure, René. 1915. *Fundamentaj reguloj de la vort-teorio en esperant. Raporto al la akademio esperantista*. Bern: Büchler.

Garvía, Roberto. 2015. *Esperanto and its rivals: The struggle for an international language*. Philadelphia: University of Pennsylvania Press.

Gordin, Michael. 2015. *Scientific Babel. How science was done before and after Scientific English*. Chicago: University of Chicago Press.

Künzli, Andy. 2001. René de Saussure (1868–1943) — tragika sed grava esperantologo kaj interlingvisto el Svislando. In Sabine Fiedler & Liu Haitao (eds.), *Studoj pri interlingvistiko/Studien zur Interlinguistik*, 234–257. Dobřichovice: Kava-Pech.

van Oostendorp, Marc. 1998. Economy of representation in the Esperanto word. In Renée van Bezooijen & René Kager (eds.), *Linguistics in the Netherlands*, 175–186. Amsterdam: Benjamins.

van Oostendorp, Marc. 2004. *Een wereldtaal: Een geschiedenis van de Esperanto-beweging*. Amsterdam: Athenaeum-Polak en Van Gennep.

Zamenhof, L. L. 1887. *Internationale Sprache. Vorrede und vollständiges Lehrbuch. Por germanoj*. Warsaw: Gebethner und Wolff.

Zamenhof, L. L. 1905. *Fundamento de esperanto*. Paris: Hachette.

Chapter 2

The morphological theory of René de Saussure's works

Stephen R. Anderson
Yale University

THE MORPHOLOGICAL THEORY PRESENTED IN THE TEXTS reproduced as Parts I and II of the present work constitutes a sort of historic landmark.[1] Although somewhat familiar to the community of students and advocates of the constructed language Esperanto, as discussed in §1, it has remained essentially unknown to scholars in the broader community of linguists. It represents a particularly explicit formulation of the sort of view that would later be associated with the theory of the Structuralist morpheme, and as such contrasts strikingly with what we can conclude about the view of internally complex words in the work of Ferdinand de Saussure.

1 René de Saussure's conception of morphology

The retrospective importance of René de Saussure's works on the nature of word formation lies in the fact that they articulate, at the very beginning of what we think of as the "modern" period in linguistics, a clear version of one of the two poles that would come to dominate discussion of this area within the field.[2] From the outset, after distinguishing simple words (e.g. French *homme* 'man', *grand* 'large, tall', etc.) from compounds (e.g. French *porte-plume* 'penholder', German *Dampfschiff* 'steamship', etc.) and derived words (e.g. French *grandeur* 'size, height', *humanité* 'humanity'), he argues that

---

[1] The material in this section has been presented in part to audiences at Mediterranean Morphology Meetings 10 (Haifa, 2015) and 11 (Cyprus, 2017). Helpful comments from the audiences on those occasions is gratefully acknowledged.

[2] For a review of this history, largely from an American point of view, see Anderson (2017; 2018). Some of the discussion below is drawn from these sources.

Stephen R. Anderson. 2018. The morphological theory of René de Saussure's works. In Stephen R. Anderson & Louis de Saussure (eds.), *René de Saussure and the theory of word formation*, 209–226. Berlin: Language Science Press. DOI:10.5281/zenodo.1306492

"il y a deux sortes d'éléments primitifs: les mots-radicaux, tels que : «homme», «grand», etc., et les affixes, tels que : «iste» (dans «violoniste»), «pré» (dans «prévenir»), etc."

[However,] "[a]u point de vue logique, il n'y a pas de différence essentielle entre un radical et un affixe; [...] On peut donc considérer les affixes comme des mots simples, et les mots dérivés au moyen d'affixes, comme de véritables mots composés. Il n'y a plus alors que deux sortes de mots : les mots simples (radicaux, préfixes, suffixes), et les mots composés par combinaison de mots simples." (de Saussure 1911: 4–5)[3]

On this view, derived words are just a class of compounds. As a consequence, affixes are to be viewed as simple sound-meaning pairs, just like simple words. Derived words are no different from compounds in that both are composed of two or more atoms in structured combination with one another. The type example Saussure gives, *violoniste* 'violinist', is thus analyzed as a compound composed of two equally basic units, both nouns: *violon* 'violin' and *-iste* 'person whose profession or habitual occupation is characterized by the root to which it is attached' with the two parts being parallel simple associations between sound and meaning.

2 Differences between René's view and that of his brother

Readers familiar with the work of René's brother Ferdinand de Saussure may be struck by the difference between this position on the structure of complex words and the one that pervades de Saussure 1916 [1974]. What matters here is the fact that René de Saussure (1911) enunciates categorically the view that all morphological elements, roots and affixes alike, constitute parallel atomic sound-meaning pairings. In this regard, such elements are uniformly of the type Ferdinand de Saussure (1916 [1974]) would analyze as *minimal signs*: arbitrary, irreducible associations of expression (sound, gesture, orthography) with content. As pointed out by Matthews (2001), the observation that such associations are a core characteristic of natural language was by no means completely original with Saussure, but his importance lies in having made them the center of attention in the study of language.

---

[3]"There are two kinds of primitive element: root words, such as *homme* 'man', *grand* 'tall', etc., and affixes, such as *-iste* (in *violoniste* 'violinist'), *pré* (in *prévenir* 'precede'), etc. From the logical point of view, there is no essential difference between a root and an affix: [...] We can therefore consider affixes as simple words, and words derived by means of an affix as real compound words. There are then only two sorts of word: *simple words* (roots, prefixes, suffixes) and *compound words* formed by combining simple words."

2 The morphological theory of René de Saussure's works

Figure 1: Ferdinand de Saussure (1857–1913)

Where the brothers part company is in the more general analysis of words. For both, simple words (e.g. *arbre* 'tree') are minimal signs, but where René saw derived words like *violoniste* 'violinist' as simply combinations of such units, Ferdinand presents a rather different view. For him, words that are not simple are also signs — of a type he refers to as *relatively* or *partially motivated*. That is, the sign relation between form and meaning obtains here, too, but in such cases it is not completely arbitrary: part of the relation is motivated by the relation between this sign and others:

> "Une unité telle que *désireux* se compose en deux sous-unités (*désir-eux*), mais ce ne sont pas deux parties indépendantes ajoutées simplement l'une à l'autre (*désir+eux*). C'est un produit, une combinaison de deux éléments solidaires, qui n'ont de valeur que par leur action réciproque dans une unité supérieure (*désir×eux*). Le suffixe, pris isolément, est inexistant; ce qui lui confère sa place dans la langue, c'est une série de termes usuels tels que *chaleur-eux*, *chanc-eux*, etc. À son tour, le radical n'est pas autonome; il n'existe que par combinaison avec un suffixe; dans *roul-is*, l'élément *roul-*

n'est rien sans le suffixe qui le suit. Le tout vaut par ses parties, les parties valent aussi en vertu de leur place dans le tout, et voilà pourquoi le rapport syntagmatique de la partie au tout est aussi important que celui des parties entre elles" (de Saussure (1916 [1974]): 176–177; cf. also de Saussure (1993): 85–90).[4]

The point to focus on here is that for Ferdinand, as opposed to René, a suffix in a derived word does not have value in and of itself as a minimal sign, but rather it obtains its significance from the fact that words of similar form are related to one another. Elsewhere in the *Cours* he gives the example of *poirier* 'pear tree'. This is obviously related to *poire* 'pear', but the meaning of *poirier* is not just a compound of two meanings 'pear' and 'tree bearing fruit specified by the root to which it is attached' (in the way René analyzes the meaning of *violoniste*). Rather, it arises because the relation between *poire* and *poirier* is similar to that of other pairs in the language: *cerise* 'cherry' / *cerisier* 'cherry tree', *pomme* 'apple' / *pommier* 'apple tree', etc. Complex words thus get their sense from their place in a constellation of relations among words.

The picture in Figure 2 is quite different from the view presented by René, who explicitly rejects such an account:

> "Il n'est donc pas besoin d'établir des *règles de dérivation* reliant l'un à l'autre le sens des mots d'une même famille (comme «homme», «humain», «humanité»; «couronne», «couronner», «couronnement»), car on crée ainsi des liens artificiels entre des atomes qui devraient rester indépendants et interchangeables comme les différentes pièces d'une machine." (de Saussure 1911: 8).[5]

We can categorize the difference between the views of the two Saussure brothers, at least roughly, in terms of two useful dimensions of theories as distinguished by Stump (2001: 1). On the first of these, theories can be lexical, and treat all form-content associations as listed; or they can be inferential, in treating form-content relations in complex words as more holistic.

---

[4] "A unit such as *desireux* is composed of two sub-units (*desire+ous*), but these are not two independent parts simply added to one another. It is a product, a combination of two linked elements which only have their value by their reciprocal relation within a larger unit. The suffix, taken in isolation, does not exist: what gives it its place in the language is a series of words like *chaleureux* 'warmth-ous, warm', *chanceux* 'fortune-ous, lucky', etc. In its turn, the root is not autonomous: it only exists through its combination with a suffix. In *roulis* 'rotation', the element *roul-* 'roll' is nothing without the suffix that follows it. The whole has value through its parts, the parts also have value through their place in the whole, and that is why the syntagmatic relation of the part to the whole is as important as that of the parts to one another."

[5] "There is thus no need to establish *rules of derivation* linking to each other the senses of words belonging to the same family (such as *homme* 'man', *humain* 'human', *humanité* 'humanity'; *couronne* 'crown (n.)', *couronner* '(to) crown', *couronnement* 'coronation'), because that would create artificial links between atoms that must remain independent and interchangeable like the different parts of a machine."

2 The morphological theory of René de Saussure's works

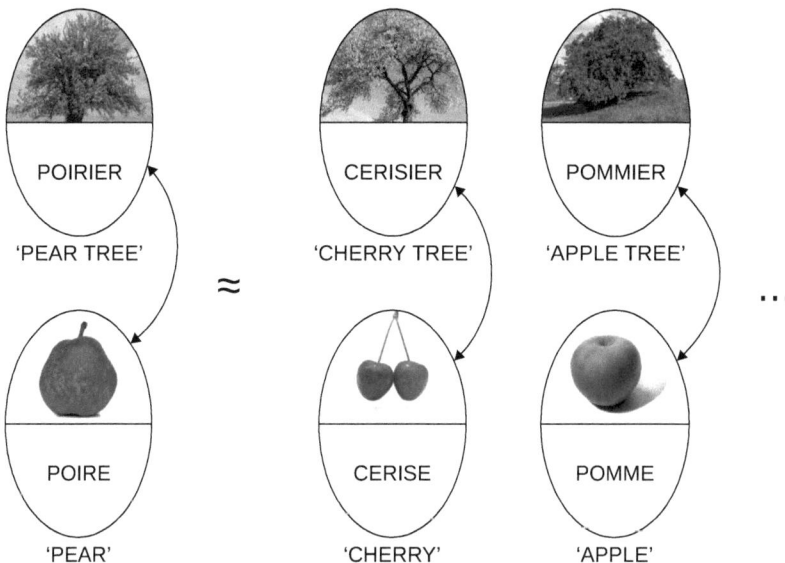

Figure 2: Relatively or partially motivated signs. Pear tree image CC-BY SA B137, Cherry tree image CC-BY SA Benjamin Gimmel, Apple tree image CC-BY SA Maseltov, Pear image in the public domain, Cherry image CC-BY SA Benjamint444, Apple image CC-BY SA PiccoloNamek.

Lexical theories are those where associations between (morphosyntactic) content and (phonological) form are listed in a lexicon. Each such association is discrete and local with respect to the rest of the lexicon, and constitutes a morpheme of the classical sort.

Inferential theories treat the associations between a word's morphosyntactic properties and its morphology as expressed by rules or formulas.

Independent of this distinction, theories can be incremental, with elements of content associated in a one-to-one fashion with elements of form, or realizational, in which the relation is less direct, such that a single element of content can be associated with one element of form, or several, or none at all, and vice versa.

Incremental theories are the ones on which a word bears a given content property exclusively as a concomitant of a specific formal realization.

Realizational theories are the ones on which the presence of a given element of content licenses a specific realization, but does not depend on it.

Stephen R. Anderson

The two dimensions are logically independent, and Stump identifies examples of all four possible combinations of values. By and large, though, most theories are either lexical and incremental or inferential and realizational. The first class sees the locus of form-content relations as a set of something like Saussurean minimal signs, identifiable generally with the classical understanding of the morpheme. Inferential/realizational theories, in contrast, see the form-content relation as rather more diffuse, and in practice continue the distinct classical tradition of "word and paradigm" analysis.

In those terms, we can categorize the Saussure brothers' views of the nature of a complex word like *poirier*: René sees this as the combination of two independent lexical elements, where each part of the meaning is associated uniquely with a specific, independently listed element of form. His theory is thus a lexical/incremental view, and the components of a complex word are essentially what would later be called morphemes.

Ferdinand, in contrast, sees the complex meaning as arising from a relation that has a status in the language. It is this rule relating *poire* and *poirier* (and also *cerise/cerisier*, etc.), not the suffix *-ier* itself, that yields the meaning 'pear tree'. His is an inferential theory, and while this example does not serve to make the point, from other sources (such as discussions of Gothic, Greek and Latin morphology in his courses on these languages) we can say that it is realizational rather than incremental.

The contrast between these somewhat different views does not seem to have attracted much attention at the time, although it represents what has historically been the basic opposition in morphological theory. René's story is an early version of what we can call a morphemic theory, one that takes internal components of complex words as the basic locus of meaning. These are combined by an extension of the syntax, and the resulting structures are compositional functions. Ferdinand's story, in contrast, is a version of what would later be called a word and paradigm theory, where whole words are the locus of meaning and an understanding of their content, as well as their form, comes from an analysis of their place in a network of relations to other words.

In the difference between the two, we can see the origins of a basic contrast between theories of morphology. In practice, however, this contrast did not become a matter of theoretical discussion immediately. René saw the decomposition of complex words into combinations of simplexes — their analysis as structured concatenations of minimal signs — as transparently obvious, a simple matter of logic, and his 1911 book and its 1919 continuation develop this picture in some detail, discussing the logical/grammatical types of simple words that we find, and

the varieties of combination of these atomic units that exist (in French, at least, and to a lesser extent in German and in English).

Although the theoretical difference between these two views was not a focus of attention in the work of either of the de Saussure brothers, that does not mean that it went unnoticed. In the conclusion to the portion of the later work included here (de Saussure 1919: 27–28), René observes that his theory attributes the same kind of structure to all languages, a type that is nicely suitable for artificial languages, but that this is not the only way to view the structure of derived words. Citing the views of his late brother, which had become available in 1916 with the publication by his students of the *Cours de linguistique générale*,[6] he notes that the structure of e.g. the made-up word *indécorable* could be analyzed in two ways. On the one hand, we could isolate component elements (*in, décor, able*) and combine these in quasi-syntactic fashion along the lines of his theory. Alternatively, we could regard it as a unit whose content is revealed by an analogical proportion:

$$pardonner: impardonnable = décorer: x$$
$$x = indécorable.$$

Discussing the contrast between these views, Ferdinand poses the question of which of them "correspond à la réalité": that is, in our terms, whether we ought to prefer a morphemic theory, which he associates with "Hindu grammar" or the work of classical Sanskrit grammarians, or an inferential-realizational one, which he identifies with "European" grammatical presentation. René's answer to this is clear and categorical: although nominally restricting himself to artificial languages, his opinion is that "the method of Hindu grammar is the only satisfying one."

In support of this opinion, he again invokes Ferdinand's opinion in the *Cours*[7] that "*abstract entities always rest, in the final analysis, on concrete entities.*" It is unclear, however, why René thought that this should imply that the structure of complex words is to be regarded as a structured concatenation of elementary atoms, rather than as systematic associations among related words. In context, Ferdinand invokes this principle in connection with abstractions such as "genitive case" in e.g. Latin, where a number of different inflectional forms all support the same function. Positing an entity "genitive case" is here based on the fact that a number of diverse concrete forms manifest it in their relation to other forms

---

[6]René cites pages 235 and 236 of the *Cours*, although the passage in question appears on pages 228–230 in the edition we use here.

[7]Cited by René as found on pages 196, 197 and 198; in the edition used here, the relevant passages are on pages 190, 191 and 192. My translation: sra.

within the paradigm of a Latin nouns, which would be illicit if there were no such concrete support for the category, but this fact does not require us to analyze case marking in Latin as exclusively a syntagmatic rather than a paradigmatic matter (in Ferdinand's terms).

Similarly, in the passage in question, he notes that English *the man I have seen* has no overt relative pronoun, but denies that in order to analyze this as a relative clause, there must be an abstract unpronounced element to represent the missing object: the material support here for the notion of relative clause structure is said to be the word order of the concrete words involved. The point at stake in this part of the *Cours* (chapter 8 of part II) is not directly relevant to a choice between the "Hindu" and "European" conceptions of word structure.

Which is not to say that in opposing those two conceptions, Ferdinand felt as strongly as René that the choice between them in developing a theory of language was clear and unambiguous. Most discussion of complex words in the *Cours* is couched in terms of analogical relations between whole words, and not as a sort of syntax of morpheme-like simple signs. In various places, however, he also recognizes that the linguistic conscience of speakers commonly includes the identification of component roots, suffixes, desinences, etc., as well as the order in which these appear within a word.

Does this fact support the claim that word formation is fundamentally a matter of arranging such pieces? It is worth noting that in the section of the *Cours* where this issue is raised (de Saussure 1916 [1974]: 228–230) Ferdinand notes the existence of facts that cast doubt on such a conclusion. In a passage skipped over in René's quote, he notes that in German

> "[d]ans un cas comme *Krantz* : *Kräntze* fait sur *Gast* : *Gäste*, la décomposition semble moins probable que la quatrième proportional, puisque le radical du modèle est tantôt *Gast*- tantôt *Gäst*-."[8]

Here part of the indication of plurality is through variation in the shape of the stem, and not only by the presence of an atom PLURAL, although he qualifies the significance of that observation by noting, in effect, the existence of contextually determined allomorphy.

Ferdinand's point here is that decomposition would only make sense if it resulted in invariants; where there is non-segmentable variation in shape associated with the formation of a morphologically complex form, the analysis based

---

[8] "in a case like *Krantz* : *Kräntze* 'wreath'/'wreaths' built on *Gast* : *Gäste* 'guest' : 'guests', decomposition seems less likely than proportional analogy, since the root of the model is sometimes *Gast*- and sometimes *Gäst*-."

2 The morphological theory of René de Saussure's works

on a rule of proportional analogy gives a more satisfactory account. This is, perhaps, the first instance in the literature of the use of non-concatenative morphology as the basis of an argument against analysis into morphemes. We can note that the argument might have been strengthened, especially given his reluctance (just noted) to posit significant zero elements, if he had cited pairs such as *Tochter : Töchter* 'daughter : daughters' or *Mantel : Mäntel* 'overcoat : overcoats' on the analogy of *Mutter : Mütter* 'mother : mothers' or *Vater : Väter* 'father : fathers' respectively, where the stem alternation is the *only* indication of the plural.

On the other hand, he did not regard the matter as entirely settled. The argument that he sees as most favorable to the analysis of complex words in terms of their components (de Saussure 1916 [1974]: 229–230) is somewhat curious, and based on a phenomenon in the history of Latin known as Lachmann's Law. As described by Jasanoff (2004: 405), this is the rule "according to which verbal roots ending in an etymological voiced stop (*-b-, *-d-, etc.), but not a voiced aspirate (*-bh-, *-dh-, etc.), lengthen their root vowel in the past participle and its derivatives (e.g. *agō* 'drive', ptcp. *āctus* (+*āctiō*, etc.), *cadō* 'fall', ptcp. *cāsus*< *cāssus*)" while similar verbs whose roots end in voiceless stops show no such lengthening (e.g. *faciō* 'make', ptcp. *făctus*, *speciō* 'watch', ptcp. *spĕctus*).

The participial forms in which the lengthening occurs were surely inherited from Proto-Indo European with the stem-final voiced stops devoiced (via regressive assimilation from the *t* of the participle ending), and thus should not contrast with root-final voiceless stops where these are unchanged from the stem form. The operation of Lachmann's Law thus requires a sensitivity on speakers' parts to a difference between roots ending in voiced stops as opposed to voiceless ones, even in inflected or derived forms where that difference was not apparent in the word's phonetic realization. And that, in turn, would seem to imply an awareness of the identity of roots independent of the specific complex words in which they appear. In de Saussure's (1916 [1974]: 230) words, "[i]l n'a pu y arriver qu'en prenant fortement conscience des unités radicales *ag- teg-*" [9][in tēctus].

A full discussion of Lachmann's Law would take us well beyond our concerns here; for a recent summary of the facts and analytic controversies, see Roberts (2009). To assess de Saussure's argument, however, it is not necessary to go into such detail. His position is that "it is necessary to suppose that *āctus* goes back to **ăgtos* and to attribute the lengthening of the vowel to the voiced consonant that follows" (de Saussure 1916 [1974]: 230 [my translation: sra]). Now we know from comparative evidence that the stem final consonants in these clusters were

---

[9] "[i]t is not possible to arrive at this without being clearly aware of the root units *ag- teg-*"

already assimilated to the following *t* in early Latin; and we also know that they were inherited as voiceless by the Romance daughter languages. In most generative phonological analyses, beginning with that of Kiparsky (1965), the voicing distinction is seen as preserved in the underlying form of the root (e.g. /ag-/), with assimilation in the participle stem but only after the required lengthening has taken place. Such an analysis was not, of course, available to de Saussure, but another possibility was, and in fact is evident in his positing of *ăgtos as the form to which lengthening applies and his subsequent discussion.

In fact, in an earlier paper, de Saussure (1889) argued that the root-final voiced consonants in these words were in fact restored in early Latin by analogy:

$$făciō : făctus = ăgō : x$$
$$x = ăgtus$$

These forms with the restored (though admittedly problematic in phonetic terms) voiced obstruents then underwent lengthening by Lachmann's Law, after which voicing assimilation again operated to produce voiceless clusters.

Ferdinand's claim that the root-final voiced obstruents were restored in early Latin just long enough for Lachmann's Law to operate has generally been rejected by subsequent scholarship, but it is far from clear that, even if we were to accept it, his account would imply that the relevant participial forms would need to be analyzed as combinations of a root and an affix. After all, the crucial step is the analogy just offered that led to the (temporary) restoration of root-final *g* in *ăgtos, but this analogy is a matter of the relation between full word forms. After the incorporation of such forms with restored voiced stops into the language, purely phonetic change could then effect the lengthening by Lachmann's Law, followed by another purely phonetic change of regressive voice assimilation. At no point in this scenario is it necessary to recognize the root /ag-/ as a structural unit, despite de Saussure's claim to the contrary.

It seems, then, that there is no real argument to be found in Ferdinand's discussion of the matter in the *Cours* that would support René's opinion that "the method of Hindu grammar is the only satisfying one." Indeed, while Ferdinand left open the possibility that languages might differ from one another as to which of the two analytic frameworks was most appropriate, his own practice generally relied on analogical (rather than compositional) operations as providing the basis for analyzing complex words. Note that it is not necessary to deny that speakers can identify stems, affixes, and desinences as these are found in complex words[10] in order to suggest that complex words are formed on the basis of rela-

---

[10] Note that in cases where part of a word's content is signalled through "non-concatenative" means, the analysis of content in terms of combinations of atoms will not be exhaustive. See Anderson (1992) and much other literature for discussion.

tions between whole words and not fundamentally by combining these elements syntagmatically. Stems are plausibly present in the lexicon on such a view, and affixal material, along with a variety of non-affixal ways of signalling morphological content, is represented in the structural changes of rules of word formation. These aspects of a grammar suffice to support the observed meta-linguistic awareness on speakers' parts of components present in complex words without requiring that the analysis of such words be grounded in the quasi-syntactic combination of "morphemes" or the atoms of René's theory.

The tension between the two views of complex words that we have been discussing, and the clear contrasting of these views in the work of René and Ferdinand de Saussure, provides important motivation for studying this neglected predecessor of the theories that would become prominent in the structuralist morphology of the mid-20th century. Significantly, de Saussure (1916 [1974]) already saw the tension between what we can call rule-based and morpheme-based accounts of the structure of complex words as a significant theoretical issue, to be resolved by empirical argument. If we are tempted to see this difference as a matter of recent morphological theory, or perhaps one that originates in Hockett's (1954) "Two models" paper, we should see that in fact it has been with us since the very earliest days of what we think of as scientific linguistics.

3 Some specific points in René's theory

If the only reason to read de Saussure (1911; 1919) were that he largely anticipates the later position of structuralist morphologists, these works might be written off as merely historical curiosities. In fact, however, René de Saussure's work on morphology develops a rather fuller and more explicit theory of word structure than just a commitment to a morpheme-like view, and a number of more specific points that arise in this theory also have importance for this area today.

3.1 Binary branching

One aspect of this theory is a limitation on the internal complexity of words to binary branching structure: "Lorsqu'un mot composé contient plus de deux éléments, son analyse peut toujours être ramenée à celle de plusieurs mots ne contenant chacun que deux éléments." (1919: 13)[11] Such a principle is presented as a substantive component of the theory of morphology by a number of writers

---

[11]"When a compound word contains more than two elements, its analysis can always be reduced to that of several words each containing only two elements." In the remainder of this section, references to de Saussure (1911) and de Saussure (1919) will be given simply as "1911" or "1919" with page reference.

(Aronoff 1976; Booij 1977; Lieber 1980; Scalise 1984), who offer arguments in favor of a binary-branching analysis of words that might be presumed to have ternary or other structure.

René shows that the way in which a multi-element word is analyzed (with flat structure or with one or another of alternative possible binary branching structures) makes a difference: thus, he argues that *international* should be analyzed as [[inter nation] al] '[that which is [between nations]]' and not as [inter [nation al]]. The reason for treating the word in this way is to provide an appropriate basis for the meaning of the complex form, since he sees semantic structure as directly represented in the morphological analysis.

René's semantically based analysis might be seen as at variance with the structure apparently motivated by form alone. In the word *international* in English,[12] the suffix *-al* is apparently more closely related to the stem *nation* than is the prefix *inter-*: cyclic analyses and their variants treat *-al* as a "level I" or stem-level affix, while *inter-* is a "level II" (or III) or word-level affix, which would seem to require the structure [inter [nation al]], contrary to René's account. For a somewhat more obvious example, consider the reading of English *criminal lawyer* as 'practitioner of criminal law', where the semantics seems to motivate [[criminal law] (y)er], while the form would seem to require [criminal [law (y)er]].

"Bracketing paradoxes" of this sort received a great deal of attention in the morphological and phonological literature of the 1980s (e.g. Williams 1981; Pesetsky 1985; Spencer 1988) and later. It is clear, however, that this issue could never arise for René, since he is quite clear that semantic considerations alone are relevant to word structure: "[l]a signification de tout mot composé résulte alors directement de l'analyse de son contenu, et non de la manière dont on suppose ce mot dérivé d'un autre" (1919: 27)[13]. Things could hardly be otherwise, since, as will be discussed below, phonological considerations of the sort that give rise to the conflict posed by "bracketing paradoxes" form no part of his theory, in which morphological structure is conceived in exclusively semantic terms.

3.2 Category, headedness and the difference between words and phrases

Internal branching is by no means all there is to the internal structure of words on René's theory. He makes it clear (1911ff.) that each of the atoms contained in

---

[12] The same issue does not arise as obviously in French.
[13] "The meaning of every compound word thus results directly from the analysis of its content, and not from the manner in which we suppose this word to be derived from another."

2 The morphological theory of René de Saussure's works

a complex word is assigned to a major word class: noun, verb or adjective, depending on its semantics. Thus, *-iste* in *violoniste* is a noun because it designates a person; *-able* in *louable* 'commendable' is an adjective, because it contains a qualifying idea; and *-is-* in *moderniser* and *-ifi-* in *béatifier* are verbs, because they contain a dynamic idea.

Atoms can also impose restrictions on the structures into which they enter based on these word classes. In an interesting passage (1911: 36–37), René argues that the word *couronnement* 'coronation' appears to contain only the atoms *couronne* 'crown' and *-ment*, but there must also be an additional verbal atom (represented here by the medial *-e-*, reduced from the infinitive ending *-er*), because nominalizing atoms such as *-ment* "ne sont employés qu'après des atomes verbaux, comme les atomes *ité, esse* ne le sont qu'après des atomes adjectifs."[14]

The categorial identity of a complex structure is determined by that of its constituent elements. Here René enunciates an important basic principle of word structure: "L'espèce grammaticale d'un mot est déterminée par son *dernier* élément; ainsi, **Schreib'tisch** est un substantif, parce que **Tisch** est un substantif."[15] This is of course the same as what Williams (1981) would propose (along with Selkirk 1982) as the "Right Hand Head Rule", a supposedly general principle of word structure, at least for English and French.

Just as the literature of the 1980s recognized the existence of exceptions to the Right Hand Head Rule, René notes that there are words like *timbre-poste* [stamp-postage] 'postage stamp' and *assurance-vieillesse* [insurance-old age] 'old age insurance' where the element that should be seen as the head from a semantic point of view is the leftmost, not the rightmost constituent. Accordingly, when words of this type are pluralized (as e.g. *timbres-poste* 'postage stamps') the plural marker appears inside the compound, on the first element.

René's account of these words is that they are not really compounds, but an rather abbreviated form of phrases. Within his theory, this is a principled solution, grounded in a proposed regular relation between complex words (compounds) and phrases. While the former, called by him "condensed molecules", conform to the principle of a structural head on the right, syntactically formed phrases (called "dissociated molecules"), in contrast, have initial heads.

This structural difference is claimed to be completely systematic, and the basis of the fundamental rule invoked for the analysis of complex words: the Law of Reversal. In general, complex words have phrasal paraphrases, and *vice versa*. The relation between these is governed by the principle that "la dissociation

---

[14] "are only used after verbal atoms, just as the atoms *ité, esse* are only used after adjectival atoms." (1911:37).
[15] "The grammatical category of an element is determined by its *final* element: thus [German] **Schreib'tisch** 'writing table' is a noun because **Tisch** 'table' is a noun." (1919: 16; cf. also 1911: 42–43)

d'une molécule condensé (ou la condensation d'une molécule dissociée) renverse l'ordre des atomes."[16] This equivalence underlies a great deal of the discussion in both of the works under discussion in the present book. The procedure for deriving a word corresponding to a complex idea is to express it in syntactic ("dissociated") form, and then reverse the order of the atoms involved to produce a corresponding "condensed" form, a compound word. Conversely, to analyze a complex word, one takes the atoms of which it is composed and reverses their order, which should yield a phrasal paraphrase (with a certain amount of unexplained footwork to provide or ignore the purely grammatical markers that may be required). Thus, German (condensed) *Schreib'tisch* 'writing table' corresponds to the dissociated form 'table (for) writing'. On this basis, if e.g. *timbre-poste* 'postage stamp' is "really" a sort of phrase, rather than a legitimate compound, the position of its head on the left is just what we would expect.

The fundamental nature of this relation undersores the fact that for René, syntax and morphology are fundamentally distinct (but systematically related) domains within the overall theory of grammar. That is, complex words are not just syntactic constructions with some kind of phonological unity, as in some modern theories, but a systematically different structure. Morphology is not simply the syntax of small domains. On the other hand, since the relation between morphology and syntax is a resolutely synchronic one (and René was at pains on several occasions to stress that his theory was intended to be purely synchronic), the difference is not to be seen as a matter of morphology preserving the syntax of an earlier historical stage of the language, as Givón's (1971) aphorism "today's morphology is yesterday's synax" would have it.

3.3 The principles of necessity and sufficiency

Central to René's view of the relation between content and morphological form are two complementary principles (1919: 13):

> **Principle of necessity.** In the construction of a compound word it is necessary to introduce (by means of the law of reversal) all of the simple elements (roots and affixes) necessary to evoke clearly the idea that the word is to express (in the given circumstances).
>
> **Principle of sufficiency:** We must also, in this construction, avoid the introduction of useless pleonasms, as well as ideas foreign to the idea that we wish to express.

---

[16] "The dissociation of a condensed molecule (or the condensation of a dissociated molecule) reverses the order of the atoms." (1911:35; cf. also 1919:11–12)

2 The morphological theory of René de Saussure's works

To accord with these two principles, a complex word constructed to express a given complex idea should contain all and only those elements whose content is contained therein, without duplication, superfluous elements or gaps. Of course, it may well be the case that the linguistic resources of a given language are not such as to make it possible to include precisely the required content: it may be that some part of the required meaning can only be introduced in conjunction with other, superfluous material. In that case it is necessary either to undershoot or to overshoot what is desired: either to leave out some component of meaning or to include some extraneous material. In this case, René invokes a Principle of Least Effort: it is better to omit (the minimum of) content than to include something irrelevant. Thus (1911: 103–104), to produce a word meaning "to put a crown on the head of someone" there is no suffix in French meaning exactly "to take an object and place it on the head of someone; the best we can do is to add a verbalizing suffix to get *couronner* 'to perform an action with a crown'. Any other suffix including more of the required meaning would also introduce additional, unmotivated material, so the Principle of Least Effort requires us to be content with this.

Here and elsewhere (cf. 1919: 6, fn. 1) we see the notion of ranked, violable constraints familiar from modern Optimality Theory (Prince & Smolensky 2004) and related frameworks: a number of principles are enunciated, but when two of these conflict, one is satisfied at the expense of the other. In the example just considered, the Principle of Sufficiency is presumed to outrank the Principle of Necessity. Elsewhere (1919: 24), with respect to the general principle that the head of a dissociated molecule is on the left, another principle is formulated to the effect that in structures with a prepositional element and its complement, the prepositional element precedes. Where these two ordering principles conflict, the regularity governing the more specific case (preposition plus complement) outranks that governing the general case of dissociated molecules.

As a consequence of the Principle of Sufficiency, the addition of an affixal element to a base is always required to introduce additional content, and not just to duplicate content already present in the base: "tout suffixe doit introduire dans le mot auquel on l'accole une idée (générale ou particulière) qui n'y était pas contenue."[17] This might seem trivial and obvious, but it allows René to get some of the same results as those that fall under the heading of BLOCKING.

Famously, Aronoff (1976: 43–44) claimed that words like *gloriosity* are excluded in English because of the prior existence in the lexicon of (essentially

---

[17] "every suffix must introduce into the word to which it is attached an idea (general or specific) which was not already contained in it." (1911: 95)

synonymous) *glory*. For René, this would follow from the fact that **gloriosity* looks like it is built on *glory*, and the suffixes *-os-ity* would not add any content. Actually, the facts here are less than clear: various online dictionaries include *gloriosity* as a word of English, but assign it a meaning distinct from that of *glory*: thus, Merriam-Webster's *Word Central* defines *gloriosity* as "a moment or experience of glory." This specific example apart, though, René gives a better example (1911: 95) from French. He notes that the word **matronine* is impossible in that language, because the content of the suffix *-ine* 'female person' is already included in the base *matrone* 'matron, older respectable woman'. **Matronine* would thus include a "useless pleonasm", and is accordingly blocked.

The effects of the Principle of Sufficiency thus include some, but surely not all of those that have been attributed to blocking in the modern literature. Nonetheless, it does have some of the flavor of principles enforcing disjunctive operation on rules in morphology of a language.

3.4 Some limitations of René's theory

While the sections above illustrate some of the ways in which René's theory of word formation anticipates later views, it would not do to exaggerate the extent to which he provides an account with coverage or adequacy equivalent to those we entertain today. There are in fact some major limitations to the works presented in this book as a comprehensive view of this domain of grammar.

One severe limitation concerns the degree of empirical coverage of René's picture. He claims that this should be universally applicable: "Les principes logiques de la formation des mots sont donc les mêmes pour toutes les langues, du moins pour toutes celles qui partent des mêmes éléments primitifs,"[18] where the limitation to languages with the same "primitive elements" simply means those that build word from roots and affixes (perhaps thereby excluding, e.g., root-and-pattern morphology of the Semitic type, which may have been familiar to him). But in fact he does not take account of any languages outside the set of very familiar ones. His examples are virtually all from French, German and English, plus a few forms from another Indo-European language, Albanian. It seems likely that he had no serious knowledge of any others, although his brother Leopold was an amateur sinologist, and Ferdinand is known to have obtained some Chinese material from him. A broader experience of the world's languages would surely have convinced René of the need to modify or abandon some of his claims.

---

[18] "The logical principles of the formation of words are thus the same for all languages, or at least for all those that begin from the same primitive elements." (1911: 4)

Another important limitation of René's theory is the complete lack of a theory of ALLOMORPHY. He generally assumes that variation in the shape of elements is due to some unformulated principles of "euphony", although he mentions various instances of variation in shape that cannot plausibly be attributed to the phonology. In fact, he had no interest in phonological variation, since his goal is the analysis of the content of complex words, and its relation to the basic elements of which these are composed. In terms of the traditional sub-parts of a theory of morphology, he is really only interested in MORPHOTACTICS, the combination of meaningful elements and their relation to meaning.

A full theory of morphology needs to take allomorphy into account too, and this does not engage his interest. An important reason for this apparent deficit was surely the fact that René was ultimately interested in the principles of word formation in natural language as a guide to the design of artificial languages, like Esperanto – and one of the guiding principles in designing such languages is to minimize or eliminate anything like allomorphic variation, so that content and form are related in as uniform a way as possible.

4 Conclusion: "Saussurean" morphology

So how much attention should we pay to what René, or indeed either of the brothers de Saussure, has to say about morphological theory? Obviously neither of them presents us with a comprehensive theory of this area of linguistic structure. Indeed, both address morphological issues against the background of other interests.

René was interested in the morphology of natural language as forming the background to the design of an artificial language like Esperanto. The aspects of natural language morphology that engage him are just those that might come into play in this other enterprise. Ferdinand, on the other hand, was primarily occupied (at least in the *Cours*) with bigger issues related to more foundational distinctions: synchrony *vs.* diachrony, *langue vs. parole*, etc. Actually we can derive much more information about his views on morphology in other work devoted to the analysis of specific linguistic material.

Both brothers, though, really do have some articulated views on the subject of word formation, views that are interesting not only as a sort of historical curiosity. And it is especially interesting, it would seem, to observe that the basic difference between views of complex words grounded in the combinatorics of morphemes *vs.* those based on rule-governed relations is already prominent, and explicitly discussed, in their work.

References

Anderson, Stephen R. 1992. *A–Morphous morphology*. Cambridge: Cambridge University Press.

Anderson, Stephen R. 2017. Words and paradigms: Peter H. Matthews and the development of morphological theory. *Transactions of the Philological Society* 115. 1–13.

Anderson, Stephen R. 2018. A short history of morphological theory. In Jenny Audring & Francesca Masini (eds.), *The Oxford handbook of morphological theory*, chap. 2. Oxford: Oxford University Press.

Aronoff, Mark. 1976. *Word formation in generative grammar*. Cambridge, MA: MIT Press.

Booij, Geert. 1977. *Dutch morphology. a study of word formation in generative grammar*. Lisse: Peter de Ridder.

de Saussure, Ferdinand. 1889. Sur un point de la phonétique des consonnes en indo-européen. *Mémoires de la Société de linguistique de Paris* 6. 246–257.

de Saussure, Ferdinand. 1993. *Troisième cours de linguistique générale (1910-1911): d'après les cahiers d'Émile Constantin / Saussure's third course of lectures on general linguistics (1910-1911): from the notebooks of Émile Constantin*. Oxford: Pergamon Press. French text edited by Eisuke Komatsu and English text edited by Roy Harris.

de Saussure, Ferdinand. 1916 [1974]. *Cours de linguistique générale*. Paris: Payot. [Critical edition prepared by Tullio de Mauro].

de Saussure, René. 1911. *Principes logiques de la formation de mots*. Geneva: Librairie Kündig.

de Saussure, René. 1919. *La structure logique des mots dans les langues naturelles, considérées au point de vue de son application aux langues artificielles*. Berne: Librairie A. Lefilleul.

Givón, Talmy. 1971. Historical syntax and synchronic morphology: an archeologist's fieldtrip. *Proceedings of the Chicago Linguistic Society* 7. 394–415.

Hockett, Charles F. 1954. Two models of grammatical description. *Word* 10. 210–34.

Jasanoff, Jay. 2004. *Plus ça change...* Lachmann's law in Latin. In J. H. W. Penney (ed.), *Indo-European perspectives: studies in honour of Anna Morpurgo Davies*, 405–416. Oxford University Press.

Kiparsky, Paul. 1965. *Phonological change*. M.I.T. dissertation. published by Indiana University Linguistics Club.

Lieber, Rochelle. 1980. *On the organization of the lexicon*. M.I.T. dissertation. Published by Indiana University Linguistics Club, 1981.

Matthews, Peter H. 2001. *A short history of structural linguistics*. Cambridge: Cambridge University Press.

Pesetsky, David. 1985. Morphology and logical form. *Linguistic Inquiry* 16. 193–246.

Prince, Alan & Paul Smolensky. 2004. *Optimality theory: constraint interaction in generative grammar*. Oxford: Blackwell.

Roberts, Philip. 2009. *An optimality theoretic analysis of Lachmann's law*. University of Oxford MPhil thesis. Available from Rutgers Optimality Archive as item ROA-1129.

Scalise, Sergio. 1984. *Generative morphology*. Dordrecht: Foris.

Selkirk, Elizabeth. 1982. *The syntax of words*. Cambridge MA: M.I.T. Press.
Spencer, Andrew. 1988. Bracketing paradoxes and the English lexicon. *Language* 64. 663–682.
Stump, Gregory T. 2001. *Inflectional morphology: a theory of paradigm structure*. Cambridge: Cambridge University Press.
Williams, Edwin S. 1981. On the notions 'lexically related' and 'head of a word'. *Linguistic Inquiry* 12. 245–74.

Chapter 3

The theory of meaning in René de Saussure's works

Louis de Saussure
Université de Neuchâtel

For a contemporary reader, the works of René de Saussure (henceforth simply "René") presented in the present volume are strongly suggestive of certain trends in modern syntactic theorizing. Even morphologically simple words are resolutely decomposed into structured combinations, reminiscent of the approach of Generative Semantics in the 1970s and some more recent Minimalist work. The positing of component atoms of meaning with no content beyond that of the basic lexical categories suggests a parallel with the "little *v, n, a*" elements of some current syntactic analyses. Pursuing these similarities, though, would be rather anachronistic, since René de Saussure's views on word structure are not articulated against the background of a theory of syntax above the word level. In the present commentary, therefore, the focus will be more narrowly on the relation between words (simple and complex) and their meanings.

In short, René de Saussure's theory of lexical meaning is compositional in a radical reductionist sense on which all words are reducible to a composition of minimal "atoms". These atoms are themselves realizations of three overarching categories signifying *being*, *property* (quality) and *action*. These basic notions are grammatical ones, as they map onto the three categories of noun, adjective and verb; but they are ultimately semantic in essence, and are labelled grammatical "ideas". This assumption that grammatical categories are fundamentally meaningful in themselves, and not mere abstract unsaturated slots to be filled with content, is a central claim of the theory and quite an original one. Elements of different types combine together to form new meanings: therefore, a word may be about a substance but nonetheless incorporate a verbal notion, as in *couronnement* 'coronation' which is a noun but still embeds a notion of action

Louis de Saussure. 2018. The theory of meaning in René de Saussure's works. In Stephen R. Anderson & Louis de Saussure (eds.), *René de Saussure and the theory of word formation*, 227–240. Berlin: Language Science Press. DOI:10.5281/zenodo.1306472

indicated by a particular morph or *atom* ('e') which is verbal in essence. More precise semantic contents are various add-ons which build upon the results of the combination of basic semantic categories.

René's approach can be linked to more classical views on language tracing back to the Stoics and is opposed in many ways to his brother Ferdinand's systemic view. However it is also reminiscent of structuralist approaches to such semantics as Hjelmslev's (1943) functional conception. The first text (de Saussure 1911) is the most developed but the second one (de Saussure 1919) adds very valuable elements of precision, elaboration and sometimes amendments to the original theory.

René's conception of language in general is oriented towards reductionism and universality. Although his assertions in the 1911 book are not claimed to be universally valid (he admits implicitly that his work might not apply to all languages), it has an overall universalist orientation, and therefore we expect him to assume some universalism in semantics in particular. In the 1919 text, he clarifies his ambitions to adopt the "international" point of view on natural languages in order to find generalities (later on to be put to work in the construction of artificial languages like Esperanto) (de Saussure 1919: 5) and he actually concludes with a strong claim about the universality of the few basic overarching semantic-grammatical categories that he identifies (de Saussure 1919: 26).

1 The theory of meaning in the scientific context

René claims at the beginning of his book: "the logical principles of the formation of words are thus the same for all languages" but further adds a nuance: "...or at least for all [languages] that start from the same primitive elements" (de Saussure 1911: 4). Unfortunately, he does not elaborate any further on the distinction between types of languages in this respect before looking at some (scarce) crosslinguistic data in the 1919 text where he strengthens his universalist claim. This is a conception that departs seriously from the more structuralist and relativist views that were soon to emerge in the structuralist trend based on some interpretations of his brother Ferdinand's (1916) *Course in General Linguistics*. This has implications at the level of semantics and places René on the side of the "naturality of meaning" hypotheses which relate categorial language to categorial thought without assuming the prevalence of language but rather that of mind (thought) as bearing universal patterns, while Ferdinand's theory is rather that languages have irreconcilable semantic systems — all built, however, upon a similar and thus natural mechanism, the "faculty" of language.

3 The theory of meaning in René de Saussure's works

It is clear in the 1911 book that René chooses to ignore linguistic variation as much as possible, and this attitude is also palpable in his conception of meaning. His general approach is one of simplification: he aims at reducing the principles in play to the strictest possible minimum (in striking similarity with Ferdinand, who goes as to posit only one overarching axiom, '*langue* is a system of signs'). It is noteworthy that Ferdinand's views also disregard linguistic variation, but only at the level of dialectal differences. René chooses to overlook differences across languages in general as much as possible. However, in the 1919 text, some contrasts are made and he takes Ferdinand's own examples (such as the famous *mouton / sheep / mutton*) in order to refine some of the claims of the 1911 text. Doing so, he explains that general principles have to be understood precisely as general, providing the big picture, while all fine-grained differences in the empirical reality ("in practice": de Saussure 1919: 15) are to be purposely ignored.

In a number of respects, his theory reminds one of the Port Royal grammar (Arnauld & Lancelot 1660) and more generally of the formal, logicist, view of semantics that begins with the Stoics and which his brother Ferdinand precisely opposed.

As a reminder: for the classical view, generally speaking, one "sign" (word or other morphological unit) means unambiguously one idea, and one grammatical category expresses one and only one particular notion — a view generally labelled that of 'logic-grammar parallelism'. This conception traces back at least to Augustine's very influential works on language (in particular *De Dialectica*[1] and *De Doctrina Christiana*[2]) which themselves refine the Stoics' semiotic theory. In short, according to the classical approach initiated notably by Augustine, language is a set of public signs which give a mental access to otherwise private "thoughts".

The Stoics' semiotic theory already assumed that a sign in general is a perceivable element that triggers an inference of a non-perceivable one. On that view, the inference from the perceivable to the non-perceivable is allowed either by causal rules, as when one infers fire from smoke, or by conventions, as when one infers a thought on the basis of a perceivable linguistic string. These conventions are based on general principles that play out on each level of language compositionality. To linguistic sentences correspond logical propositions, to "words" – not only words in the conceptual lexicon but also non-inflectional affixes – correspond concepts ("conceptions") of various kinds depending on the grammatical category. Finally, functional categories and in particular "grammatical

---
[1] Augustine 1975.
[2] Augustine 1996.

words", such as conjunctions, correspond to types of mental operations. With regard to words proper, the logical-grammatical parallelism approach classifies concepts, or "conceptions", mainly as substances (objects), signified by "substantive nouns" (nouns) and as accidents, or qualities, i.e. properties predicated about the substance (adjectives).

In this tradition, another important dimension is the reductionist conception of meaning, where each meaningful combination is actually a synthesis from more general but also more developed notions. For example, a verb such as *briller* 'to shine' is reducible to an ontological hidden verb of being, and therefore carries existentiality: *briller* is a linguistic reduction of a notion of *être brillant* 'be shining', actually 'be [sun-shining]', so that *Le soleil brille* 'The sun shines' actually means 'The sun is being sun-shining'.

René, knowingly or not, adopts a similar approach in several respects and would probably be happy to be labelled a Stoic, which may not be very surprising given that he was a mathematician. His brother Ferdinand, on the contrary, fiercely rejected this logical tradition, at least in the formulation of the *Course in General Linguistics*. There he famously says that the classical conception, which "supposes ready-made thoughts pre-existing to words", is a "simplistic view" (de Saussure 1916 [1974]: 97). Even though it is usually assumed that Ferdinand de Saussure had no real semantic theory of his own, he had at least a theory about the source of lexical meaning: each word or "sign" is a mental pairing of a concept with an *image acoustique*, an imprint of sounds in memory, and the meaning of that sign results from the complex relations of oppositions and associations it enters into within the whole system of interdependent signs – to be later described as a "structure": the *langue*.

For Ferdinand, meaning exists only as it results from "value", that is, from differentiation within the system. This postulate derives from his thorough knowledge of the history of languages, which he views as involving breakings off of previous, more general signs, so that new signs begin to exist through oppositive relations with one another. On that view, whatever the degree of morphological compositionality eventually involved (as in the famous example of *poirier* as composed of *poire* 'pear' and *-ier* 'tree'; cf. §2 above), the whole lexical meaning stems from this dynamic of oppositive relationships. For René, on the contrary, compositionality is central to the meaning of words, in line with the former idea that words evoke *ex-ante* ideas and notions. Where Ferdinand insists on the contrasts between languages, connecting with more cultural and conventionalist views about meaning and reference, René insists on the similarities between words across languages or at least across the languages that he compares (mostly French and German, but also English and a few others in the 1919 text).

Furthermore, René radically opposes his brother's view that meaning depends on the linguistic environment, whether real ("syntagmatic" relations in Ferdinand's terminology) or abstract ("paradigmatic", associative relations). The following quote, which uses some of his brother's own terminology, seems precisely directed against Ferdinand's view: "The logical analysis of words is only possible if the symbols with which we work are invariant elements; thus the sense, the value of an atom, must depend only on itself and not at all on the sense or the value of the atoms that surround it" (de Saussure 1911: 8). While Ferdinand has a top-down view of meaning, imposed by the idea that the "value" of any element itself involves the whole "system of signs" within a given language, which then differs radically from those of other languages, René has a bottom-up conception of meaning where blocks with fixed, invariant and *a priori* meanings are combined together in the making-up of more complex meanings. He has a clearly analytic methodology which consists in explaining "compound words by simple words, and simple words by the basic words" (de Saussure 1919: 21).

2 The elements of meaning

His notion of "atoms" of meaning which combine together in order to generate more complex "molecules" is interestingly comparable to what Louis Hjelmslev (1943) would later propose as a theory of structural functional semiotics, although this was presented as a continuation of Ferdinand de Saussure's pre-structuralism. The technical notions of structural semantics such as SEMES (atoms of meaning or *semantic traits*), SEMEMES (aggregations of semes corresponding to a lexical item), ARCHISEMEMES (those particular semes that have overarching value in a semantic paradigm), seem also to resonate with René's approach of "molecular" meaning, even though René's notion of atom is about morphs whereas the structuralist notion of semantic traits is about abstract concepts, not linguistic realizations.

However, whereas structural semantics assumes that semantic elements combine together within a system of oppositions, mirroring structural phonology, René does not hold that "atoms" should exist because of some system of oppositions relative to one particular language. What René advocates is rather the idea that "molecules" are like sets of ideas, each of which is realized linguistically by an "atom". When none of these atoms is sufficient to fully express a particular idea, a morphological composition of the basic atoms is needed. This, interestingly, is again comparable to some extent to what mainstream structural semantics would propose.

For René, there are two kinds of words: simple words and compound words, the latter being either compounds of autonomous words or morphological constructions involving affixes. Since simple words and affixes fall within the same general notion of bearers of simple meanings — that is, both affixes and words have a single, atomic meaning — the two morphological categories reduce to the same general semantic type. This approach is a typical reductionist conception of language which ignores cross-linguistic disparities as much as possible.

The only difference between simple words and affixes is that, according to René, affixes tend to represent more general ideas than lexical roots, since, as he ventures to suggest, the more general an idea, the more frequent it is in discourse, and the more frequent a meaning, the more likely it is to aggregate in an affix. This is of course a debatable claim, but it does in a way prefigure some approaches within the contemporary conceptions of grammaticalisation and lexicalisation, which suggest a general pattern for the production by a language of grammatical morphemes on the basis of archaic conceptual lexical words.

These atoms, in any case, are considered by René the 'basic material for word formation' (de Saussure 1911: 5) and are assumed to be stable across contexts and also across compositions. Their individual content is supposedly known and identified. René insists in a footnote that this principle of invariability of atoms is not about their form but about their meaning, but his comments on the formal variation of morphemes shows substantial ignorance both of the nature of allomorphic variation and of linguistic diversity (de Saussure 1911: 6).

Just as for the Port-Royal grammarians and for most of the formal tradition in semantics, meaning according to René is fundamentally compositional, not inferential. He even dismisses the need for 'rules of derivation' (de Saussure 1911: 8) (but the picture is somewhat different in the 1919 text, see below). However, intellectually speaking, his approach is organized in a slightly different way than what existed on the market at his time. Notably, his view of the way in which meanings combine is an original one. This is most of all because words, according to him, involve not only hierarchical meanings (i.e. the meaning of a word includes the meaning of the superordinate, as *horse* means 'horse' but also 'animal' and so on[3]). Furthermore, the top-most superordinate meanings are actually those of abstract grammatical categories *themselves*, breaking into pieces the traditional distinction that opposes conceptual-declarative and grammatical-functional meaning. More precisely, for René de Saussure, the meaning of a word has several layers: an "explicit" meaning (the particular idea) and a series of im-

---

[3] That René takes the example of *horse* ironically echoes Ferdinand's mention (de Saussure 1916 [1974]: 97)97 of the word *horse* when he criticizes the classical tradition.

3 The theory of meaning in René de Saussure's works

plicit meanings (the more general ideas) (de Saussure 1911: 10). Interestingly, the most general, the most abstract idea is a *grammatical* one. 'Horse' involves not only 'mammal', 'vertebrate', 'animal' (which all have to be substantive, de Saussure 1911: 13) but even the "substantive idea" itself.

There are three such fundamental, overarching grammatical elements of meaning: the nominal idea (ontologies), the adjective idea (qualities, properties) and the verbal idea (states of affairs and (other) actions). The "nominal idea" corresponds to the abstract notion of "being" itself (de Saussure 1911: 10); this resonates again with the philosophical tradition of Port-Royal. Through this abstract notion of being, which is semantically attached to the grammatical category as a whole and to all its members, a word like *horse* entails therefore a meaning of 'some being'. This "nominal idea" is implied not only by concrete real beings such as 'horse' but also for abstractions like "theory" or "type". Therefore, it is not only the case that substantives indicate one class of concepts (substances) and adjectives another one (accidents or qualities), as in traditional grammar, but also, and much more interestingly, that there is a grammatical notion that semantically encodes the very notions of being (substance) and of quality, as top-most overarching semantic elements. And of course, the same holds for the "verbal idea".

He explains: "The nominal idea, the adjectival idea and the verbal idea are thus ideas completely like other ideas: they are simply those of our ideas that are the most general and as a consequence, the most abstract. [...] I will call them grammatical ideas" (de Saussure 1911: 12).

These grammatical ideas are represented in language by a number of linguistic items, the basic grammatical atoms, which bear only the function of evoking the grammatical idea. There may be various linguistics markers of one grammatical idea but still they all encode that particular grammatical idea. An adjectival suffix, for example, encodes the grammatical idea of quality ('hum-*an*'), since all morphological indicators of a grammatical category encode the semantic notion behind it. In some cases a particular grammatical item operates a shift of categorization, as when *riche* 'rich' becomes *un riche* 'a rich [person]' (de Saussure 1911: 19). In such cases, as with *ce* and *le* (see de Saussure 1911: 28), he explains that the determiner is the "nominalizing atom", the maker of substantivity, which might recall a very contemporary view (introduced in Abney 1987) on which noun phrases are actually headed grammatically by the determiner, not the noun (in René's theory the definite determiner is more abstract than the indefinite: cf. de Saussure 1911: 27–28).

The "adjective idea" can be found not only in grammatical adjectives (typically because of a variety of affixes which themselves bear the "adjective idea"), but also, curiously, in some prepositions, which René treats as "dissociated suffixes", such as French *de* 'of' in *d'homme* 'of man' where it "plays the same role" as *ain* in *humain* (i.e. as 'an' in 'hum*an*'). The same property is attributed to some pronouns, such as *qui* 'that, which' in *qui diffère* 'that differs' as an equivalent to *différent* 'different'. Needless to say, the latter claim both recalls Port-Royal again, but once again with differences: ultimately, in René's approach, *qui diffère* and *différent* have the same meaning (but then what happens to the verbal idea in such a composition is unclear).

René acknowledges the existence of other types of "atoms" which do not belong to the nominal, adjectival or verbal type: adverbs, prepositions, etc. However René considers any attempt to classify them pointless because they do not, according to him, contain any general ideas of their own, but only particular ones (e.g. time or place etc. when considering adverbs) (de Saussure 1911: 117).

3 Meaning, composition of meaning, and grammar

These fundamental grammatical ideas have compositional properties. René considers that "the noun cannot function alone any more than a body without limbs" (de Saussure 1911: 75) and thus needs verbal and adjectival atoms in order to construct not only sentences but even "molecules". This suggests that René, unlike Frege, does not have a referential conception of meaning, since nouns are unlike verbs in that they can refer without need of anything else, whereas verbs need arguments to refer to actual eventualities.

The relationship between grammar and semantics in René's work is somewhat ambivalent. On the one hand, all conceptual meanings are subordinate to some grammatical notion, but, on the other hand, since all grammatical notions are ideas, the grammar is ultimately a matter of meaning, and therefore bears a semantic essence. This brings the two brothers close: Ferdinand, looking at the "system of signs", does not really discriminate between the world of the conceptual and that of the functional. All these elements are signs with values. For example, according to Ferdinand, systems with masculine and feminine genders only differ from those that have a neuter gender because of the mutual oppositions of these genders inside the system of gender that they form together.

However, contrary to Ferdinand's views, for whom *langue* resides in the community of speakers,[4] René clearly holds an internalist conception, even though

---

[4]However Ferdinand's views are more complicated. *Langue* as specific to one particular language exists in the corresponding community of speakers and thus is perhaps "external", but *langue* as a principle of organisation is true of all languages and is thus internal, as a cognitive feature of the brain.

unfortunately he does not elaborate on the ontology of language. Language, for René, is neither a mere indicator of thoughts (with reference to external objects) as in Port-Royal grammar, nor a thought-maker as it is in Ferdinand's account at the other end of the spectrum. Language for René is rather an apparatus which imposes its principles on the referential lexicon and thus belongs itself to the domain of thought, since the grammar is, ultimately, conceptual.

When René discusses the notion of the "verbal idea", he faces a problem of categorization, since it is not intuitive to unite stative and dynamic notions in a single general type (de Saussure 1911: 17). At first, he represents not one but two quite distinct verbal ideas: "ag" for "active verbs", i.e. verbs indicating dynamic aspect, and "sta" for stative verbs. But further on, René elaborates a unifying solution which has the merits of being already aspectual, years before the seminal works by Otto Jespersen on that notion outside the Slavic domain in the twenties (e.g. Jespersen 1924).

René's knowledge of physics is clearly recruited to discuss the status of verbality and of eventualities. He claims that states are a subtype of dynamic events: "the static idea is however only a special case of the dynamic idea. The latter implies forces in activity: if the forces are not in equilibrium, we have the proper dynamic idea (action), which is the general case; if the forces are in equilibrium, we have the static idea (state). And indeed as soon the state changes, we fall back into action" (de Saussure 1911: 32–33).[5] An issue with this conception of the "verbal idea" could be that "state" looks pretty much like a "nominal idea" since it also involves a notion of being. However, whereas the nominal idea concerns the ontology of substances, the verbal idea concerns some particular property that a substance may bear at some particular time.

In the 1911 text, René seems to leave aside the possibility that words do gain some semantic autonomy when they are incorporated into the lexicon as units; he mentions the movement from compounding to units in the 1919 book but only to suggest that this does not impact the analysis because it is a historical, evolutive, problem (de Saussure 1919: 5). In a footnote (de Saussure 1911: 37) he acknowledges a suggestion by Charles Bally to consider the autonomy of lexical items (Bally was the successor of Ferdinand de Saussure at the University of Geneva and editor of the *Cours*), but René abstains from a conclusion here, saying that he only aims at developing the logical point of view. Yet in the 1919 text, he actually moves on and recognizes that each word, despite being possibly compositional, "is in itself its own structure" (de Saussure 1919: 27).

---

[5]This view, which René imports from physics into linguistics, is problematic when it comes to the way language represents facts: that states are particular instances of non-states does not look right linguistically, and René seems to be lacking some more precise knowledge of sub-categories. What is more, the complements of an atelic verb may turn it into a telic verb phrase, a problem that could hinder René's "principle of invariability of atoms" (de Saussure 1911: 21).

However, René does not always avoid such discussions, as when he compares *doux* 'sweet' and *doucereux* 'smooth, unctuous', saying that the meaning from the logical point of view is the same but "superfluous atoms" of meaning are added on top of the logical meaning of *doucereux* to express a nuance (de Saussure 1911: 61–62).

The 1919 text provides an interesting philosophical development of these primitive categories of meaning ("grammatical ideas"). In just a few words, which, however prefigure later conceptions of the relation between language and cognition ("thought"), René relates natural language to the nature of the human mind much more deeply than what one finds in the canonical version of Ferdinand's *Cours*. René even places it in the context of human evolution: " "grammatical" categories correspond to "logical" categories, and since the former are the same for all languages, language must therefore be the expression of a certain philosophical conception of the world, the popular conception if you will, but one that must have very deep roots, because it emanates so to speak from within natural evolution." (de Saussure 1919: 26).

Leaving aside the *Cours*, which does not do full justice to Ferdinand's actual thoughts on the matter, it is likely that such considerations have their roots in the debates and discussions the two brothers certainly used to have about language. There may even be a trace here of Ferdinand's own influence, since he is reported to have clearly affirmed, notably during his third course of General Linguistics in Geneva, that language is an "instinct" (a notion that echoes that of "faculty" found in the *Cours*) and that it has to do with the "folders of the brains" (de Saussure 1993: 80).

René asserts two major principles with regard to the 'synthesis of words', that is, the construction of words composed of more than one atom of meaning (de Saussure 1911: 99); these principles are very interesting inasmuch as they suggest an economical view of meaning construction which goes well with many scholars' positions across various linguistic domains of investigation: for example, the Prague school in phonology, but also Martinet's view on linguistic change, and of course the well-known principles of economy at play in pragmatics according to most authors in the Gricean tradition.

On the one hand, René posits a *principle of necessity* which requires that a certain quantity of information is provided by the word in order that clarity and completeness of meaning are ensured. Conversely, a *principle of sufficiency* requires that an idea is expressed only once in a word, and that no idea foreign to the meaning of the word is incorporated. These two principles limit each other: the principle of sufficiency imposes a restriction on the degree of linguistic pre-

3 The theory of meaning in René de Saussure's works

cision of an item, avoiding superfluous meanings or redundancy, whereas the principle of necessity imposes the requirement to go as far as possible in the linguistic marking of meaning.

The equilibrium between these principles results in the fact that "the meaning of a word depends only on its own content, and on all of its content and not on the manner in which one supposes this word to be derived from another" (de Saussure 1911: 99). In passing, we note once again René's opposition to derivational theories, even though he acknowledges that derivations take place in the history of languages (de Saussure 1911: 120). In this respect, the theory is perhaps made clearer in the 1919 text, as René (after noticing the behavioural similarity between verbs and adjectives) considers that there exist constructions like adjectivalizations, which he recognizes as derivations. But still, this does not change the whole picture inasmuch as this type of derivation is (probably) to be understood as historically and not synchronically relevant.

In some cases, the two principles cannot both be met adequately. This typically happens when the idea becomes too precise for expression as the result only of the composition of more basic items. Two options are possible in theory: *excess*, if some notion is needed but its linguistic marking would extend to additional extraneous meanings, and *rounding down*, if some necessary idea is however omitted from expression for lack of appropriate atom; René claims that languages always choose rounding down because it is economical since it avoids more confusions than excess. *Couronner* 'to crown' is an example of a process by rounding down: in this word, there is a notion of an object (the crown) and of an undetermined action, but *couronner* involves more than just any action performable with a crown: a notion of a patient and of a particular positioning of the crown (de Saussure 1911: 109).

"Rounding down" cases force René to open the theory of meaning to some degree of contextual determination and of sematic underspecification; unfortunately he does not elaborate on this important aspect of meaning.[6]

---

[6] Also, René uses only his own lay semantic intuition, and fails sometimes to pursue further semantic investigation. The example of 'coronation' could for instance be challenged: first, isn't the notion of an individual's head already "contained" in some way in the object itself? In other words, isn't the function of an object part of its meaning? After all, a crown is made in such a shape that it ought to fit specifically on a head. There could be room for a notion of typicality here: a typical action performed with a crown is to put it one one's head in the way it is made to be employed. As a result, it is very hard to imagine different usages of 'to crown' than this one (except of course non-literal usages). If this is correct, then there is no need for a notion of usage or context here and René seems to have trapped himself into problematic consequences of his claims about "rounding down", at least with unambiguous words like the one he chooses to illustrate it.

Some further elaborations of the theory concern "synonyms" (with interesting ideas such as that the linguistic variation observable for some meanings has the function of selecting the proper grammatical idea for the former), ambiguous atoms (which he names 'double-sense atoms' and views as phonetic accidents irrelevant for the logical analysis), etc.

The 1919 text adds a few elements to the picture elaborated in 1911, notably some nuances. His brother Ferdinand is now universally acclaimed and the tone of the text is closer to reconciliation with his recently deceased brother than the 1911 text was. This is true even though the 1919 book seems to continue in some way the discussions with Ferdinand: the *Cours* is abundantly cited and René attempts to bridge a few elements of his approach to what he finds there. For example, he tries to relate Ferdinand's principle of the arbitrariness of the sign *vs.* motivation to the distinction between simple and compound words in his own theory (de Saussure 1919: 6). Although some very interesting clarifications, elaborations and adaptations are provided by the 1919 text, (for example about the "law of reversal" which establishes the relationship between morphology and syntax, (de Saussure 1919: 11), the essence of the 1911 theory remains unchanged and still opposed to Ferdinand's systemic view.

René's compositional theory achieves a considerable degree of descriptive adequacy. Some of the examples which he analyses show that many subtleties of meaning composition can be accounted for within the theory, as when he compares *brossier* (someone who sells brushes, in a somewhat archaic French) and *brosseur* (someone who brushes) (de Saussure 1911: 112): only the second case contains the verbal idea of action. The assumptions driving this analysis may push theorizing further: while we intuitively tend to define the word *brossier* as someone who *sells* brushes, thus using a verbal notion in the definition, it might more accurate to define it as someone who *has brushes* (for sale).

Similarly, his approach to word composition accounts for the fact that verbs constructed on the basis of nouns (e.g. *couronner*) are semantically of a different type than "simple verbs" such as *frapper* 'to beat'; however such compositions as *couronner* are not, he insists, derivations from a noun into a verbal derivative but compositions of atoms of different kinds, even though the anti-derivational stance is attenuated in some way in the 1919 text where he suggests that some words (like *musique*, 'music') "giving rise to new adjectives" such as *musical* "where the root *music* plays the role of a simple element" (de Saussure 1919: 5).

4 Conclusion

All in all, the most important feature of René de Saussure's theory of meaning is the assumption that grammatical categories as such are not only semantic types but are also meaningful, corresponding to the overarching concepts (of being, or qualities or to actions) that serve as the foundation of all possible particular lexical meanings. This is perhaps a consequence of his particular interest in morphology and its role in the constitution of meaning. In this perspective, syntax, then, should perhaps be considered as a formal apparatus that governs the arrangements of meanings, not of pure abstract labels.

References

Abney, Steven. 1987. *The English noun phrase in its sentential aspect*. MIT dissertation.

Arnauld, Antoine & Claude Lancelot. 1660. *Grammaire générale et raisonnée*. Paris: Chez Pierre le Petit.

Augustine, Saint. 1975. *De dialectica*. Dordrecht/Boston: D. Reidel Publishing Co. English translation with introduction and notes by B. Darrell Jackson of text edited by Jan Pinborg.

Augustine, Saint. 1996. *De doctrina Christiana* (Oxford Early Christian Texts). Clarendon Press. English Translation by R. P. H. Green.

de Saussure, Ferdinand. 1916. *Cours de linguistiique générale*. Lausanne: Librairie Payot. Edited by Charles Bally and Albert Sechehaye, with the collaboration of Albert Riedlinger.

de Saussure, Ferdinand. 1993. *Troisième cours de linguistique générale (1910-1911): d'après les cahiers d'Émile Constantin / Saussure's third course of lectures on general linguistics (1910-1911): from the notebooks of Émile Constantin*. Oxford: Pergamon Press. French text edited by Eisuke Komatsu and English text edited by Roy Harris.

de Saussure, Ferdinand. 1916 [1974]. *Cours de linguistique générale*. Paris: Payot. [Critical edition prepared by Tullio de Mauro].

de Saussure, René. 1911. *Principes logiques de la formation de mots*. Geneva: Librairie Kündig.

de Saussure, René. 1919. *La structure logique des mots dans les langues naturelles, considérées au point de vue de son application aux langues artificielles*. Berne: Librairie A. Lefilleul.

Hjelmslev, Louis. 1943. *Omkring sprogteoriens grundlæggelse*. Copenhagen: Ejnar Munksgaard. Translated 1953 by Francis Whitfield as *Prolegomena to a Theory of Language*; revised edition published 1963 by University of Wisconsin Press.

Jespersen, Otto. 1924. *The philosophy of grammar*. New York: Henry Holt & Company.